PUBLIC DOLLARS, COMMON SENSE: NEW ROLES FOR FINANCIAL MANAGERS

By
William R. Phillips
Bonnie L. Brown
C. Morgan Kinghorn
Andrew C. West

Coopers & Lybrand L.L.P.
Washington, D.C.

William R. Phillips, Bonnie L. Brown, C. Morgan Kinghorn, Andrew C. West

Public Dollars, Common Sense: New Roles for Financial Managers

Library of Congress Catalog No. 96-86563

ISBN 0-944533-24-8

Bulk quantities of this book may be obtained from:

Bookmasters, Inc.
Distribution Center
1444 State Rt. 42
RD 11
Mansfield, Ohio 44903
Telephone: 1-800-247-6553
Fax: 419-281-6883

60705

TABLE OF CONTENTS

It's a Jungle Out There

Sorry, Wrong Numbers

Federal Financial Management Has Not Motivated Improvements

"Accountancy--that is government!," Said Louis Brandeis

A New Breed of Financial Leaders

From Money Police to Business Partners: Changing the Financial Culture

Systems Challenges

Riding the Audit Trail

What Audits Reveal, Best Practices Can Heal

Measuring Government Performance

Managerial Accounting: Putting Financial Numbers to Work

Private Sector Precursors of the New Reform Legislation

Crises in City Government and Federal Largess Prompt Extension of Rules

Domestic and Defense Federal Spending Goes Ballistic

What Federal Accounting Practices Really Do, and Do Not Do

First Steps in a New Era of Federal Fiscal Reform

The Need for Legislative Mandates

The Letter of the Law

The Spirit of the Law

Federal Comptroller Adds Value to Agency Operations

Personal Leadership Roles

Financial Process Improvement: Key to Credibility in the New Roles

Gauging the Maturity of the Financial Organization

ABBREVIATIONS AND ACRONYMS

ABC: Activity-based costing
ABEST II: Automated Budget and Evaluation System of Texas
AGA: Association of Government Accountants
AICPA: American Institute of Certified Public Accountants
BPR: Business process redesign or reengineering
CFO: Chief financial officer
CIO: Chief information officer
COSO: Committee of Sponsoring Organizations of the Treadway Commission
COTS: Commercial off-the-shelf software
CPA: Certified public accountant
CSF: Critical success factor
DISC: Defense Industrial Supply Center
DOE: U.S. Department of Energy
DSO: Days sales outstanding
EDI: Electronic data interchange
FASAB: Federal Accounting Standards Advisory Board
FASB: Financial Accounting Standards Board
FBI: Federal Bureau of Investigation
FFMIA-96: Federal Financial Management Improvement Act of 1996
FMFIA: Federal Managers' Financial Integrity Act of 1982
FMS: Financial Management Service of the U.S. Department of the Treasury
FTE: Full-time equivalent
FY: Fiscal year
GAAP: Generally accepted accounting principles
GAO: U.S. General Accounting Office
GASB: Government Accounting Standards Board
GMRA: Government Management Reform Act of 1994
GOPB: Texas Governor's Office of Budget and Planning
GPRA: Government Performance and Results Act of 1993
GSA: General Services Administration
HUD: U.S. Department of Housing and Urban Development
IG: Inspector General
IRS: Internal Revenue Service
IT: Information technology

JAD: Joint application design
JFMIP: Joint Financial Management Improvement Program
LLB: Texas Legislative Budget Board
MIS: Management information system
NIST: National Institute of Standards and Technology
NPR: National Performance Review
NSA: National Security Agency
OIG: Office of the Inspector General
OMB: U.S. Office of Management and Budget
PBO: Performance-based organization
PCIE: President's Council on Integrity and Efficiency
R&D: Research and development
RIF: Reductions in force
SEF: Standard exchange format
SFFAS: Statement of Federal Financial Accounting Standards
SSA: Social Security Administration
T&E: Time and expense
VA: U.S. Department of Veterans Affairs

ACKNOWLEDGMENTS

Public Dollars, Common Sense would not have been possible without the assistance of dozens of government officials and Coopers & Lybrand professionals and support staff.

We begin by thanking the federal financial executives who participated in the focus group we convened in April 1996, which helped us to identify subjects of most interest to the federal financial community:

> Steven App, Deputy Chief Financial Officer, Department of the Treasury
> Ted David, Acting Chief Financial Officer, Department of Agriculture
> Vincette Goerl, Chief Financial Officer, Customs Service
> Sky Lesher, Deputy Chief Financial Officer, Department of the Interior
> Ron Longo, Deputy to the Chief Financial Officer for Policy and Planning, Department of the Treasury
> Tony Musick, Chief Financial Officer, Internal Revenue Service
> John Nethery, Deputy Assistant Secretary for Financial Operations, United States Air Force
> Jack Nutter, Special Assistant to the Deputy Program Manager for Defense Systems, Defense Finance and Accounting Service
> Alvin Tucker, Deputy Chief Financial Officer, Department of Defense
> Edwin Vurberg, Associate Administrator for Administration, Federal Aviation Administration

We conducted in-depth interviews with many government officials to gather background information and examples. We thank the following officials for graciously giving time for these interviews:

> Charles Bowsher, (former) Comptroller General, General Accounting Office

Jay Brixey, Chief Financial Officer, Federal Bureau of Investigation

Donald Chapin, Chief Accountant, General Accounting Office

Ed DeSeve, Controller, Office of Management and Budget

Dennis Fischer, Chief Financial Officer, General Services Administration

Louise Frankel Stoll, Chief Financial Officer, Department of Transportation

The Honorable John Glenn, U.S. Senate

Ernest Gregory, Deputy Assistant Secretary of the Army for Financial Operations

John Hamre, Under Secretary of Defense–Comptroller, Department of Defense

Sallyanne Harper, Acting Chief Financial Officer, Environmental Protection Agency

The Honorable Stephen Horn, U.S. House of Representatives

Elaine Kamarck, Senior Policy Advisor to the Vice President, National Performance Review, Office of the Vice President

Valerie Lau, Inspector General, Department of the Treasury

John Mercer, Majority Counsel, Senate Committee on Governmental Affairs

George Muñoz, Assistant Secretary (Management) and Chief Financial Officer, Department of the Treasury

Kevin Sabo, General Counsel, House Committee on Government Reform and Oversight

Members of the federal CFO Council participated in a May 1996 round-table discussion of topics for the book, including Messrs. App, DeSeve, Fischer, Muñoz, and Frank Sullivan, Deputy CFO of the Department of Veterans Affairs.

A special word of thanks goes to the Association of Government Accountants for partnering with us in the summer of 1995 to conduct a survey of federal CFO offices, inspectors general offices, and program managers.

We appreciate the fine technical insights of Coopers & Lybrand partners Jim Dillard and Larry Farmer; Jay Gremillion for his substantial contributions to Chapters 5 and 6; Dan Noss and David Ramseyer for diligence in assembling Appendices A and B; and Beverly Bell, Christopher Butler, Tom Cocozza, Jim Durnil, Gregg Gullickson, Joe Lewis, Cathy Presnell, Denise Rabun, and Mike Reeb for their valuable contributions. Pam Bayliss and Karen Portman deserve a special word of thanks for their help in project communications, scheduling, and budgeting. Portions of Chapter 3 and 7 are adapted from *Reinventing the CFO: Moving from Financial Management to Strategic Management*, by Coopers & Lybrand partners Thomas Walther, John Dunleavy, and Henry Johansson and Elizabeth Hjelm.

We had the benefit of superb editorial support from chief editor Steve Clyburn and editor Saïdeh Pakravan, and Grammarians, Inc. technical writers Lyndi Schrecengost and Peter Adam, copy editor and proofreader Mellen Candage, and indexer Winfield Swanson. For an excellent job in producing the book, we thank production chief Mike Clover, word processors Anna Fano and Lucia Gladchtein, and graphic artist Patrick Scroggins.

INTRODUCTION

Unnoticed by most citizens, fundamental financial management reform is happening throughout government, driven by both need and opportunity. New laws mandate this reform in the federal government, such as the Chief Financial Officers Act of 1990 (CFO Act), the Government Performance and Results Act of 1993 (GPRA), and the Government Management Reform Act of 1994 (GMRA). Behind the laws is a government desperately seeking solutions for major deficits in revenue, performance, and public confidence. Yet, in some departments and agencies, desperation is giving way to hope and pride. There, financial managers have taken command of the opportunities afforded by the new reform legislation. Once labeled as back room bean counters, these financial managers now are on the front lines of reform.

Chief financial officers (CFOs), once found only in industry, now help lead the way to fiscally sound, cost-effective public service. Financial managers and audit professionals, no longer content simply to be "money police," are becoming partners with program managers to enhance service to citizens. Inspectors general are spending less time on reactive investigations and more on proactive searches for improvement opportunities. While legislation defines and mandates these new roles, the innovational energy of government financial professionals is turning the law into reality.

Public Dollars, Common Sense is about these professionals, new laws, and other government initiatives that are the engines of reform. Our goal is to describe the roles played by forward-looking financial leaders as they make progress in reform, including the personal skills and technical methods that are critical to their success.

Although we offer the reader some strategic methodologies for improving financial operations and measuring results, this book does not contain bromides without ballast. Much of the information we present is gleaned from interviews with financial managers at work in agencies today. These are the people who are in the trenches, and it is their learning experiences, successes and failures, criticism and caution, hopefulness and confidence that inform this book.

Sources of Information

Coopers & Lybrand is a Big Six accounting and management consulting firm, working with thousands of private sector companies and federal, state, and local government agencies. Our public clients often ask, "How do you make government more dynamic, responsive, and willing to take risks? What roles do financial managers play in the process?" To answer these questions for this book, we turned to a number of sources:

- **Extensive one-on-one and group interviews** with leaders who have been applying private sector methods to government, conducted in the spring and summer of 1996. They include federal CFOs and deputy CFOs, inspectors general, members of Congress and their staffs, and senior officials of the U.S. Office of Management and Budget (OMB), the General Accounting Office, (GAO), and the National Performance Review.

- **A spring 1996 focus group session** with federal CFOs and representatives from GAO and OMB, in which they identified, ranked, and discussed the important issues confronting government financial professionals. These issues form the framework of this book.

- **The new financial and management reform rules and regulations** themselves, including the laws listed at the start of this introduction, federal Executive Orders, OMB circulars, and standards of the Federal Accounting Standards Advisory Board. Please see Appendix B for the full text of the laws and a summary of key regulations.

- **A summer 1995 survey** of financial managers, inspectors general, and program managers in nearly 100 federal agencies, concerning progress and problems in implementing the new reform legislation. The survey was conducted by Coopers & Lybrand and the Association of Government Accountants.

- **Published and unpublished literature** on private and public sector financial management and performance measurement issues, including internal reports of government agencies.
- **Coopers & Lybrand's government and industry experience** in financial management, accounting, and management.

Everyone we interviewed was eager to participate and enthusiastic about the current move in government toward financial reform. To them we owe a great debt; there would not be a book without them—at least not a very good one.

Our hope is that this book furthers the current reinvention effort in government. In our attempt to get at the heart of the matter in a way that exhorts rather than condemns, we echo the words of America's great pragmatic eighteenth-century philosopher, Thomas Paine, in his pamphlet *Common Sense*:

> In the following pages I offer nothing more than simple facts, plain arguments, and common sense; and have no other preliminaries to settle with the reader, than that he will divest himself of prejudice and prepossession, and suffer his reason and his feelings to determine for themselves; that he will put on, or rather that he will not put off, the true character of a man and generously enlarge his views beyond the present day.

William R. Phillips
Bonnie L. Brown
C. Morgan Kinghorn
Andrew C. West
December 1996

Chapter

1

WHY NOW? THE NEW FOCUS ON ACCOUNTABILITY

This chapter is an overview of the challenges faced by government financial managers as well as a summary of *Public Dollars, Common Sense.* Topics include:

- Underlying problems of public sector financial accounting and performance measurement
- Laws that are transforming government financial and management practices
- The new breed of government financial executives and managers
- Results and analysis of a survey of the federal financial and inspectors general communities that shows their chief challenge to be lack of integrated systems
- Why the culture of government financial professionals must change
- Why government program managers do not use available financial information and how to solve this problem
- How audit requirements are reshaping federal financial accounting
- Appropriate use of performance measurement, best practices benchmarking, business process redesign or reengineering, and activity-based costing to improve financial and operations functions.

The federal government is accounting's last new frontier. Once it has been conquered, we are destined to have a government that is fully accountable and that provides quality goods and services.
—Stuart L. Graff, in *Management Accounting*

In 1893, when the Census Bureau announced that the western frontier was officially closed, historian Frederick Jackson Turner wrote that, with the nation complete from coast to coast, national characteristics and identity would become clear and magnified. Though it may seem odd to link Turner's thesis with accounting and financial management reform, those engaged in taming the federal fiscal frontier know otherwise. Much of the world of government numbers is only recently settled and quite primitive. Some parts are still treacherous wilderness.

It's a Jungle Out There

How treacherous? Well, consider the well-known case of the $450 hammer. This is the tool that inspired Vice President Al Gore's Hammer Award, which he gives to federal organizations for eliminating waste in government. Most recently, the hammer was alluded to in the 1996 science fiction film *Independence Day: The 4th of July,* this time with a much higher price tag and the implication of fraud and abuse (President: "How could this secret facility exist without my knowledge?" Scientist: "Remember those $20,000 hammers?").

In fact, the primary cause of the hammer's price was accounting, not fraud, waste, or abuse. In the 1980s, a defense agency bought an electronic device (let's call it a "black box") along with a tool kit for it. The invoice for this package of goods equally divided and allocated the contractor's total overhead costs to each line item in it, a standard practice in government purchasing. The $20,000 black box (a line item) was allocated $445 in overhead, as was each item in the tool box, including a $5 hammer. Total overhead for black box plus tools was reasonable.

The Myth of the $450 Hammer   Figure 1-1

Accounting practices that
distorted reality left the
buying agency open to
career-busting criticism.

Misunderstanding the numbers, someone thought the
hammer's loaded cost of $450 ($5 direct cost plus $445
overhead) reflected how much it had really cost the government. Irate, they leaked this to the media, which of course
had a field day. Defense officials pleaded in vain that the
hammer did not really cost $450, but the scandal helped
trigger congressional and Executive Branch investigations
of alleged fraud, waste, and abuse throughout the military
procurement system. People wrote reams of new procurement regulations to solve problems that did not exist, which
made buying more costly. More recently, the federal
National Performance Review (NPR) advocated getting rid
of many of these regulations, and Congress and the
Executive Branch responded by streamlining them away.

Now, the treachery in the story is that most of the people who beat up those poor Pentagon bureaucrats knew
what that hammer really cost—but that's business as usual
in the wilderness of government accounting. The moral:
How you count your numbers has to be rational and clear to
everyone inside and outside your organization.

Sorry, Wrong Numbers

This is not to say that governments do not have plenty of numbers on finance and performance; no institution on earth measures more things. They range from gargantuan (the federal debt) to gnat-sized (the cost of inspecting a chicken at a poultry processing plant). Unfortunately, these are often the wrong numbers. For example, according to the NPR in 1993, the federal government's hundreds of rules, 120,000 financial management employees, and millions of lines of reports had not produced helpful, accurate information for program managers* to use in financial decision making. The NPR pointed out that this had nothing to do with a lack of commitment or hard work among federal employees responsible for delivering direct services to the public. Instead, according to a September 1993 report of the NPR, it was the result of decades of uncoordinated, budget-obsessed focus on line items that were unrelated to any measures of achieving a mission, compounded by multiple procedures that created the illusion of control.

So, despite such enormous investment in integer infrastructure, no one really knows how much government functions cost, how well they are carried out, and with what results. Thus, the numbers that citizens read in the newspaper, plus hearsay and their personal experience, have fostered a burgeoning cynicism about their government's twin deficits—fiscal and performance. How cynical? According to Vice President Gore, analysis of public opinion poll data shows that in 1994 only 10 percent of Americans agreed that government generally tries to do the right thing—down from 60 percent in 1965. This is why many want government to privatize or even abandon some public services.

Is the federal government so inept and misguided as to deserve such low esteem? Of course not. True, there are plenty of problems, grave ones that threaten national solvency and well-being. But we know of many agencies where productivity and efficiency equal or surpass those of

---

*Throughout the book the term "program managers" refers to managers of program, line, or operations processes

private sector counterparts. Every day, we read about and take part in major government improvement projects that cut costs by billions of dollars while improving services to citizens, exemplifying the NPR's "Do More With Less" spirit. Why does the federal government receive so little credit for these successes, and why aren't there even more of them? Poor accounting and performance measurement practices are part of the reason.

Federal Financial Management Has Not Motivated Improvements

Unless the federal government measures and reports accurately the cost, value, and results of public services, assets, and improvements, its accountability to citizens is not clear and it is wide open for both earned and unearned criticism. Lacking timely, useful financial and performance data that help predict future trends as well as record historical ones, government program managers find it difficult to make cost-effective decisions. After all, how can you do more with less if you cannot even measure "more" and "less?"

For example, financial management in the federal government has largely been a system of budgets and full-time equivalent (FTE) or personnel head counts. Under the FTE system, an $18,000-per-year clerk and a $55,000-per-year professional each represent one FTE in a budget. One potential (and all too often actual) outcome of the FTE system is that managers have no incentive to transfer simple, routine tasks from professionals to clerks. To the managers, it all "costs" the same, even though the value created by a class of employee may be considerably less than the salary.

Many agencies still use FTE as their main method of managing financial resources, and their funds follow FTE allocations or some related methodology. Also, in most agencies, budget staff and the systems that support the full gamut of resources, including FTE, are located in regional or national offices. Therefore, most field organizations, which use resources to do the actual work of implementing programs, have little knowledge or incentive to manage their programs in a cost-effective manner. Organizations that are more sophisticated in resource management authorize more flexibility to field and other operating units and have designed information systems that provide field managers with the appropriate financial data. Such organizations find that, if given flexibility in return for accountability, field offices tend to manage their money more efficiently than do headquarters personnel.

Thus, under the current system, one big question federal managers always have is, "What is our head count?" The other is "How much is left in that line item in our budget?" Often, federal managers are forced to make ineffective—even nonsensical—decisions when playing by the rules of inflexible line item budgets. For example, awhile ago a repairman came to our office to fix a portable computer's burned-out screen. A replacement screen would have cost $1,000, but he said that for a bit more we could buy a new computer with better features than the old portable. We said that of course we would buy a new machine, and asked him who would be so foolish as to do otherwise. "Well," he said, "I sell a lot of this old model's replacement screens to federal offices that have exhausted their computer purchase budget but still have lots of money left in the computer repair budget."

Finally, the major federal financial process is preparing annual budgets, which consumes billions of dollars a year that might better be invested in improving other areas of financial management. Hundreds of thousands of federal personnel devote major portions of their time to formulating budgets, yet despite such a huge investment, federal financial management has lacked the key ingredients of cost-effective decisions and sound fiscal stewardship.

"Accountancy—that is government!" Said Louis Brandeis

U.S. Supreme Court Justice Louis Brandeis made that remark in congressional testimony back in 1914, and it was a good prophecy. As discussed in detail in Chapter 2, for the past sixty years the U.S. Congress has been imposing accounting regulations on commerce and governments.

Why laws, instead of self-regulation by those covered in this legislation? Well, crises like the stock market crash of 1929 and the Great Depression were clear signs that self-regulation was not enough to tame the frontiers of accounting.

Federal laws regarding financial statements began with the Securities Acts of 1933 and 1934, which established reporting and accounting standards for public corporations. One of the key requirements of these laws was that corporations publish annual audited financial statements that complied with generally accepted accounting principles (GAAP). This helped to ensure that the average investor received reliable information on stocks and bonds before buying them.

Such legislation was the underlying concept of more recent laws like the Single Audit Act of 1984, which required state and local governments that receive federal funds to improve their financial reporting, including publishing annual audited financial statements. The laws, along with fiscal crises such as the federal bail-out of New York City, prompted many state and local governments to begin other financial and management reforms. At this time, the link between public sector financial stability and public management practices gained widespread visibility. One has only to peruse the state and local examples in the book *Reinventing Government* to understand that the most recent wave of government reform started outside the Washington, D.C. Beltway.

Congress tried to bring more discipline in federal finance through the Federal Managers' Financial Integrity Act of 1982 (FMFIA), which required federal agencies to assess their systems and financial controls. However, FMFIA lacked the structure and teeth to force fundamental reform. A growing deficit crisis and the apparent success of the state and local reforms inspired new, stronger laws. They include the Chief Financial Officers Act of 1990 (CFO Act), the Government Performance and Results Act of 1993 (GPRA), and the Government Management Reform Act of

1994 (GMRA). These laws are the central legislation addressed in this book; we discuss them in detail in Chapter 2 and provide their full text in Appendix B. Rounding out the new reform legislation are the Chief Information Officer (CIO) Act of 1996, intended to rationalize and improve the information systems that are essential to modern financial and management control, and the Federal Financial Management Improvement Act of 1996 (FFMIA-96), which requires agency financial systems to support controlling the cost of government.

The federal Executive Branch also has been taking action to improve financial management. The Federal Accounting Standards Advisory Board (FASAB) was established in 1990 to create common accounting rules for federal entities (*see* Chapters 5 and 6). The National Performance Review, intended to reinvent the federal government, was created by President Bill Clinton to inspire and coordinate financial and management reform.

A New Breed of Financial Leaders

New laws and initiatives provide the impetus for accelerated government reform, but they do not tame frontiers. Pioneers do, people willing to take on new risks and roles to make change happen. In Chapter 3, we discuss how a new breed of financial managers is leading the way through the fiscal wilderness of federal accounting.

Their objectives are twofold: to enhance the efficiency of existing fiduciary, internal control, accounting, and transaction functions and to add services that increase the effectiveness of the office of the CFO. These new services include strategic planning, performance measurement, assisting program managers in making cost-effective decisions, and leading major financial initiatives. Indeed, the new financial managers are becoming business partners with their counterparts in operations, while many CFOs are now part of the inner circle of executives who make agency policy.

This new emphasis makes eminent sense. Many traditional financial functions are being automated, reengineered, and outsourced, whittling away the cadres of accountants and clerks responsible for them. The future of financial management is to help agencies develop innovative business strategies, and financial leaders will be chosen because they know how to use the strategies to add value to an agency's products and services.

From Money Police to Business Partners: Changing the Financial Culture

Great leaders need great followers, and therein lies a formidable task for government CFOs. Every organization and profession has its own culture, made up of written and unwritten rules, norms, values, beliefs, and even myths that are collectively held by their members. Much of the old government financial community's culture hinders rather than helps the current wave of fiscal reform. The current cadre of financial professionals may have started their careers with the same progressive visions as their new CFO leaders, but for many, "the system" has long since ground away such aspirations. Often, they have an adversarial relationship with program managers, playing the part of nay-saying "money police" instead of partners in bettering the system. Many have either forgotten or never learned the basics of managerial accounting, so their effectiveness as partners is doubtful.

This cultural problem is not limited to financial professionals. Many program managers also have spent their careers boxed in by overly bureaucratic and budgetary boundaries. In their culture, underspending budgets is a strong taboo—indeed, a prime objective is to spend 100 percent of the money allocated.

As discussed in Chapters 3 and 10, overcoming these barriers to progress requires financial leaders to become change managers. This means investing much of their time aligning the human, organizational, and cultural elements of their agencies with new ways of doing business. Training is one answer, as are incentives, rewards, and the opportunity to expand professional horizons, making an otherwise routine career more interesting. Communicating the compelling need for change is a critical task for leaders, as is ensuring that those affected by change are involved in helping make it happen.

Also, change management is needed to help an agency align its people with the new information systems—systems that many financial managers and inspectors general see as the greatest challenge to fiscal progress.

Systems Challenges

In 1995, Coopers & Lybrand and the Association of Government Accountants conducted a survey of federal financial managers, inspectors general, and program managers to determine progress and barriers in implementing the new financial reform legislation. As shown in Figure 1-2, the survey showed that financial managers and inspectors general agree that lack of *integrated systems* is the number one challenge they face.

Figure 1-2

Federal Finance Managers and Inspectors General Opinions on Barriers to Implementing the CFO Acts

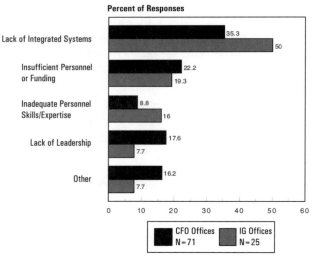

Percent of Responses

Lack of Integrated Systems	35.3 / 50
Insufficient Personnel or Funding	22.2 / 19.3
Inadequate Personnel Skills/Expertise	8.8 / 16
Lack of Leadership	17.6 / 7.7
Other	16.2 / 7.7

CFO Offices N=71
IG Offices N=25

Source: CFO Act Survey, 1995

Much of the data produced by government financial and performance measurement systems at best comes too late for corrective action and at worst is meaningless. Easy solutions that meet immediate demands address only the symptoms of these problems. Further, simply automating existing financial systems is no answer, and it usually creates more problems than solutions. As we discuss in Chapters 4 and 10, introducing information systems must be accompanied by changes in financial processes; otherwise, agencies face the risk of "paving the cowpaths" of outmoded ways of doing business. Often, people find it difficult to adjust to new ways of working, and may even resist these changes. Thus, effective change management is a critical part of implementing new systems. Business process redesign or reengineering (BPR) has lately become the accepted best practice approach to major systems development—but only when it integrates systems engineering, process redesign, change management, and strong leadership from the top. We discuss change management and BPR at length in Chapter 10.

Riding the Audit Trail

Commenting on the history of auditing in government, DoD Inspector General Eleanor J. Hill told a House subcommittee in 1995: "In 1779 the Continental Congress purchased thousands of preprinted pro forma ledger pages for use by Army commissary officers. Quartermaster Jacob Greene balked at this attempt to create an audit trail which would facilitate Congressional oversight. The Quartermaster claimed the paperwork required by the Treasury Board was unreasonable and told Congress that his purchasers could not be expected to itemize expenditures or provide delivery certifications from suppliers. He further stated that the Quartermaster Department could not be run like the 'plain business of the common storekeeper.' Two hundred and sixteen years later in the computer age, the government cannot supply Congress with an acceptable accounting of expenditures."

This long chapter in federal fiscal history is finally coming to a close. Today, the CFO Act and GMRA require that departments prepare annual audited financial statements and otherwise shape up their financial reporting. But if you think traveling the Oregon Trail was tough, ask any CFO about the hardships of the audit trail. It takes courage for a large government entity to go through an initial financial audit. Almost invariably, first-time audits reveal billions of dollars in errors such as overstated or understated accounts receivable or payable, contractor overpayments, bad loans, unfunded liabilities, and similar problems. Departmental secretaries and CFOs, their backsides already bruised by the normal wrath of oversight committees, have had to take many more licks because of the audit revelations.

Unlike Quartermaster Greene, federal CFOs welcome this opportunity to get their financial houses in order. As discussed in Chapters 5, 6, and 7, many are applying pre-audit, audit, and post-audit processes to discover and permanently correct long-standing deficiencies in the accounting of public funds. Even more, forward-looking CFOs understand that failure to obtain a clean opinion is a powerful stimulus for change, even to an organization's culture. For example, rectifying the deficiencies uncovered by initial audits led the Army to break down the traditional stovepipe barriers between functional and financial managers, prompting them to work together to fix Army problems and to improve stewardship.

What Audits Reveal, Best Practices Can Heal

". . .and there is no new thing under the sun."
—Ecclesiastes 1:9, The *Bible*

Federal financial pioneers can take heart that other fiscal frontiers have been explored, tamed, settled, and civilized, because much can be learned from them. While the public and private sectors have some significant differences in products and purpose, most of their financial processes are the same. Rather than waste time and money developing financial solutions from scratch, more and more agencies are using *benchmarking* to borrow the best practices of corporations and other government entities.

Chapter 9 discusses the ins and outs of best practices benchmarking, which is a system for identifying, analyzing, adopting, and adapting the high performance processes of external organizations. This system is quite different from old-style performance comparison studies or the "visiting fireman" junket to study similar organizations. Experienced best practice benchmarkers will quickly tell you the two key differences:

1. They thoroughly analyze internal processes before looking outside for better ones. Often, improvement opportunities found by this analysis push up performance standards that drive the search for better ways of doing business.

2. Instead of looking within their industry for the exact same process, they investigate processes in other areas that perform the same general function, even if the end products are different.

Best practices benchmarking is a key tool for fixing government processes. Already, it has been applied to financial functions in organizations ranging from service giants like the Government Services Administration (GSA) to small agencies in local and state governments. Also, financial managers can play an important role on the benchmarking teams formed by program managers. A major challenge in benchmarking is to develop apples-to-apples cost comparisons between an internal process and candidate external processes, and to carry out cost/benefit analyses of implementing alternative best practices.

Measuring Government Performance

Many CFOs have been tasked with the job of developing performance measures for their agencies. As we discuss in Chapter 8, a measurement system everyone in an agency will find useful has the following characteristics:

- It measures for customer and stakeholder satisfaction and expectations, financial and program performance, and external factors that affect an agency's ability to meet its mission.

- It allows trend analyses and helps identify areas for improvement.
- People understand the business processes for which measures are developed.
- Everyone shares the same measurement data base.
- Top management is committed to the measurement process.

Such a system will help equip agencies to meet GPRA requirements for planning and reporting on performance. As important, it will enable financial and other managers to apply leading-edge performance improvement tools that work best when supplied with hard data.

Managerial Accounting: Putting Financial Numbers to Work

Most of our book is about financial accounting, which is the most pressing concern of much of the government financial community. However, financial statements are rarely useful to program managers, who make the decisions that ultimately determine the results recorded in the statements and in annual agency performance reports. As noted earlier, most government program managers do not use traditional cost and managerial accounting information to make decisions.

And it is just as well that they do not. Among other problems, the traditional methods rely primarily on allocation to assign indirect or overhead costs to activities, products, and services, which distorts their true costs (remember the $450 hammer?). Also, these methods are not aligned with process-oriented thinking and decision making, which is becoming the norm in most federal and many state and local agencies. Such problems plague industry as well as government, and there is a growing trend to switch to better alternatives.

We suggest in Chapter 10 that *activity-based costing* (ABC) is one of the best alternatives for government. ABC is a process-based set of managerial accounting methods used to identify and describe cost objects (products, services, work units, processes, groups of customers), the activities or processes they consume, and the amount of resources the activities consume. ABC traces indirect costs to activities based on their actual consumption of these costs, instead of allocating them by some formula that distorts true costs.

Regardless of which forms of managerial accounting agencies select, CFOs will need to devote even more time and resources to making them part of business as usual than they are now investing in financial accounting. Managerial accounting is one of the toughest challenges of the fiscal frontier, because it involves fundamental changes in the thinking and culture of all people in an organization.

Arming for the Expedition

Appendix A of *Public Dollars, Common Sense* includes references and resource groups that will be useful to financial managers. The appendix includes a list and abstracts of relevant books and periodicals, contact information on government accounting and financial management professional associations and advisory groups, and Internet sites of finance and accounting information.

At the request of CFOs interviewed for this book, we have included in Appendix B the complete, indexed text of the key laws of the modern era of federal financial reform. Abstracts of relevant U.S. Office of Management and Budget (OMB) circulars and FASAB standards are also in the appendix. Separate from the book, we have created a searchable CD-ROM and computer diskette set of the full text of all these laws, circulars, and standards, along with other information on financial management implementation methods. Information on how to obtain this software is in Appendix A.

Bon Voyage

While the rest of this book is somewhat technical, we hope that readers starting their journey into the last fiscal frontier—or those who already live there—will not forget the basic philosophy of *Public Dollars, Common Sense.* We believe that the most sensible way out of public debt and citizen cynicism about government is a long-term commitment to prudence and common sense. Although there are many places where budgets can and should be cut, more will be gained by improving financial and management practices. Creating fundamental change always is harder than stop-gap solutions, but that's the pioneer way.

Chapter

2

EVOLUTION OF THE NEW REFORM LEGISLATION

Reform laws that work do more than specify policy changes. They create new roles, open up lines of communications, construct frameworks, and introduce innovative concepts to government. This chapter reviews the history and the content of a set of laws that are truly reforming how the federal government manages its finances:

- Chief Financial Officers Act of 1990 (the CFO Act)
- Government Performance and Results Act of 1993 (GPRA)
- Government Management Reform Act of 1994 (GMRA)
- Chief Information Officers Act of 1996 (the CIO Act)
- Federal Financial Management Improvement Act of 1996 (FFMIA-96).

Like earlier federal legislation on private sector and state and local government accounting and financial reporting, these laws were stimulated by fiscal and performance crises. The new reform legislation differs from earlier attempts to improve federal financial and management practices because these laws:

- Are mandated by Congress and have strong bipartisan support
- Are based on sound principles of good stewardship
- Provide a structure for accountability
- Force a union among politics, economics, and programs
- Authorize a strong role for agency CFOs.

I don't see any legislation before the CFO Act that involved a sincere planting of a seed that was going to mature. Everything has its timing. The CFO Act's time has come.

—CFO George Muñoz, U.S. Treasury Department

Every process has drivers: the forces that cause it to perform in a given way. Recent laws on financial, management, and information systems practices are among the new drivers of the federal reform process, because they are causing agencies to take a hard look at how they perform their missions. However, the new laws are but the latest chapter in the legislative history of public accountability and performance improvement. This has been an evolutionary history, with one set of laws forming the foundation for the next. Each stage of the evolution was prompted by fiscal or performance crises.

Private Sector Precursors of the New Reform Legislation

The CFO Act of 1990 evolved in part from the concepts and practices of the Securities Acts of 1933 and 1934, and there are many parallels between them. Yet we tend to forget the similarity in circumstances that prompted Congress to enact these laws: crisis and lack of citizen confidence.

Anyone who questions the role of government in promoting standard accounting and financial reporting rules ignores the 1929 stock market crash. Then, the economy crumbled under a mad mixture of wild speculation, debt, and questionable financial reporting practices—a deadly stew, nourishing only to ruin, depression, and war.

In the Great Depression that followed, 30 percent of the American work force was unemployed. Still, 70 percent had jobs, so there was at least some investment money available. Why didn't this capital move into the stock and bond markets or at least into banks, where it could hasten economic recovery? The reason was lack of confidence. The average investor violently distrusted Wall Street and felt safer hiding money in a coffee can than trusting it to bank that might fail, as did hundreds of financial institutions in the 1930s.

Restoring confidence in the economy took more than President Franklin D. Roosevelt's fireside chats on radio. FDR knew that the stock and bond markets had to be reformed in order to attract back investors whose money would help revive the economy. Voluntary measures alone were not enough. The crisis in confidence needed the stronger medicine of laws with criminal sanctions: the Securities Acts of 1933 and 1934.

Figure 2-1

The Securities Acts of 1933 & 1934 required the private sector to adopt uniform standards of accounting and financial reporting.

Among other things, these laws imposed extensive disclosure and public reporting requirements on entities that traded shares across state lines. These requirements included preparing a prospectus with financial statements that had been audited by a certified public accountant who attested to their fairness in representing the financial status of a company. The laws also prompted development of accounting and financial control standards, a task undertaken by the American Institute of Certified Public Accountants (AICPA). These became generally accepted accounting principles. A requirement to publish annual audited financial statements assembled according to GAAP helped bring more honesty and clarity to private sector financial reports.

A basic regulatory system, chiefly embodied in the Securities and Exchange Commission, gave enforcement teeth to the new laws.

All this gave investors more reliable information for their decisions, which increased their confidence in companies and financial institutions. Money began to move from coffee cans back into markets, which helped the economy start recovering. By protecting investors for more than sixty years, the new securities laws have done much to prevent us from concocting another deadly stew of economic ruin.

Public Confidence in Government Ran High, So Pressure to Reform Was Low

However, the nation's largest interstate bond seller—the federal government itself—was excused from the laws for nearly all those 60 years, until the CFO Act was passed in 1990. Public and political support for fundamental financial reform in government were not strong during the Great Depression, World War II, and the postwar boom years. After all, the federal government had quite literally saved the lives and hopes of many Americans in the 1930s, then rescued and rebuilt much of the world in the 1940s and 1950s. The massive public debt accumulated during this period was considered the dues for survival and prosperity, and was duly paid back. Besides, people trusted their government. As late as 1965, about 60 percent of citizens said that government generally tries to do the right thing, according to a September 1993 report by the National Performance Review.

As a result, federal action was slow and intermittent in extending to governments the financial disclosure and uniform accounting standards requirements of the Securities Acts. A few more financial calamities were needed to prompt serious reform in this area.

Crises in City Government and Federal Largess Prompt Extension of Rules

Not until New York City experienced severe financial problems in the 1970s did Congress seriously think about increasing the accountability for federal assistance to states and local government entities. Virtually bankrupt and in danger of defaulting on its bond interest payments, the city required a federal bailout. Other cities had similar problems, and most state and local governments were receiving massive infusions of federal funding as part of Great Society and other programs.

Figure 2-2

The Inspector General Act of 1978 and the Single Audit Act of 1984 extended accounting and reporting requirements to entities receiving federal funds and to state and local governments.

As keeper of the largest purse strings in the nation, the federal government had a vested interest in the financial management practices of the beneficiaries of its largess. It showed that interest by requiring organizations that received federal funds to adopt a uniform set of accounting standards and prepare audited financial statements. First, the Inspector General Act of 1978 (P.L. 95-452) augmented the reporting requirements of federal fund recipients. Later, the Single Audit Act of 1984 (P.L. 98-502) required state and local governments receiving $25,000 or more a year in federal aid to produce audited financial statements annually.

For the states, cities, towns, and regional authorities that already accessed the capital markets, conforming to reporting and accounting requirements was not entirely new. Debt rating agencies demanded it, and without good ratings these governments could not sell bonds. Also, unlike the federal government, many state and local governments are bound by law to balance their books, which is a strong incentive to use sound accounting practices and implement proper financial control procedures.

Once again, as was the case with the Securities Acts, the Single Audit Act did not apply to the federal government. But extending financial disclosure and reporting requirements to state and local governments set the stage for results-oriented management reform throughout the public sector. Later, the success of these efforts helped prompt the federal government to take stronger action for reforming its own financial management and performance measurement.

Domestic and Defense Federal Spending Goes Ballistic

In the 1960s, President Lyndon B. Johnson's policy of fighting a foreign war against communism and a domestic war against poverty started to increase the annual federal deficit. President Richard M. Nixon, however, was able to balance the budget in the early 1970s, probably for the last time in this century. But soon thereafter the earlier guns and butter policy caused an enormous increase in the flow of red ink into Washington's account books.

As for the guns, in the 1980s, President Ronald Reagan and Congress began a massive military buildup in a final Cold War campaign that was won in part by outspending the Soviet Union and driving it to ruin. During the Reagan presidency the national debt began its steep climb to today's current levels, but the Cold War was not entirely to blame. At the same time the grinding demographics of entitlements such as Social Security and Medicare started to gear up, and this butter greased the skids for a potential slide into federal insolvency.

As they entered or approached retirement age, each successive generation of Americans grew increasingly afraid that the social compacts of Medicare and Social Security would be breached. What amounted to congressional "borrowing" against these funds did nothing to reassure them. By the 1990s, citizens started to get really worried. The national debt was so large and increasing so rapidly that no one believed it could be paid off during their or their children's lifetimes.

With no wars or national emergencies to justify it, the looming federal financial calamity drew increased public attention. Support grew for extending disclosure and financial reporting requirements yet again, this time to the entire Executive Branch of the U.S. government.

What Federal Accounting Practices Really Do, and Do Not Do

Before the CFO Act, most federal agencies did not have to produce annual audited financial statements like those of industry and other governments. Also, unlike nonfederal organizations of any consequence, the federal government had been keeping its books on a cash rather than an accrual basis, and used a system of fund accounting in which each department or agency maintained separate accounts. The main purpose of these systems is to enable political leaders to ensure that money is used only for authorized purposes. Thus, federal accounting practices are in essence information systems for budget formulation and execution. They are of little use to the average citizen who wants to know the true cost of services, the value of government assets and liabilities, or the value added by one program versus another.

In 1985, Charles Bowsher, then U.S. Comptroller General, listed the major problems with the federal financial management system: "Federal finances are managed through an elaborate structure of decision processes and information systems. Many of these processes and systems, now obsolete, face ever-increasing difficulties in comparison with the demands placed upon them. The most visible evidence of difficulties is the enormous cost in time, energy, and public confidence involved in the annual search for consensus on the budget."

He enumerated the structural problems with this system as follows:

- The processes by which the federal government decides how much to spend, and for what purposes, are cumbersome, repetitive, and time-consuming.
- Controls over how federal money is spent are detailed and burdensome, but they are routinely found to be ineffective in preventing abuses.
- Budgeting, accounting, and management information systems often yield data that are unreliable, inconsistent, and too often irrelevant.

That eleven years later these problems remain is not for lack of trying. Instead, their continued presence reflects the difficulty of turning around decades of inattention to basic financial and program management. We trace the attempts to remedy the problems back to the early 1980s.

First Steps in a New Era of Federal Fiscal Reform

At a 1996 conference of the Joint Financial Management Improvement Program, Bowsher said that as early as 1981, the General Accounting Office (GAO) started working with a major public accounting firm to develop a conceptual framework for integrating government financial systems. GAO representatives met with Office of Management and Budget and Treasury officials to discuss the concept. Treasury first, and then OMB later under Richard Darman and Frank Hodsoll, favored moving ahead.

Federal Managers' Financial Integrity Act of 1982: Getting Started

Frank Hodsoll, former Deputy Director for Management at OMB, said in 1991 that the political system had not, until very recently, been particularly interested in accounting, financial management, and internal controls. There was never a precedent or tradition for such an interest. As Hodsoll explained it: "Budget execution was 'handled' at least in obligating budget authority. There [were] criminal sanctions for exceeding the limits under the Anti-Deficiency Act (31 U.S.C. 1341-42; 1511-1519). But what actually happened to the money, the condition of our assets, the extent of our liability, the performance outputs and outcomes of our policies and programs—these were all matters that I assumed were also 'handled'...What a shock it was to discover that many program managers didn't know the results of their outlays, the location and value of their inventories, the wear and tear on their buildings, the aging of their receivables, and the souring of their loan portfolios."

As Hodsoll implies, the real impediments to financial reform initiatives like the CFO Act are tradition and long historical practice. Breaking strongly held traditions requires strong measures. But during the 1980s neither the Legislative nor Executive Branch of the federal government was quite ready to force federal agencies to knuckle under the same requirements imposed by Washington on all other legal entities.

Even the first attempt by Congress to create financial reform was half-hearted and without teeth. True, the Federal Managers' Financial Integrity Act of 1982 (FMFIA, P.L. 97-255), required agencies to assess their systems and financial controls. Yet the act did not provide any consistent structure, leadership mandates, or specific tools with which financial managers could bring about fundamental reform. Like many other well-meaning but complex statutes, FMFIA is a paper exercise in many organizations and a massive one at that.

Still, said Bowsher in 1996, FMFIA started the financial federal reform process rolling. Yet it would not be until the next decade that an aroused public's concern about the swelling deficit would be sufficient to pressure Congress into acting with dispatch in this area. In the interim, the Executive Branch was starting to take action.

Reform 88: Making Progress

Reform 88, a major Reagan Administration management initiative, marked the start of this action, according to Gerald R. Riso, former OMB Director of Management. As part of it, the OMB Director, Treasury Secretary, and Comptroller General issued a set of core financial systems requirements. The requirement built upon the experience of several major departments in improving their primary accounting systems and was a significant milestone in establishing guidelines and standards for federal financial systems such as:

- Establishing standards to ensure consistency of data and processing function in all systems
- Installing a single, primary financial system in each major agency to aggregate budget and accounting information for all management levels
- Eliminating redundant systems through system consolidation and promoting cross-servicing agreements through which some agencies would purchase accounting and related services from those agencies with more efficient and better-performing systems
- Promoting the use of commercial off-the-shelf software (COTS) to keep system development costs and schedules to a minimum.

In addition, Reform 88:

- Designated a CFO within OMB, requested agencies to do likewise, and established a federal CFO Council
- Called for installation of comprehensive cash management systems in order to enhance return on the government's then $2 trillion cash flow
- Attempted to achieve compliance with FMFIA requirements
- Promoted extensive daily cooperation and collaboration between OMB and Treasury staff that led to progress in all the areas above.

OMB financial management staff were made responsible for taking the lead in setting ambitious program objectives and schedules and for working directly and assiduously with individual departments to make sure they met implementation objectives and schedules. This was a good opening salvo on the war against insolvency, setting the stage for future legislative action. Promoting the appointment of CFOs eventually led to the CFO Act. Also,

OMB at one point began to use agency report cards on basic performance in several financial and program areas. That did not last long because no consistent measurement framework was developed, nor were agency leaders prepared for the consequences of being measured this way. However, this presaged provisions of the Government Performance and Results Act passed only a few years later.

The Need for Legislative Mandates

Those involved in Reform 88 realized that, though it was a good start, it was not strong and consistent enough to motivate all federal organizations. Legislation was needed to recreate a strong, permanent, and widespread CFO and financial management structure in the federal government. According to the Management Report of the President accompanying the 1990 budget, "A permanent organization structure for the CFO is necessary to provide critical continuity of financial operations and improvement programs and provide a sufficiently high level of policy and leadership from the Executive Office of the President to assure long-term success." CFOs with excellent financial skills and experience were particularly important to providing this leadership.

About this time several major financial scandals occurred, including at the Department of Housing and Urban Development and with the nation's savings and loan institutions. The latter eventually became the single most costly government bailout in history; it persists to this day. This increased Darman's and Hodsoll's support for financial reform to help prevent even more calamities.

Bowsher said in 1996 that a 1990 meeting at the White House resulted in agreement that the Secretary of the Treasury, the Director of OMB, and the Comptroller General should establish a Federal Accounting Standards Advisory Board to consider and recommend accounting principles for the federal government; the nine-member board was authorized in October 1990. Also at the meeting, it was agreed to support legislation that resulted in the CFO Act.

This legislation had strong, bipartisan support on Capitol Hill. Senator John Glenn (D-Ohio), who as Chairman of the Committee on Government Affairs had long been a proponent of such legislation, introduced the CFO Act. Under the CFO Act, a few departments were mandated to start pilot projects that involved developing annual audited financial statements. Early successes in these pilots promoted the subsequent passage of the Government Management Reform Act of 1994, which extended the audit requirements to nearly all federal agencies.

Not content for Uncle Sam simply to keep his books properly, Capitol Hill would soon impose performance measurement requirements on agencies and bureaus (in the form of the Government Performance and Results Act of 1993) and tie them into the budget process. In 1996, Congress passed the Chief Information Officers Act and the Federal Financial Management Improvement Act partly because of the critical importance of technology to sound financial and performance management systems.

The Letter of the Law

Texts of the CFO Act, GPRA, GMRA, and FFMIA-96 may be found in Appendix B. The following highlights of the new reform legislation set the stage for a discussion of new roles for federal financial managers.

The Chief Financial Officers Act of 1990 (The CFO Act, P.L. 101-576, 104 Stat. 2838, as amended)

The CFO Act designated the Deputy Director for Management of OMB as the chief financial officer of the United States and required that a controller be appointed to direct the OMB Office of Federal Financial Management. In addition, a CFO and deputy CFO were to be designated at 16 of the 23 major executive agencies (later, the Social Security Administration [SSA] was added, to make 24).Ten pilot project agencies were selected to prepare agency-wide financial statements, to be audited by either an agency inspector general (IG), a public accounting firm, the GAO, or, for the military departments, their own audit agencies. The act has several objectives:

- To focus responsibility and authority for financial management in the position of CFO and, for continuity, in the statutory position of a career deputy CFO at the department level
- To provide for the improvement of agency accounting and financial management systems
- To establish a requirement for audited financial statements.

The act also addressed the need for performance measurement, laying the groundwork for the GPRA, and codified the federal CFO Council, which ensures continuity to financial management initiatives even as political leadership changes.

The Government Performance and Results Act of 1993 (GPRA, P.L. 103-62, 107 Stat. 285)

GPRA amends the Budget and Accounting Act of 1921 (P.L. 67-13, 42 Stat. 20) and is one of the few major amendments to that law dealing with performance as it relates to budgeting. GPRA is the primary legislative framework through which agencies will be required to set strategic goals, measure performance, and report on the degree to which goals were met. GPRA requires each federal agency to develop a strategic plan that covers a period of at least five years. This plan should include the agency's mission statement and identify its long-term goals. The act requires each agency, beginning in 1999, to submit an annual performance plan to OMB. GPRA also creates a process for each executive agency to use in measuring its annual financial and program performance by identifying four key performance indicators: output, outcome, efficiency, and effectiveness. Like the CFO Act, it sets up pilot projects that will give agencies experience in defining and reporting performance measures and goals. This includes pilot projects in performance budgeting in which, the law says, "Such budgets shall present, for one or more of the major functions and operations of the agency, the varying levels of performance, including outcome-related performance, that would result from different budgeted amounts."

GPRA adds a new dimension and character to the budget dialogue—funding decisions can be made on the objective measurement of program effectiveness instead of supposition. This will give congressional decision makers better information for allocating resources. Also, GPRA offers citizens the comfort that objective measurement may help cut through some of the politics surrounding budget issues.

The Government Management Reform Act of 1994 (GMRA, P.L. 103-356, 108 Stat. 3410)

GMRA amends the CFO Act to extend the agency-wide audited financial statement requirement to all 24 major executive agencies (including SSA) and their component agencies starting with FY 1996. The audited financial statements should present a picture of the overall financial position of each office bureau's assets and liabilities and a clear accounting of the results of operations. In addition, GMRA mandates that a consolidated financial statement for the entire Executive Branch be prepared by the Treasury Department and audited by the Comptroller General beginning in FY 1997.

The Chief Information Officers Act of 1996 (The CIO Act, P.L. 104-106, 110 Stat. 679)

This law is discussed in more detail in Chapter 4, so here we will focus on its place in the legislative history of federal financial management. On its surface this act may not appear to be a financial management statute, yet it is critical to the success of fiscal reform. To summarize, the CIO Act gives agencies more flexibility in acquiring information technology and mandates that an agency's CIO and CFO work together to develop financial and performance measurement systems.

The Federal Financial Management Improvement Act of 1996 (FFMIA-96, P.L. 104-208)

We abbreviate this law as FFMIA-96 to distinguish it from the Federal Managers' Financial Integrity Act (FMFIA).

Passed in September 1996, FFMIA-96 requires that agencies develop and maintain financial management systems that comply substantially with federal requirements for those types of systems. Agency systems are to be audited for compliance with the act, and agency heads are to report to the Congress on the implementation of remedial actions needed to bring systems in compliance. We discuss FFMIA-96 more in Chapter 4.

The Spirit of the Law

While the new reform legislation makes important structural and technical changes to the federal financial structure, the effect of the laws on people within that structure is equally important. Kevin Sabo, General Counsel to the House Subcommittee on Government Reform and Oversight, told us that "The CFO Act has certainly made a difference in that it rejuvenated hordes of government accountants at all levels. They are buoyed by the fact that government actually cares about financial management. If you had looked at a list of agencies that were dragging their feet four years ago, it would have been three times as long as it is today. Five years from now, we will find all agencies complying with the law as a matter of routine." In addition to the accountants, the new laws appear to be giving new life to sound management practices concepts such as strategic planning; customer-focused, results-oriented performance measurement; and useful managerial and cost accounting.

Having worked closely with many of the new federal CFOs, we believe that the reasons for their enthusiasm include the bipartisan support for the new laws, the structure of accountability they require, the sound principles of good stewardship they espouse, and the unified approach to politics, economics, and programs that the reforms force.

The Reforms Are Bipartisan Congressional Mandates

Democrats and Republicans in Congress and the Executive Branch support these laws. As bipartisan legislation, they stand outside overt political agendas and do not depend on personalities or specific administrations. For example, the

CFO Act was conceived in the Reagan Administration, born during Bush's, and strongly sustained and supported under Clinton's.

In addition, the reforms have never been touted as quick fixes. They are understood by supporters to require congressional and Executive Branch commitments well beyond the normal two-, four-, and six-year terms of office. Such long-term commitment is critical. According to Marion Harmon, when Vice President Gore asked several corporate executives to determine how long it takes to bring about cultural change in a private sector organization, they agreed on ten years.

In short, unless policy conforms with how Congress wants to manage the federal government, it is difficult for reform initiatives to succeed. However, because the power of such mandates springs from Congress, its members are ultimately responsible for sustaining the initiatives they create. A good way to do this is to continue oversight of the implementation of the reforms. The best way is actually to use the financial and performance information the reforms create for policy and budget decisions.

The Reforms Provide a Structure for Accountability

One of the limitations of Reform 88, FMFIA, and other initiatives was that they focused on compliance and reporting but did not really address systemic reforms and process improvement. The CFO Act develops accounting and reporting standards; requires annual audited financial statements; and creates an infrastructure of accountable officials throughout government. This and the other reform acts together create a new structure of government accountability at the OMB and agency levels.

The Reforms Are Based on Sound Principles of Good Stewardship

These new laws are not based on some academic or political thinktank notion of how to run a government. Instead, their foundation is a half-century of business and government experience in financial accounting and management. Indeed, most senior agency officials with whom we have worked stress the importance of the reforms in helping them to learn more about their business processes. This is certainly a fundamental principle of sound stewardship of the public trust. Indeed, nearly everyone accepts that meeting the requirements of the laws is not an end in and of itself. The focus on stewardship is the ultimate reward.

The Reforms Force a Union Among Politics, Economics, and Programs

CFO Ed DeSeve of the OMB says that the CFO Act, GMRA, and GPRA integrate economic realities with political proclivities by "forcing people to articulate thoroughly and thoughtfully the mission of an organization, its overall objectives, and its particular goals. As allocation decisions are made, as resources are connected to results, people will have a framework that is very clear. There is no murkiness." By creating this framework and clarity, the new reforms lay the groundwork for a true reinvention of how the federal government does business.

The Reforms Authorize CFOs to Take On Top Leadership Roles

The new reform legislation gives the top financial manager in a department or agency a position of authority equal to that of any other executive who reports to the organization's director. However, this is only an opportunity for leadership. To turn opportunity into reality, CFOs and their staffs must become partners with other agency executives and managers. To do this, they must learn new value-creating roles that go beyond the traditional functions of financial management. This is the subject of our next chapter.

Chapter

3

NEW ROLES FOR FINANCIAL MANAGERS

The CFO Act initiated a process of financial management reform aimed at improving how the federal government does business. For the process to succeed, agencies will require a new set of skills and capabilities best set forth in seven new roles for CFOs and financial managers:

1. **Strategist/visionary**, creating the future of the agency by working with teams of top executives during the strategic planning process
2. **Information manager**, providing everyone in the organization with critical information and analysis needed for sound business decisions
3. **Networker**, delivering hands-on service to managers and forming liaisons with key people and stakeholders outside the agency
4. **Innovator/entrepreneur**, applying new ideas and technology to both financial and operations processes
5. **Asset manager**, ensuring the quality and timeliness of systems for property, inventory, and other asset management and control
6. **Change manager**, helping to align the agency to new ways of doing business
7. **Policy maker**, taking a well-earned place in the highest forums of policy formulation.

These are personal roles. As an organization, the CFO office should strive for the role of Team Leader for financial aspects of agency improvement by:

- Producing sophisticated financial, performance, and strategic analyses
- Sharing the values of the rest of the agency
- Focusing on creating value for customers
- Fully integrating financial and performance data
- Giving program managers the financial skills and information they need for daily cost-effective decision making.

Once glorified bookkeepers, the best chief financial officers are now rounded players who orchestrate megadeals, fix troubled companies, and hatch creative ideas.
– Shawn Tully, in *Fortune,* November 13, 1995

The new reform legislation opened a window of opportunity for financial managers to become equal partners with other managers in the tough task of righting the federal government's fiscal ills. To go through the window, financial managers must, at a minimum, have the set of core competencies outlined in the box below; the set was developed by the federal CFO Council and the Joint Financial Management Improvement Program (JFMIP). This chapter discusses some of those competencies and the many roles financial managers must play in order to create value for agencies. Also, the CFO's organization must progress through several levels of competence before the group can achieve what we call the Team Leader role in financial management. We will start with an example of how a pre-CFO Act federal financial management pioneer and his staff started increasing the value they created for their agency.

**Core Competencies of Federal Financial Managers
(as Set Forth by the Federal CFO Council and the JFMIP)**
I. Strategic Vision
- Knowledge of applicable legislative, administrative, and regulatory requirements. Agency planning to include those of the GPRA and the impact of those requirements on external organizations and agency operations
- Knowledge of the strategic planning process and how it relates to the budget formulation process
- Ability to develop creative and innovative solutions to complex financial, budget, and program management issues
- Ability to identify problems and potential concerns, provide leadership, and involve others in decision-making process and build support for options that provide solutions

---

II. Resource and Program Management

- Knowledge of all applicable agency, legislative, administrative, and regulatory requirements that define resource management functions and their impacts on external organizations and agency operations
- Knowledge of structure of appropriations and other funds that support programs and mission of the agency and how fund management affects program achievement
- Ability to implement management control systems with the agency (including a quality assurance program and effective support for program auditors) respond to findings, and harness audit information to program improvement
- Knowledge of management and evaluation systems that use performance measurement and cost accounting and ability to use them to achieve program objectives
- Ability to acquire and administer financial information and ability to establish and administer management controls to provide information to and acquire information from appropriate systems and to disseminate that information to appropriate users
- Ability to prepare budget submissions according to prescribed format and specifications
- Detailed knowledge of assigned program/account areas
- Knowledge of and ability to use principles, methods, techniques, and systems of financial management to improve program effectiveness and customer service
- Skill at assessing customer needs and modifying program management to improve the delivery of goods and services to customers

III. Human Resource Management

- Knowledge of how human resources policies and practices support the missions and functions of the agency; applicable legislative, administrative, and regulatory requirements; and effects of human resources policies on external organizations and agency operations
- Ability to manage human resource planning, recruitment, and selection processes to acquire and maintain a diverse workforce in support of the agency's mission and to meet customer needs
- Skill at building teams and fostering cooperation throughout the organization

---

- Ability to organize workforce potential to meet the agency's strategic vision

IV. General

- Knowledge of the basic missions and functions of the agency; applicable legislative, administrative, and regulatory requirements; and effects of the office on external organizations and agency operations
- Ability to advocate positions, communicate information, and present ideas and instruction both orally and in writing to internal and external groups
- Ability to identify key internal and external contacts and maintain appropriate personal networks in support of organization's information needs and interests

Source: *Framework for Financial Management Personnel in the Federal Government,* Federal CFO Council, and Joint Financial Management Improvement Program, November 1995.

Federal Comptroller Adds Value to Agency Operations

In 1989, as Comptroller of the Defense Industrial Supply Center (DISC), George Allen told Coopers & Lybrand, "Operations managers here used to have to get permission from my office to use employee overtime, sometimes for only one hour, which might cost $15. Now, who in my office is qualified to say whether a manager needs the extra hour? And the approval paperwork cost us another $15.

"So we stopped doing that—it's the managers' job now. Instead, we've moved our accountants and analysts into management teams located in division offices, where they identify projects with savings potential and help managers solve problems. Now, about all we do in the comptroller's central office relates to specific appropriated and other accounts, and I need very few people for this.

"This was a common sense business decision. If I'm paying people a professional wage, they can't just approve overtime. I changed their job from one that did not add value to DISC's services to one that did. Besides, the guys in the comptroller shop were not happy approving forms and pushing paper. Out in the divisions, they work on meaningful things and see results measured in millions of dollars."

Once a rarity, executives like Allen are now forming a critical mass of champions for change in federal financial management—and they love their jobs. According to CFO SallyAnne Harper of the Environmental Protection Agency, "Because we are on the cutting edge of CFO development many of us have the faith of true believers, so I think we bring somewhat of an extra zeal to the work that we do." Enthused about the frontier they are taming, government's top money managers define their new roles in terms normally found in commerce: strategist, visionary, networker, innovator—in short, *leader.*

Personal Leadership Roles

Forward-looking senior financial executives play seven personal leadership roles in their quest to add value to agency services: strategist/visionary, information manager, networker, innovator/entrepreneur, asset manager, change manager, and policy maker. In doing so, they take a rightful place among the senior decision makers of their organizations.

Strategist and Visionary

By the end of FY 1997, nearly all federal agencies with funding of more than $20 million a year are required by the Government Performance and Results Act to develop five-year strategic plans. CFOs and other senior financial executives are in a unique position to add value to the strategic planning process for several reasons. First, given fiscal constraints, a significant portion of agency strategizing must focus on the most cost-effective way to achieve agency goals. Second, good strategy must be linked to financial management, budget formulation and execution, and internal controls, all of which are most CFOs' anchors in an agency. Third, a senior financial executive's work touches all parts of an agency. Next to the agency chief and deputy chief, a CFO must be more broadly knowledgeable about an agency's operations, issues, problems, and opportunities than anyone else.

Often, none of the above is true in government. C&L consultants in our government practice have participated in hundreds of federal strategic planning sessions and have observed two disturbing things about them. First, executives in most agencies rarely discuss issues of sound financial management when developing agency strategy. Second, they rarely use financial analysis when deciding on strategy options—even when the CFO or other senior financial executives take part in the strategy sessions.

Typically, the financial executives remain largely silent throughout the planning meetings, occasionally responding to questions from other executives such as, "Do we have the budget for that?" but not "What is the most cost-effective strategy?" or "What are your ideas for a strategy in this area?" In this situation, a financial executive is a simply a source of moderately useful technical information, not a strategist. The dynamic of the meetings makes it clear that, in many organizations, financial executives are not yet considered equal partners with other senior leaders of their organizations.

Financial executives wanting a value-creating role in strategic planning start by providing the type of financial and other information needed to give it a solid foundation. This includes analyses of financial trends, cost/benefit comparisons of alternate strategies, and other financial data that will inform and focus strategic decisions (see Chapter 7 for more on this subject). By doing this, a financial executive becomes intimately familiar, from a financial perspective, with an agency's most important business issues. Then, he or she can contribute this sorely needed fiscal view not only to strategy discussions, but also to projects designed to execute strategy. For example, methods such as activity-based costing and business process redesign offer an opportunity for CFOs and financial managers to become knowledgeable quickly about an agency's key processes while at the same time contributing their financial analysis skills to improvement initiatives. (See Chapter 10 for a discussion of these methods.)

As important as these contributions are, CFOs have to go beyond them to win their way into the small, powerful circle of executives who make the really tough strategy decisions. The price of admission is vision. Referring to the private sector, Treasury Department CFO George Muñoz told us, "The CFOs are leaders in terms of having a vision of where the company is going, they have input into how to meet strategies and goals, and many times they are seen as potential successors to CEOs because they have the same attributes as the top executive." Rising to the top of an agency is rare for a government financial manager, but not without precedent. As cost-effective governance grows more important in the eyes of Congress and citizens, we expect to see more strategist/visionary CFOs take the helm of their organizations.

Information Manager

Providing information has become a pivotal role in all organizations. Traditionally, it is one of the core roles of financial managers, who either "own" much of an agency's information or use it in annual financial statements. The new reform legislation creates more demand for information, but not necessarily for traditional financial data delivered well after events in formats that do not meet the needs of program managers.

As discussed in Chapter 9, an ability to match agency results to costs is an underlying assumption behind the performance-based organization (PBO) concept now being tested in several federal organizations. A PBO is to operate with greater flexibility and freedom than other agencies, provided it meets its performance goals and standards. This elevates the importance of measuring financial and operational results and demands that the measures be integrated.

The most useful information for a program manager is that which solves a problem, creates an opportunity, or predicts future problems and opportunities. Most financial managers can produce historical measures, but few can explain how to apply the data to identifying and evaluating operational problems, and fewer still know how to predict cost trends. When asked "Where should we focus improvement investments to save the most money?" most financial managers are discovering that they cannot calculate the costs of processes and rank them in order of resource consumption. Nor do most financial systems provide the data needed for make/buy decisions, apples-to-apples comparisons of internal versus contractor service offers, or accurate unit costs for agency products and services, without which a PBO cannot prove its effectiveness.

Providing timely information is as critical as is being accurate, according to CFO Dennis Fischer of the General Services Administration. He told us "Even after receiving a clean audit opinion* in 1994, I felt we had a material weakness in our own backyard because we couldn't provide managers with information on a timely basis to manage with during the year. There are all these indicators, but we don't provide the managers with the information they need on an ongoing basis. Clean audit opinions don't help the manager who is out there wondering how much money he has left to spend. So I declared it as a material weakness. And we have done some things that now make that data available and accessible to managers." Fischer has been pushing up the timeline for producing GSA's annual financial reports by one month every year. He believes the agency can get close to what he perceives as the private sector benchmark of 30 days following the end of the fiscal year. The tighter the date and the better the data, the more useful the information will be. "The management payoff to me," says Fischer, "is when a program manager who is thinking about making an investment gets information out of our accounting system and doesn't even consider that the information might be inaccurate."

---

*An unqualified audit opinion, indicating that auditors believe that financial statements fairly present the operations and financial condition of the reporting entity

We believe that financial managers must be proactive in providing this information, asking their program manager customer what is required, when, and in what form. This will do more to forge the desired partnership between financial and program managers than any other single effort.

Figure 3-1

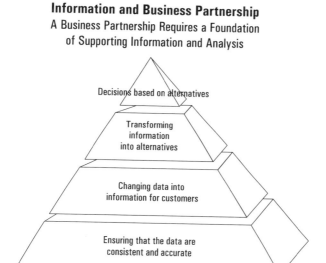

Information and Business Partnership
A Business Partnership Requires a Foundation
of Supporting Information and Analysis

Decisions based on alternatives

Transforming
information
into alternatives

Changing data into
information for customers

Ensuring that the data are
consistent and accurate

Networker

As CFOs step out of their offices and into executive board rooms, they must start honing their communication and networking skills. The same is true for financial managers who work on teams with program managers. Successful financial managers understand their organizations, establish credibility within them, and create liaisons both within and without the agency. A keen understanding of an agency's culture and internal politics is critical to leveraging opportunities and moving into areas where financial managers have not traditionally tread.

An agency's culture can be based on upwards of two centuries of operation, or on the nature of its business or the primary professionals who work within its walls—most of whom are not financial specialists. Politically, an agency can be seen as a network of personal relationships that can go back for decades. If a financial manager has not grown up, professionally speaking, in this environment, then he or she must talk to people, learn, and understand an agency's intricacies. Financial managers must focus on building relationships that will keep them from walking over a cliff, and also build up reservoirs of good will for protection for when things get tough.

GSA's Fischer told us, "You have to be hands-on and you've got to just be there. You need to try to help the organization in its basic mission. We touch customers through my colleagues in a lots of places, so I find it extremely important to network with the customers, to be a representative of GSA's programs. But most important is just being there and being involved, so that you can respond with some credibility and say, 'This is my view from a management perspective.'" Indeed, financial managers make a critical mistake when they have a narrow perspective focused only on financial issues. When co-author Morgan Kinghorn became CFO of the Internal Revenue Service, he told his staff, "We are not here to do financial management per se, but rather to help improve tax administration."

External networking is critical, too, and not just when an agency or program faces a budget cut or negative report from an oversight organization or committee. At the top, value-creating CFOs and senior financial executives network with key congressional staff and Executive Branch senior leaders. They work with executives in other agencies to develop joint projects such as shared services and franchising. They actively support the federal CFO Council agenda and participate in its activities. They are in touch with their professional colleagues in both government and industry; financial managers at lower levels do the same in order to maintain their competencies and gain new ideas. Building such networks helps the CFO maintain a leadership position in an agency and helps the agency become a leader in its field.

Innovator/Entrepreneur

Financial managers must be innovative, constantly looking for new tools and opportunities. This means not accepting restrictions as givens, but instead searching for ways to overcome them.

Recently, the CFO of one of our federal agency clients was asked by the departmental secretary to be a financial innovator in supporting the strategic planning process and its resulting improvement initiatives. Wall Street analysts sit up and take notice when private sector CFOs assume this role. If the Internal Revenue Service were a private corporation, the analysts would have made a star of Carl Moravitz, the IRS Budget Director who used his knowledge and experience with budgeting rules that some might see as restrictive to assemble an innovative $2 billion package of additional investments to increase tax compliance. Wall Street analysts also are hot to invest in entrepreneurial companies that find new ways to make money. They would recommend buying stock in the Patent and Trademark Office, which has been operating without appropriated funds since 1991 because user fees made the agency self-sufficient. Ditto for the Immigration and Naturalization Service and the Veterans Benefits Administration, where entrepreneurial financial managers are leading the way in creating solid fee structures to pay for some services. The analysts are keen to alert investors to companies that break outmoded traditions to become more competitive. A cash-only business for 200 years, the U.S. Postal Service was convinced that accepting credit and debit cards at Post Office counters would cost more than handling cash. Spurred by its treasurer, the organization conducted activity-based costing analyses and learned that the cards actually cost less, so that now postal patrons can buy stamps with plastic. Anyone who thinks that financial managers are too conservative to be entrepreneurs needs to pay a visit to these federal organizations.

To be innovative and entrepreneurial, financial managers need to arm themselves with tools for creative thinking. These include computerized process and financial model and simulations that test assumptions of growth and the fiscal impact of alternative solutions for process improvement. More basically, financial managers must be able to supply the financial data needed for such models, and to help identify what drives costs and performance in existing processes. Activity-based costing is a sound approach for developing this type of information.

Asset Manager

Asset manager is a radically new role for most agency CFOs, although a few have been playing it for years. For example, as the agency asset manager, a CFO works with logistics managers to ensure the quality and timeliness of systems for property and inventory management and control. Other asset areas, such as credit, loan portfolios, and other forms of debt, also must be high on the list of some CFOs' priorities. Financial auditors are deeply interested in the valuation and control of assets, so there is a natural fit between the asset manager role and a CFO's other fiscal stewardship responsibilities.

At the Federal Bureau of Investigation (FBI), the CFO is the head of the Financial Division, which has a property, procurement, and management section responsible for property and inventory. However, most other agencies have a separate logistics and procurement division that handles these functions. In such cases, initially there may be misunderstanding and even turf battles between the CFO and acquisitions or logistics managers. To overcome this barrier, CFOs must find ways to demonstrate clearly how they can add value to logistics processes, thus winning the cooperation and coordination of logistics managers.

We have seen many benefits to this new role. One is a dramatic increase in communications and coordination between CFO offices and other agency components that work with assets. Another is a net improvement in asset management. As CFOs become more involved in this area, they are finding many problems, such as asset management processes that are insufficient, outmoded, even nonexistent. Inefficiencies in these areas can tie up millions of dollars, and CFOs are taking the lead in correcting them. For example, at the Department of Education, financial and program improvements almost doubled the amount collected on defaulted student loans—an extra $1 billion in 1995.

Change Manager

CFOs newly appointed must understand there are limitations and barriers to establishing a broader role for the financial organization. The culture of the financial organization or of other parts of an agency may not be supportive of these new roles, at least at first. Some financial managers do not want to change their old ways, and many program officials simply do not want financial managers "mucking in their business."

The first step is to gain support from the very top of the organization. If top leaders support a proactive CFO, then he or she can move on to working with the program managers. If top support is uncertain, then the CFO must manage upwards, providing convincing evidence of the value of the finance organization's involvement in business affairs. In the private sector, CFOs are considered partners and advisors to CEOs because the financial executives provide information and insight valuable in making critical decisions. Federal CFOs who do this can expect the same level of support from the top as their colleagues in business.

Next, the CFO must work on changing the culture and processes of the financial organization, to align these with the mission, goals, and objectives of the parent agency. This is a continuing task, because financial processes will undergo substantial changes as governments move further into the Information Age.

Having started the change process within the financial organization, the CFO's next target is the agency's other managers. One way to bring them aboard is through the daily value-creating contributions to their operations by the new breed of financial managers. Another is to carefully plan for a culture change among program managers that will make cost-effectiveness one of their primary values. This is discussed more in Chapter 10 under change management.

Policy Maker

The CFO Act sets the legislative groundwork that helps move the CFO from simply observing the execution of policy to helping develop it. Transportation Department CFO Louise Frankel Stoll says "What the CFO Act did was to empower somebody like me to move quite freely through an organization where there were troublesome financial issues and force reconsideration of the issues in order to make them manageable. From a content point of view, I wouldn't presume what should be on an air traffic controller's desk, but I can be given options and help make decisions about that as a policy-oriented person."

While the CFO Act provides the CFO a chair at the policy table, simply focusing on basic finance functions is not enough to fill it. CFOs become policy partners by developing their financial organizations into business partners at lower levels, and by providing top executives with information and insights that otherwise would not be available to them. Private sector CEOs expect this of their CFOs; it should be no different in the public sector.

Ultimately, it is the political savvy of the policy maker that distinguishes the public sector CFO from his or her corporate colleagues. Says Kevin Sabo, General Counsel for the House Committee on Government Reform and Oversight, "I used to think that private sector experience should be a prerequisite for the job of CFO, but I no longer feel that way. It takes a whole different breed of individual to know how to come up to Capitol Hill and sway a committee."

Policy and Budget Control

Budgets are the most important manifestation of policy. When CFOs have responsibility for the budget process, they gain access to everything an agency does and have an authoritative voice in policy decisions. Says Fischer, "I think it is important for the federal CFO to have responsibility for the budget function. Some of my colleagues might disagree; I think their organizations and their jobs suffer as a consequence. Your budget function brings you visibility; it gives you clout."

From the very beginning stages of the development of the CFO Act, OMB emphasized that a CFO cannot function effectively without a strong budgetary role. Even more, we believe that an agency's success in implementing financial reforms is directly linked to how well and pervasively a CFO influences and controls the budget.

These, then, are the personal roles that CFOs and financial managers must play to succeed. A CFO should periodically evaluate his or her personal abilities and those of the financial staff against these roles. No one is likely to be strong in all roles, but collectively the strength of the financial organization should make it a leader among all other components in an agency. In a moment, we will discuss the organizational leadership role of the CFO office, but first want to emphasize that none of the new roles will be accepted if financial managers lack credibility.

Financial Process Improvement: Key to Credibility in the New Roles

Financial managers start to improve agency operations by first focusing on the efficiency and effectiveness of their own traditional financial functions (fiduciary accounting, internal controls, transaction processing). Usually, these functions can be done better and for less money. Success in improving them builds credibility with other parts of an agency. Financial managers have specific responsibilities for improving their own processes:

- Reviewing financial policies and procedures for their practicality and relevance, and designing them to increase their efficiency and effectiveness
- Working with program managers to build internal controls into processes, which transforms the controls into value-creating enablers of process control and improvement

- Reducing the cost and cycle time of financial processes, while improving their effectiveness in providing information for business decisions.

There are good reasons for focusing on process improvement during the early stages of transforming a financial organization. Tangible results such as cost savings and other improvements will free up funds for other financial initiatives or simply reduce an agency's cost of meeting its mission. Working on improvements will introduce financial managers to the concepts of processes and process-based management, making them more valuable to program management teams using similar approaches.

Increasingly, these program managers are becoming concerned with financial analysis and information capabilities, and will develop them with or without leadership from their agency's financial professionals. For example, federal agencies are just starting to develop managerial cost accounting systems, the standards for which were developed by financial professionals in the FASAB. It is up to internal financial organizations to lead the way in implementing the systems, but to do so they must achieve a level of financial management maturity not normally found among federal agencies.

Gauging the Maturity of the Financial Organization

In some societies, a person is said to have reached maturity when, in the judgment of other adults, he or she has successfully carried out adult roles and responsibilities. Likewise, a financial organization is mature when managers in other parts of an agency consider it an equal, value-creating partner. Gauging the maturity of a financial organization means evaluating answers to the following questions:

- What is the financial organization's primary role now, and what should it be in the future?
- Is the financial organization involved and knowledgeable about the business of its agency?
- How can financial managers become business partners with operations managers?

Below, we suggest some ways for determining the answers.

A Vision of Maturity

Working toward maturity means that a financial organization has developed or is developing among its people the qualities and characteristics discussed earlier under personal roles. Most successful CFOs start with the visionary role, developing a view toward the future of what their financial organizations will become. Figure 3-2 is a private sector example of such a vision, from Johnson & Johnson's finance group. Except for tax management, the vision covers virtually every area of what a typical federal financial group does.

Vision of the Johnson & Johnson Finance Group

Figure 3-2

Business partnership. Act as a business partner and be productive and innovative in the application of financial knowledge and techniques to help solve business problems and maximize business opportunities.

Organizational excellence. Achieve organizational excellence by developing and maintaining a strong organization with self-perpetuating characteristics and high standards in a creative and productive atmosphere.

Technological leadership. Maintain technological leadership by ensuring optimal efficiency in our systems and computer operations and build strategic business alliances with our customers and suppliers. Capitalize on advancements in information technology.

Cash and tax management. Take a leadership role in the conservation of assets, control of spending, management of taxes, and management of cash flow.

Audit and control. Maintain an internal control environment that will provide management with reasonable assurances that assets are safeguarded from unauthorized use or disposition and that financial records are accurate and reliable. Ensure that the requirements are met in an effective and efficient manner and are flexible enough to adapt to changing business conditions or requirements. Due consideration should be given to appropriate automation applications and resource limitations.

Source: *Reinventing the CFO.*

Gauging Maturity

Figure 3-3 is a Coopers & Lybrand QuikGrid for gauging the maturity of a financial organization in the role of business partner with other parts of an agency. We use this primarily with private sector CFO organizations, and have adapted it somewhat for the public sector. The bold titles at the top of the figure show the maturity of the financial organization that is best defined by the characteristics of each

Figure 3-3

Financial Organization Maturity QuikGrid

Lagging *Conformer*	Behind *Reactor*	Median *Controller*	Ahead *Team Player*	Leading *Team Leader*
• Basic finance functions • CFO spends 90%-100% of time on basic functions • Financial functions separate from operations • Focus on control and compliance • Regulations • Bureaucratic • Isolated "silo" structure with primary loyalties to parent organization financial types	• Basics, occasional special analyses • CFO time on basics = 70%-90% resources • Reluctant participant in operations decisions • Exercises veto power based on budget rules • Occasional team member • Aloof, "we-they" attitude • Centralized services	• Basics, some routine analyses • CFO time on basics = 50%-70% • Financial control of operations • Traditional oversight • Frequently involved in team projects • Team leader in finance-oriented projects • Improves financial processes • Centralized services • Some integrated financial data bases	• Basics, many routine analyses of finance and performance • CFO time on basics = 30%-50% • Financial managers are team workers who help create value • Integrated financial information • Cross-functional training • Shared goals with operations units • Some finance professionals work in cross-functional process teams • Most financial data are integrated • Accepts project responsibility • Operations managers assuming more financial roles	• Basics, many sophisticated analyses on finance, performance, and strategy • CFO time on basics = 20%-30% • Shared values with entire agency • Focus on value creation • Delivers results • Market focus • Sought out for business knowledge • Most financial professionals work cross-functional teams • Financial and performance data fully integrated • Operations managers capable of most routine financial analyses

column. The italicized roles below the titles refer to the organization, not the individuals in it.

There are two basic trends in this shift from old to new roles:

From separate to shared structure and values. In the Conformer and Reactor roles on the left columns of Figure 3-3, the financial organization is a structure separate and apart from the rest of the agency. The goals and values of the financial organization are aligned with another, higher-level financial office in a parent agency or department, not with those of the operations managers of the rest of the agency. This is a key reason why operations managers distrust financial organizations—in a very real sense, the latter work for somebody else. In the Team Player and Team Leader roles in the right columns, the financial organization's goals and values are the same as those of the rest of the agency.

From basic to advanced services. As the financial organization matures, it offers ever more sophisticated services to the rest of the agency. Many are advanced analyses needed for strategic decisions. Starting at the Ahead stage on the right side of the figure, financial professionals also are teaching operations managers the basics of management accounting, and assuring that data that link finance and performances are available when needed. One good measure of progress in this area is the time the CFO or other senior financial executives spend on basic financial functions. The more time they devote to advanced services and team leadership, the more likely the financial organization is maturing.

Devices such as the QuikGrid are meant to help guide discussion of the future role of a financial organization. The most value can be derived from this and other types of assessment tools by finding out how internal customers would rate their financial organizations. Ways to do this include surveys and focus groups of managers from different components in an agency. A written survey of the managers might include the questions shown in Figure 3-4. Note

Figure 3-4

Sample Questions from the Coopers & Lybrand Finance Alignment Survey

Circle the Number that Applies:

My agency's finance organization:	**Disagree**	**Agree**	**Not a Priority**	**Top Priority**
Makes accurate financial assumptions in agency-wide and business unit strategic planning processes	1 2 3 4 5		1 2 3 4 5	
Tracks and analyses information that is predictive and actionable	1 2 3 4 5		1 2 3 4 5	
Assists management in measuring its performance against the approved strategic and operating plans	1 2 3 4 5		1 2 3 4 5	
Effectively builds financial controls into business processes	1 2 3 4 5		1 2 3 4 5	

From your perspective, is your finance organization more concerned with managing cost relative to value or simply cutting costs?

Describe initiatives your business unit has taken to manage costs. Describe the role the finance organization has played in these initiatives.

From your perspective, what is the CFO's primary role in supporting your business unit's operations? In what ways would you like to see that role evolve?

Source: Adapted from *Reinventing the CFO*

that the questionnaire asks a manager's perception of the financial organization's performance in a particular area and the relative importance of the area to the manager. A CFO's plans for improvement should focus on areas that are most important to managers, but where they think performance is lowest. Also, averaging the scores of the numeric response questions in Figure 3-4 provides baseline data on levels of customer satisfaction, against which a financial organization can measure its improvement progress. Open-ended queries like those at the bottom of the figure are good for collecting more detailed information from customers.

Becoming a Team Leader

To achieve the Team Player level of maturity in the area of business involvement and knowledge, financial organizations provide several types of services:

- Analyze financial and performance information that is predictive and actionable
- Reduce the time between an event and the availability to program managers of measures related to the event
- Participate with program managers in the development of planning models that reflect key drivers of value. This requires financial managers to understand an agency's processes and what causes process performance to vary
- Maintain awareness of and constantly incorporate leading-edge financial and business processes from outside the agency
- Make valuable, acknowledged contributions while serving on cross-functional teams with operations and other managers
- Build sensible and sensitive internal controls into processes so that process managers can prevent undesirable risk and detect problems early
- Quickly adapt financial systems to program requirements and business needs
- Work with teams to identify, quantify, and reduce the amount of non-value-added activities in nonfinancial processes
- Assist management in measuring performance against strategic goals and objectives.
- Provide reliable product or service cost information, both for existing and planned products; also, provide information on the cost differences of serving specific external customers or customer groups

- Teach operations managers to use basic financial analysis tools and techniques as part of their normal work.

In the rest of this book we will describe and discuss methods and tools that financial managers have been using in government and industry to deliver these services. There is much good technical information in the following chapters, along with examples and insights from the experiences of federal CFOs, legislators, ourselves, and others. However, our key message to the federal financial community is in this chapter on new roles: Have a bias for action, be willing to learn, and embrace the changes required for partnership and leadership.

Chapter

4

SYSTEMS AND SOLUTIONS

Federal financial managers and inspectors general say that lack of integrated systems is the major barrier to implementing the CFO Act. Indeed, up to 80 percent of the data needed for tasks such as preparing financial statements is located outside financial information systems. However, some organizations have achieved clean financial audits despite systems limitations. Thus, systems integration is only part of the solution to CFOs' data requirements.

- Recent federal rules, especially the CIO Act, give CFOs more flexibility in developing new systems.
- Operating under a strategic information plan helps prevent an unfocused approach to financial systems development.
- Understanding financial processes and how organizational culture relates to use of financial information must precede development of new systems.
- Overcoming resistance to new systems and to using new types of information requires leadership and user involvement.
- Instead of a single financial management system, many organizations may need to think in terms of a unified set of systems.
- Commercial off-the-shelf software offers solutions with many advantages over customized software, but few agencies are using it.

The information we have is not what we want.
The information we want is not what we need.
The information we need is not available.
                    —John Peers, Logical Machine Corp.

It's a two-part process. Without modern systems, you cannot
achieve integration. Without integration, you cannot achieve CFO.
          —Jack Nutter, Defense Finance and Accounting Service

Today, developing and mastering integrated information systems are the keys to organizing information—and such control is what gives managers the facts they need to make cost-effective decisions. If the financial organization is mired in yesterday's technology, it will lose its information-based leverage in policy making and business partnership.

It should come as no surprise, then, that our 1995 survey showed that about one-third of federal senior financial managers and one-half of IG offices said that *lack of integrated financial systems* was the greatest barrier to implementing the CFO Act. As shown in Figure 1-2 in Chapter 1, this problem far surpassed any other. In this chapter, we look at why this problem came to be and how it is being solved.

The Federal Financial Data Archipelago

As of the end of FY 1995, the agencies covered by the CFO Act reported that they had 820 financial information systems consisting of 1,181 applications in operation, and 106 systems under development or being phased in. Figure 4-1 summarizes some of the characteristics of and plans for these systems. Only one-third of the applications shown are part of a single, integrated financial management system. Thus, they cannot share data easily, making it difficult to communicate about cross-functional financial issues or create consolidated information.

The systems shown in the figure are for financial management information. Savvy financial managers know that up to 80 percent of the data they need for activities such as preparing CFO Act financial statements reside in *non*financial systems, as we discuss in Chapter 5. Unfortunately, a significant portion of the data is ferreted away in countless unofficial systems that exist as one-of-a-kind written ledgers or computer spreadsheets. Individual managers often develop the invisible systems to track budgets and to make deci-

Figure 4-1

Financial Systems in Agencies Covered by the CFO Act, FY 1992-95	FY 1992	FY 1993	FY 1994	FY 1995
Agency financial management systems in operation	878	804	816	820
Agency financial management applications in operation	1,306	1,273	1,183	1,181
Part of single, integrated financial management system*	N/A	N/A	29%	34%
Designated as standard application for the department	N/A	26%	29%	34%
Planned to be replaced within five years	24%	29%	31%	29%
Planned to be upgraded	25%	23%	24%	26%
More than ten years old	30%	34%	39%	44%
Implemented or upgraded during the year	23%	19%	19%	10%
Using commercial off-the-shelf software (COTS)	13%	12%	10%	10%
Fully implementing the federal standard general ledger	30%	31%	34%	40%
Meeting agency standards for computing environment	55%	52%	63%	66%

*As defined by OMB Circular A-127.
Source: Federal Financial Management Status Report & Five-Year Plan, U.S. Office of Management & Budget and the federal CFO Council, June 1996.

sions about costs, because the official systems produce data that are outdated or just plain meaningless.

Thus, much of the body of federal financial and performance information is uncharted frontier—no one really knows what is out there. If charted, it would likely resemble the Indonesian archipelago, because the federal financial information frontier is made up of thousands of isolated database islands. Many have a distinctive language, ranging from Stone Age to Space Age in sophistication, and they rarely communicate with each other or the central government. It is not unusual to find systems within the same

Figure 4-2

The Federal Financial Data Archipelago

agency—even the same office—that cannot share data without costly, duplicative, error-prone rekeying.

Archipelagos are heaven for anthropologists, but hell on accountants. Realizing this, OMB has a long-term goal of unifying or integrating a common set of federal financial information. Given the diversity of financial information needs among the many federal agencies, Uncle Sam will probably never achieve a single, unified financial *system,* but has a good chance of *integrating* the national government's financial *systems.* This integration will take years, but agency-level progress in financial management and reporting need not wait. How to progress is critical. Since the mid-1980s both military and civilian agencies have seen

computing power available at ever lower costs, yet computer use has increased without proportionally higher benefits.

Are Systems the Solution?

While we agree with federal CFO and IG offices that lack
of systems integration is a major barrier, it is a symptom of
more serious problems that prevent agencies from producing useful and reliable financial information. According to
Ernest Gregory, Deputy Assistant Secretary of the Army for
Financial Operatons, "It's about information, not about systems. Information is the answer, not systems." For decades
very large private organizations obtained clean audit opinions without benefit of computers. Federal agencies with
antiquated financial information systems, as was the case at
the Social Security Administration, have been able to garner
a clean opinion, while some agencies with modern systems
have not yet done so.

The difference among these agencies, CFO Dennis
Fischer of GSA believes, is an attitude and operational ethic
that says "Even though our system is not the greatest, we
are going to get the right results." He continues, "Every
agency has problems. Some will be fixed by systems.
Others will be fixed by just taking a process apart and
putting it back together. A good example of that at GSA is
in the area of travel, which is pretty straightforward and
simple. But we did not rush in and acquire an automation
package for travel. We can reengineer travel processes
enough so that when we finish we won't need an automated
system at all. We will rely on other pieces already in place,
like using the time-keeping system to reimburse for miscellaneous expenses, so that we are not going to require
automation that is specific to travel processes. This comes
from looking at a process from start to finish and asking
'Why?'" (*See* Chapter 9 for a discussion of GSA's reengineered travel system.)

Understanding Precedes Systems Development
Financial managers have to learn to ask the right "whys" so
that they and their subordinates can understand the issues

involved in systems development *before* undertaking such projects. For example, OMB Controller Ed DeSeve thinks that generating an auditable financial statement should *precede* systems integration. The discipline of and insights derived from producing an auditable statement will help guide the improvement of that process and the development of systems that support it. Typically, the designers of financial systems "determine" what information is needed by asking users what information they require or would like to have. This practice is based on the often erroneous assumption that users know what information they need, actually want it, and will use it in the desired way. Frequently, users and financial managers are caught in the paradigm represented by the type of information that has been available in the past, instead of new information that would help them create value for customers or comply with new fiscal regulations. Until users and financial managers understand their processes, their own information needs, and those of their customers, they cannot answer the fundamental systems design questions: What do you need to know? Why do you need that information, and how will you use it? When do you need the information, and in what format?

Culture, Numbers, and Systems

Understanding how new systems may change an organization's culture is critical, because this will affect systems design and usage. For example, if an agency has a culture in which program managers trust only their gut feelings to make decisions, why should better, more timely information by *itself* cause them to behave any differently? An overly bureaucratic culture can subvert the best designed system. A case in point is the use of agency credit cards. According to Elaine Kamarck, senior National Performance Review policy advisor to Vice President Al Gore: "Here we have the ability to use a government-wide credit card for small purchases. It is very simple to use this card. It is slightly more complicated than using your own personal credit card, because with the government card you have to shop around for the lowest price, but it is not terribly complicated. Yet some agencies are putting lower limits on purchases made with it, which is nuts. Other agencies are requiring pages of documentation for card purchases, when the whole purpose of it is that you don't need that level of documentation. The credit card company statement shows what you bought, for how much, on what day, etc. These agencies are recreating the procurement system that we got rid of legislatively—increasingly, the barriers are internal, a terrible problem."

Cowpaths versus Transformational Technology

Finally, the issue of paving cowpaths versus using transformation technology requires keen executive attention. Paving cowpaths means using information technology to automate existing processes without improving the workflows or other components of these operations. Often, the result is to do the wrong things faster. A natural tendency exists for financial personnel to want to automate processes exactly the way they are now. They may reject changes brought about by new technology as unproved, unfriendly, or even as being against regulation. Financial executives must be alert to this tendency in order to prevent it from causing an agency to miss the transformational benefits of technology.

Transformational technology is that which completely changes an operation so that it performs at vastly higher levels of efficiency and effectiveness than before. Credit cards are transformational technology when they eliminate the need for petty cash funds and paper work, capture purchase data once at the source for many uses, and create audit trails that make IGs happy. Other examples include communications groupware such as Lotus Notes™, data warehouses, bar codes, artificial intelligence systems, and electronic commerce and data interchange technology. Beyond just saving costs and improving financial systems, these technologies frequently offer ways to create new value in an agency's most important products and services. Such technology changes so rapidly that forward-looking CFOs often set up teams to stay abreast of new developments.

Performance Measurement and Financial Information Systems Face Similar Issues

Financial system issues also apply to performance measurement systems, the development of which is a major task required by the GPRA. Agency leaders should not delay performance measurement that brings valuable information to headquarters and program managers in the field simply because existing systems cannot produce 100 percent reliable data. Delay means losing valuable experience with the performance measurement process and the opportunity to start integrating it immediately in an agency's culture. Chapter 8 is a detailed discussion of federal performance measurement requirements and issues.

CFOs Should Not Delegate Responsibilities for Systems Development and Implementation

There can be major problems if the information technology resources needed to develop and implement financial systems are not directly controlled by the CFO office or if the CFO is not seen as the primary customer of such systems. Although they espouse the need to integrate systems, most organizations are uncomfortable doing this because it involves tradeoffs, compromises, and internal politics. More seriously, integration means making information from one work unit or function available to others, which makes some managers nervous. Because of this, the CFO office's interests are best served by controlling the requirements and resources of financial systems development and implementation. The exception may be when there are excellent institutional linkages and working relationships between financial and information managers, but even then the CFO must have strong control over the effort.

One reason for this is that there are too many nontechnology issues, such as process and culture, involved in the success of financial and performance measurement systems for CFOs to delegate their responsibilities completely to information specialists. CIOs and systems engineers are important partners in financial and performance measurement information initiatives, but they may not be capable of addressing all the issues.

For example, CFOs and other financial executives must see to it that financial managers and employees understand, need, receive, and use the information and capabilities new systems can deliver, and that the information complies with the law. This is a critical task, because often users will be receiving the information for the first time. Also, financial executives must ensure that changes to financial processes and systems are coordinated and aligned. Finally, the huge price tags of many financial information systems often make them a CFO's largest incremental cost. Sound stewardship requires intimate understanding and control of the details of the full spectrum of activities needed for success.

Relevant Laws and Guidance for Financial Management Information Systems

The CFO Act makes an agency CFO responsible for all agency financial management operations, activities, and personnel, including producing financial information, establishing an integrated financial management system, developing cost information, and conducting systematic performance measurement.

The CIO Act provides that the chief information officer and CFO, or a comparable official of each agency, develop an accounting, financial, and asset management system that is reliable, consistent, and timely.

The Federal Financial Management Improvement Act requires agencies to establish financial management systems to support full disclosure of financial data; to report on how they now or will comply with the act; and to have their financial systems audited for compliance with this act.

OMB Circular A-127, *Financial Management Systems,* prescribes policies and standards for executive departments and agencies to follow in developing, operating, evaluating, and reporting on financial management systems. These policies and standards must be satisfied in setting requirements for cost accounting systems.

Framework for Federal Financial Management Systems, Joint Financial Management Improvement Program (JFMIP). This document defines what is meant by a single, integrated agency financial management system and describes the framework for establishing and maintaining such a system.

Federal Accounting Standards Advisory Board recommendations, especially the *Managerial Cost Accounting Standards,* require that each reporting entity accumulate and report the costs of its activities using a cost accounting system. The FASAB is working on cost accounting systems requirements that will build upon and provide the means to implement requirements arising out of GPRA, the FASAB, OMB circulars, and other sources.

Other OMB Circulars. Financial systems should be designed to meet the information reporting and other requirements outlined in the following OMB circulars:

- **A-11,** *Preparation and Submission of Budget*, establishes policies and procedures for the preparation and submission of budget estimates to the OMB.
- **A-25,** *User Changes*, establishes guidelines for federal agencies to determine fees assessed for government services and prices for the sale or use of government property and resources.
- **A-34,** *Instructions on Budget Execution*, establishes requirements for apportionment of funds and reports on budget execution.
- **A-76,** *Performance of Commercial Activities*, provides guidelines for comparing costs of internal commercial-like operations to the costs of those offered by vendors.
- **A-123,** *Management Accountability and Control*, provides guidance on improving the accountability and effectiveness of federal programs and operations by establishing, assessing, correcting, and reporting on management controls.
- **A-130,** *Management of Federal Information Resources*, establishes policies for managing information, information systems, and information technology.

Federal Mandates and Guidelines on Financial Management Information Systems

Four or five decades ago, a well-respected expert in the field predicted that all U.S. data processing requirements could be met by six large computers. Today, there are many more computers in America than people, if you count the ubiquitous chips found in everything from aircraft to toasters. This has caused a profound transformation in the way we think about computing and systems, from centralization to decentralization. Nowhere is this more evident than in the Chief Information Officers Act, which governs information technology (IT) acquisition and establishes requirements for information systems.

The predecessor to the CIO Act was the Automatic Data Processing Equipment Act of 1965, or the Brooks Act after its author, then Representative Jack Brooks (D-Tex). According to a July 1996 report by the Congressional Research Service, the Brooks Act was intended to centralize and coordinate the acquisition of ADP equipment through the GSA. This requirement made sense in a large mainframe ADP environment characterized by centralized operations and shared services. In the ensuing years, however, many thought that this type of acquisition policy caused procurement delays, imposed standardized technology and application solutions, and mismatched technological solutions with agencies' missions. Also, the nature of IT changed during this period, producing more and more custom solutions at ever lower costs. The best example of the change is the personal computer, which obviated the need for much of the work done by mainframes.

CIO Act Gives More Flexibility to Agencies, Creates CFO/CIO Partnership

The CIO Act, authored by Senator William Cohen (R-Me), though not a complete 180-degree shift from the centralization of the Brooks Act, strips GSA of its central policy role in information technology acquisition. Each federal agency is given more flexibility in IT product and service acquisitions, with OMB assuming a coordinating role. While national security systems are exempted from the act, security and defense agencies' routine payroll and finance information systems are covered by it. Several provisions of the act are of particular importance to CFOs and other senior financial managers:

- **OMB and agency roles in IT capital investments.** OMB will use its budgetary authority to help develop methods for federal agencies to track and analyze risks and results of their major IT capital investments. Agencies will design processes for reporting on capital planning and investment control of IT acquisition, consistent with their financial and budgetary management criteria. Agency systems are to be evaluated on their performance and results in how they help agencies to serve the public, carry out missions, and reach goals.

- **NIST standards and guidelines.** The National Institute of Standards and Technology (NIST) of the Department of Commerce will provide standards and guidelines for federal information systems. Agencies can use more stringent standards if required for the security and privacy of sensitive information.

- **IT acquisition.** Agency heads have broad power to acquire, enter into contracts with, and work with other federal agencies where appropriate. (The exception is FTS 2000, the federal government's telecommunication system, which remains under GSA central control.)

- **Chief Information Officer.** Each agency will appoint a CIO to advise and recommend policy to the agency head and develop, maintain, facilitate, evaluate, and assess information systems.

- **Financial systems development.** An agency's CIO and CFO (or comparable officials) are to develop an accounting, financial, and asset management system that is reliable, consistent, and timely.

In some organizations, the CIO "owns" all systems, including those for financial management. In others, the CFO may "own" the systems, and the CIO may report to the CFO. In both cases, the CFO–CIO relationship is reciprocal. The CFO is the CIO's customer for planning and implementation assistance in designing and implementing financial information systems that meet new requirements. The CIO is the customer for the CFO's financial analysis and other related services that are essential to IT acquisition, use, and evaluation. Both face a formidable challenge in straightening out the slow, inconsistent, and unreliable jumble that constitutes many agencies' information resources.

The Federal Financial Management Improvement Act of 1996

Attention CFOs and IGs: Congress listened to your complaints and, through FFMIA-96, elevated efforts to solve financial management systems problems to a higher level of importance. The act passed in September 1996 as we prepared to go to press, so we will only highlight its key points.

First, FFMIA-96's most important purposes relevant to financial systems are to:

- Provide for consistency of accounting by an agency from one year to the next, and uniform accounting standards throughout the federal government
- Require financial management systems to support full disclosure of financial data, including the full costs of programs and activities, in order to provide citizens, Congress, and agency managers with accurate financial information
- Improve performance, productivity, and efficiency in financial management
- Build on and complement the CFO Act, GPRA, and GMRA
- Increase the ability of agencies to compare spending to results of activities.

FFMIA-96 demonstrates congressional concern with the importance of systems by requiring that:

- Agencies comply substantially with federal financial management systems requirements, applicable accounting standards, and the U.S. government standard general ledger at the transaction level
- Agency financial systems be audited for compliance as part of their annual financial statement audits
- Should systems be found not to comply, agency heads establish a remediation plan that includes resources, remedies, and intermediate target dates necessary to bring the systems into substantial compliance (the period for coming into compliance is three years after the systems audit determination, unless good cause can be shown for taking longer)
- Inspectors general report to Congress instances and reasons when an agency does not meet intermediate target dates set forth in the remediation plan
- The OMB Director report to Congress on progress in implementing the act.

We believe the FFMIA-96 requirements to be just what some CFOs need to inspire agency heads to take immediate action to improve financial systems. And immediate action is needed: FFMIA-96 requirements go into effect in 1997.

What Does a Reliable, Consistent, and Timely Financial System Look Like?

Developing a reliable, consistent, and timely financial management system starts with understanding what a good system might look like. OMB Circular A-127, *Financial Management Systems,* and the JFMIP *Framework for Federal Financial Management Systems* describe it as a unified set of financial management systems with common data elements, common transaction processing, consistent internal controls, and efficient transaction entry.

We believe that these characteristics are basic foundations that are essential to building systems that will be able to share information efficiently without redundant rekeying of data or expensive generating of one-time special reports.

The concept of a unified, integrated set of systems recognizes that no single system will meet specialized financial information needs that occur horizontally across an agency's large processes or vertically down through its divisions, branches, and field offices.

Next, we believe that an agency's integrated set of financial accounting and management systems should be able to:

- Produce useful information for agency executives, lower-level managers, and stakeholders such as the Congress, oversight agencies, and citizens. This requirement demands common data elements and sources, and systems capable of supporting both financial reporting and managerial accounting.

- Develop cost data that accurately calculate the total cost of units of production, processes, and other components of operations that consume resources. Thus, cost accounting systems must be built into the overall integrated system.

- Generate financial and program data that can be used in measuring performance and results. These data have two important uses: 1) for executives and stakeholders to monitor operations, and 2) as starting points for lower-level managers and employees to diagnose and solve operations problems and identify opportunities. Such data must be generated and reported to the right personnel in a time frame that allows for corrective action before problems become critical.

- Integrate proprietary and budgetary information at the source, and incorporate financial management requirements.

- Contribute to the success of sound internal controls and financial stewardship.

If, as a set, an agency's financial systems fail to do all these things, then the results of the whole set may be suboptimal. For example, program managers may be required to spend time developing data they do not use locally, so that it can be fed to a headquarters-mandated financial reporting system that adds no value to the managers' products and services. Conversely, program managers may create their own subsystems for financial management information that is not consistent with headquarters numbers, assumptions, and procedures. Both examples reduce an agency's productivity, and possibly the quality of its outputs, because managers spend less time on quality issues and agency-wide process issues. Many of these problems can be prevented by a good strategic information plan.

Strategic Planning for Information Systems

The genesis of a good strategic information plan is a review of the agency-wide strategic plan. The actions prescribed in the information plan should be designed to help achieve the goals of both the agency strategic plan and the CFO office's strategic plan. Also, information collected during the assessment phase of agency or CFO office strategic planning may be useful in information planning. For more information on strategic planning for agencies and their internal financial organizations, please see Chapter 5.

Below, we show the key tasks of strategic information planning as they are applied to developing systems used agency-wide and by CFO offices. We recommend combining the planning for *all* systems, including those for financial and nonfinancial operations, because doing otherwise risks uncoordinated development. Typically, the tasks involved are done by a team headed by the agency CIO; a CFO must insist that representatives of the internal financial management organization be on this team.

Early assessment. The planning process starts with a brief analysis of the agency's and CFO office's business, competitive IT position, and current IT environment. The competitive analysis is important, because it shows whether existing IT resources are a help or a hindrance in competing with other agencies or the private sector for programs and their support functions. This is an initial, high-level view of opportunities and directions for IT. The results are set forth in a brief vision statement that ensures that the rest of the planning will focus on significant issues.

Strategic vision (business focus). Planners review and analyze the vision statement of the agency-wide and CFO office strategic plans, which helps to align information planning with organizational goals. Careful thinking during this task will help reveal the business opportunities for IT, which may include new services or improved efficiency within existing operations. Also, the review will help focus long-term technology directions, illustrating the likely long-term effect of technology on the agency and CFO office.

Business architecture and logical information systems architecture. This task provides a complete representation of the agency's or CFO office's current and future process and information requirements. First, the requirements are represented in the business architecture, which relates them to the geography, organization, and critical components of the agency's or CFO office's business. Second, the requirements are shown in the logical information systems architecture, which provides a structure for the business systems and information groupings necessary to meet those needs.

Strategic vision (IT focus). This vision identifies the future state of information resources and how they will be aligned with the agency-wide and CFO office strategic visions and goals. As part of developing the vision, planners rank the opportunities for using IT and establish preliminary views for each of the goal IT architectures.

Current IT effectiveness. Planners now evaluate in detail the ability of the agency's existing IT architecture to meet current needs and how the architecture might provide a foundation for meeting future requirements.

Goal IT architecture. Planners establish measurable goals for the proposed future role and position of IT within the agency and CFO office, and for goal architectures for applications, data, technology infrastructure, and IT organizations and management. The goal architecture provides the long-term view of how IT should be employed to the agency's and CFO office's best advantage.

Transition and strategic justification. Now, planners develop a recommended strategy for transition from the current to the target IT environment and a proposed sequence for implementation. This is accompanied by the justification for the IT strategy as a whole and an evaluation of its impact on the organization and its relevance to major programs and directions.

Strategic IT plan. The final product of planning is a document that compiles the information developed in the earlier tasks, supported by plans and projects for implementation.

A good strategic information plan is central to making a business case for investing in new IT resources. Also, the plan helps prevent the fragmented development of IT systems that produce the current information archipelagos that characterize most federal systems.

Issues in Developing Optimal Financial Management Systems

Legacy Systems and Legacy Data

In FY 1995, 44 percent of 810 federal agency financial systems were reported to be more than ten years old. Some of these systems are legacies of an archaic architecture that devours substantial portions of management information systems (MIS) maintenance budgets, yet still does not meet today's needs. Immediate replacement of the older systems can be a budget buster, but this should not preclude a more gradual upgrade based on a long-term strategic information plan. A complete upgrade will likely take longer than the average tenure of a federal CFO or CIO, but working together they can create a strategic information plan and the supporting planning systems and monitoring processes in just a few months.

Legacy data are somewhat different from legacy systems. They are historical data that are no longer collected but that an agency still must maintain, either because it needs to or is required to. Legacy data can gnaw away at MIS budgets, prolong the life of legacy systems, and needlessly complicate the development of new systems. An objective assessment of the risk of not maintaining such data may lead to its quiet interment in off-site storage. Likewise, an agency must periodically re-examine any mandates for maintaining legacy data. Such mandates may have expired or, upon careful review, may be determined to have been strictly internal requirements that can be eliminated without violating statutory regulations.

Meeting All Requests, Making Quick Fixes, and the Temptation to Tinker

Many times, agencies will insist that their financial management systems meet every need specified by users. Given free reign, users will develop long laundry lists of the things they want the new technology to accomplish in the hope of covering every nook and cranny of operations.

Unfortunately, many items on the lists are often added without considering their costs and benefits. The result is an overly large, spaghetti-like system that has been asked to do too much and that may end up missing the most important objectives. The same is true for a system that is reactionary, or designed in fits and starts to put out fires and meet one-time needs. Both types of systems will eventually become costly and cumbersome to operate.

Replacing or tinkering with one part of the system can cause problems in others. Michael Yoemans, Director of Functional Process Improvement at the Office of the Secretary of Defense, gives a good example in an article by Heather Hayes in the February 1996 issue of *Government Executive:* "[(I)]f we wanted to take all the payroll systems [(in DoD)] and get them all down to one, it sounds pretty simple. Payroll's payroll, right? But when you look inside an organization's payroll system, you see interfaces to their labor distribution, project management, personnel, and so forth. It's like one internal organ in a body. You can't just rip it out and expect for everything to be all right. You have to reattach the organ. So instead of it being just one system,

it's actually an infrastructure with many tentacles."
Concerns like this will only increase in the future. More and more, operational, financial, and performance measurement systems are being used together by managers and employees at all levels of an organization for applications most can't even imagine today.

Custom versus Commercial Off-the-Shelf Solutions

At one time, all financial systems were customized, one-of-a-kind programs, almost exactly matching the manual processes they replaced. However, most custom financial systems are costly to code, maintain, and upgrade, and their documentation often sparse, if available at all. Despite this, many people like custom solutions because they are convinced that their organization has unique processes or informational needs—and because they do not have to change the way they work.

Commercial off-the-shelf software, on the other hand, usually is less costly than custom software to develop, install, maintain, and upgrade. COTS documentation is almost always better than custom systems, and vendors have an economic motivation to enhance their products continually. In our 1995 CFO survey, 59 percent of financial managers said that COTS offers a feasible, relatively low-cost solution to many of their financial system needs. Only one in four felt that their organization was so individual that it could not be served by COTS solutions. In its most recent catalogue, the GSA Financial Management System Software schedule lists seven vendors of COTS software for core financial systems; their products have been validated for government requirements.

Given the advantages of COTS and the positive attitude toward it by financial managers, it is as yet but a small part of the national government's computing power. As shown in Figure 4-1, of 1,181 federal financial management applications in operation during FY 1995, only 10 percent were COTS. Why is this so?

Many organizations in the public sector are uncomfortable using COTS because they think that no "canned" system can possibly meet their requirements or operating environment. Unfortunately, often such requirements arise from cowpath-like processes that have grown, spread, and mutated without conscious planning over long periods. As a result, the processes are inefficient, redundant, and costly, and information systems have to be jerry-rigged to fit them. Naturally, no COTS solution will fit this situation—but custom solutions serve only to institutionalize the problem further. COTS is not the answer to all system problems, but all agencies must consider COTS when exploring systems solutions.

COTS at FBI shows need to change work methods to accommodate new systems. As late as the 1970s, parts of the Federal Bureau of Investigation budget and accounting processes were charmingly and alarmingly anachronistic. Budgets were put on 3x5 cards. Anytime anyone wanted to buy something, he would take the requisition down to purchasing. Purchasing would look at the budget card, and if there was any money left on it, subtract out the cost of the purchase. The only internal control was the initials of the purchasing agent on the card.

CFO Jay Brixey played a key role in developing a new accounting system that started out modestly as a means of keeping track of how agents were spending their time. Implementing an automated financial system was problematic because the FBI's automation group did not have the right expertise. Though it was an unpopular decision at the time, the bureau opted for COTS. Instead of forcing the COTS system to do things for which it was not designed, Brixey trained employees to change how they worked to accommodate the new system. For example, the system uses corporate world terminology; rather than change the software and revise the screens, employees were taught what the corporate terms meant. Through accommodations like these, the bureau implemented the new accounting system with few people and at minimal cost.

Keys to COTS. In the June 1996 *Federal Financial Management Status Report and Five-Year Plan,* the OMB and CFO Council set as an objective for the federal government to make better use of COTS. To meet this objective, the JFMIP is charged with issuing management cost accounting system requirements. Also, the CFO Council and GSA are to promote development by vendors of COTS that meet agency needs without major agency modifications, and to identify standard processes and requirements for selected functional financial systems. This will facilitate agencies' acquisition and use of COTS.

Within each agency, we believe that the keys to the effective implementation of COTS solutions include:

- Thoroughly understanding core accounting and financial processes and their requirements before selecting a COTS package
- Understanding important requirements outside the core, including information needs of other processes and systems
- Selecting COTS packages that can be tailored to fulfill critical requirements that cannot be met by their standard programs.

Resistance to New Technology, Systems, and to Change in General

Changes in systems and technology frequently generate resistance by users. We provide a general framework for managing change in Chapter 10, and here we will discuss a few specific change issues related to technology.

Senior Management, New Technology, and New Information

New information technology can be personally and professionally daunting for some CFOs and senior financial managers. As noted at the start of this chapter, IT is the key to developing and mastering the types of integrated financial systems that give people the information they need to make decisions. If financial executives want their personnel to use these systems, they need to lead the way by mastering the technology themselves. Also, financial executives need to take the lead in educating operations executives, including departmental secretaries, about how to use newly available technology to access financial information. Make no mistake: If those executives use the technology, their direct reports and everyone else will be eager to do the same.

Involving Users in the System Development Process

There are many points of view about what a process or related system is or does, including those of the office of the CFO, operations executives and managers, customers, auditors, and many others. Another perspective is strictly technical: documentation of the process or system with flow charts, reports, and performance measures related to cycle time, accuracy, and other characteristics. Obtaining these many viewpoints during systems design is critical; otherwise, systems will serve some vital needs but not others.

Earlier attempts at involvement. Going back a decade or so, most information systems were designed by systems engineers and IT specialists, with only cursory input from users, who often did not look beyond their own immediate needs. Gradually, organizations came to understand the importance of gaining user input into systems design, and introduced user surveys and Joint Application Design (JAD) workshops for this purpose. In JAD, a skilled IT specialist/facilitator works with a group of users to define and design the various elements and screens of a new system. JAD serves an important change management purpose, lowering resistance to new technology because user representatives feel they have contributed to the system design.

Requirements definition alone is not sufficient for designing most new federal financial systems. For example, a poorly planned JAD or other system development effort can produce a very nicely consolidated wish list instead of validated requirements and needs. Also, the processes served by the new systems are undergoing major change, so that users may not yet understand them. In these cases, requirements definition may be preceded by process design or redesign workshops in which user representatives and others develop high-level process and systems plans before moving into actual systems design.

For example, until recently, each of NASA's space research centers had its own financial system. Previous attempts to centralize operations and considate the systems had resulted in failure. In 1995, the agency began a new initiative that is succeeding, in part because NASA invited representatives from each research center to participate in the design process, making it a cooperative, participative effort. The representatives were required to come to the design table with business processes they wanted to see incorporated in the new system. The representatives were grouped into teams of ten who focused on different systems modules, for a total of more than 100 people contributing their insight and expertise. The first task for each module team was to focus on the redesigned processes of the new way of working. This helped them understand the type, format, and frequency of information the new system needed to produce. This future focus enabled the teams to avoid paving the cowpaths of the existing processes.

Success Factors in Systems Planning and Implementation

Our experience in working with many government agencies to plan and implement financial systems is that five factors are most important to success: 1) gaining senior management support, 2) setting priorities, 3) defining expectations, 4) communicating, and 5) celebrating success. As well, there are a host of minor but still important tips we would like to share.

Senior Management Support

A CFO needs absolute, unwavering support from the very top of an agency or department. He or she must ensure that senior executives understand the complexities of the project and the likelihood, because of its comprehensive nature, that there will be some discontent, turf battles, and resourcing challenges along the way. CFOs must build that support before starting a project and sustain it until the project is completed. The support helps overcome the roadblocks that constantly pop up, and helps focus an agency on its information goals.

For example, when co-author Morgan Kinghorn was being interviewed for the job of IRS Controller (he later became CFO), the IRS Commissioner asked him, "What one thing could we do for you if you decided to undertake the challenge of implementing a major COTS system in our organization?" Kinghorn answered "Don't blink! It will take three to five years to bring in the new system *and* begin using it effectively, including decentralizing all budget execution to the field. If you blink—even if mistakes are made—I'm dead." The commissioner responded "You've got it." That support lasted during the tenure of three IRS commissioners, extended upward to the Treasury Department, and was so strong that failure to be seen an active supporter of the process was cause for job security concerns. Using a COTS approach, IRS went on to replace eight local financial management systems with a new system that was successfully completed on time.

Establish Priorities

Focusing on first things first is an important character trait for CFOs, especially when they are pressured from all sides to meet expectations with limited resources. Few federal departments and large agencies can hope to revitalize all their financial systems at once. Naturally, the first priority is anything that is needed to support an agency in meeting its mission. For the office of the CFO, this will likely be core financial systems, followed by the interface with other systems such as procurement, personnel, payroll, facilities, or logistics.

There are no standard rankings of priorities, however; each CFO must set his or her own. For example, John Hamre, DoD Under Secretary and CFO, said: "So far, we've done a good job of getting a master plan on consolidating our disbursing systems and our finance systems, but not our accounting systems. Accounting is our third priority, because the accounting systems don't have the immediate payoff of the other two, and I can't produce a good, auditable financial statement until I deal with all three. So really, the audit is by default almost a fourth priority. It is still important, but we have to go through these other things first."

Define Expectations, Then Plan and Manage the Effort
Anticipate complaints and objections by making it clear that a new system is not all things to all people. Also, let people know that systems implementation requires much work up front, and that they may need to change the way they work. Then, develop a clear project plan, publish the rollout schedule, and stick to it.

System implementation failures have often been traced to poor project management resulting from these problems:

- **Requirements creep,** or constant additions and changes to system specifications. For combat weapons systems, requirements creep often results from changes in threats and advancing technology. Financial and performance measurement system design does not require the type of rocket science needed for complex weapons, though. Most of these systems' requirements creep comes from failure to understand early on how an agency wants to operate its business.
- **Dragging it out,** or taking too long to implement systems. Installing some financial systems through-out an agency can take years. Such a schedule can result in requirements creep due to changing needs. Also, lengthy implementation leaves a system vul-nerable to future unanticipated budget cuts that will stall progress or even kill the effort entirely. Finally, technology improves so rapidly that today's lead-ing-edge solution is tomorrow's drag on productivi-ty. A flexible, modular, and phased approach to implementation helps to ensure at least partial suc-cess and prevents total failure.
- **Inadequate postimplementation monitoring,** which is especially important when taking a modu-lar or phased approach. Monitoring includes con-

firming original cost-benefit analyses, monitoring risks, and ensuring that users apply the system as planned and are satisfied with its results. Failing to monitor may allow counterproductive practices to creep back into the system, as happened with the credit card example Elaine Kamarck described earlier in this chapter.

Communicate, Communicate, Communicate

With financial system implementation, like many other things in life, reality is nine parts perception and one part truth. Define a network of key users, keep them informed, listen to them, and address and try to resolve their issues and concerns. Be sure that people understand the reasons that all their desires cannot be met immediately, and that there is a schedule for future implementation for their most important needs.

Celebrate Success

This stuff is difficult! When a system meets a key implementation milestone, take time out to celebrate with those who deserve it. It helps build support when times get tough—and they will—and broadcasts that the process is working. When the system is installed in the first location or pilot site, make that a major success and invite program managers and other site leadership to celebrate.

Other Tips for Success

Prepare for problems associated with the financial audit. All federal financial and performance measurement systems should be planned with financial audits in mind. Otherwise, financial managers will find themselves falling months behind schedule in preparing for audits and risk losing a clean opinion. This includes deciding early on what to do about reconciliation and keeping an eye on the conversion process. Scheduling new systems to go "live" in the middle of a fiscal year can create problems for the annual audit, so try to avoid doing this.

Many organizations involve their auditors in financial system and process design and reengineering. In this way, the auditors are drawn into a consultative role that both improves the systems and wins their support for new ways of working.

Training and other personnel issues. Usually, new systems mean that financial personnel need training in new IT skills, so it is wise to include funds for user training in any systems initiative. Many organizations create user groups to guide system usage; including field personnel in these groups ensures that ultimate users have a say.

Immediate help. Having an *immediate response* hotline for users is critical during the early postimplementation period. Often, it is important to have an on-site contractor to respond to crisis situations.

System integrity. Protect the basic integrity of the system. People like exceptions and overrides, and even COTS systems can be overridden by changing business processes. In some cases, overrides will be absolutely necessary to manage an exception or a particular issue. But be wary of building in overrides as an essential element of a system and of making this a habit. The result will be a jerry-rigged system, just like the custom system that COTS replaces. For example, before IRS implemented a COTS system, the bureau had a practice of charging to an "Appropriation Nine." However, IRS didn't have nine appropriations; number nine was really a holding file for problem transactions such as those without the right code or appropriation information. The new COTS system did not have such a category, and there was intense pressure to create one by modifying the system. Then-CFO Kinghorn prohibited such a change and required that managerial and process discipline be instituted to minimize any such uncertainties. This maintained both systems and management integrity.

Beware of bleeding-edge technology. Leading-edge technology is proven by others, while bleeding-edge technology requires its first users to go through the trials and tribulations of proof. A wise rule is to be neither the first nor last to adopt a new generation of technology (although investigating new releases of an organization's existing technology is always a good idea).

And You Thought It Was Over

The hard work of managing and marketing a new system begins when it is finally operational, because that's when the confusion starts, and we do not mean the piddling problem of learning to use new software and screens. If a CFO has used new systems development as an opportunity to redesign financial operations, then people within and without the financial organization will suddenly come up against new processes. This includes customers, parent and partner organizations, vendors, and auditors. For months, perhaps years, after the system goes live, senior financial managers must maintain their presence and vigilance to ensure that people use the new way of working.

Chapter

5

AUDIT ANGST

The federal government had, as of mid-1996, gone through five rounds of annual audits on agency financial statements. Obtaining an unqualified or clean audit opinion on these statements is a rite of passage for most agencies, marking the start of their journey toward excellence in financial management.

- The CFO Act and GMRA, which require annual financial statements and audits for most federal agencies, are helping to lay the foundation for a better way of fiscal management.

- The form and content of a federal financial statement is based on private sector models. However, the federal government is developing new standards and formats that are even more in keeping with public sector missions and funding mechanisms.

- The process of developing and auditing financial statements is more important for improvement than the audit opinions themselves.

- An effective audit involves considerable advance planning by both CFOs and their auditors, and postaudit work is needed to get in shape for the next year's audit.

- Most federal entities will require several annual audits before receiving an unqualified opinion, but each attempt produces opportunities for improving fiscal stewardship.

I think it an object of great importance...to simplify our system of finance and to bring it within the comprehension of every member of Congress...the whole system (has been) involved in impenetrable fog. (T)here is a point...on which I should wish to keep my eye...a simplification of the form of accounts...so as to bring everything to a single center; we might hope to see the finance of the Union as clear and intelligible as a merchant's books, so that every member of Congress, and every man of any mind in the Union, should be able to comprehend them to investigate abuses, and consequently to control them.

— Thomas Jefferson, 1802

In 1996, almost 200 years after Jefferson's comment, Senator John Glenn told us: "What amazes me is that we went this long in the history of our country without requiring bottom-line audits at the end of every year from departments of the government. The angst to agencies caused by having to prepare financial statements and undergo independent audits has heightened attention and pressure to fix longstanding problems that for so long have plagued us."

Although the U.S. federal government is the largest financial entity in the world, throughout most of its history it has operated without annual financial statements developed in accordance with GAAP. These statements are part of the foundation of sound financial management.

Obtaining an unqualified or clean audit opinion on the statements is a threshold event, indicating a baseline ability to achieve fiscal maturity. Anthropologists might call an organization's first such audit a "rite of passage," much the same as the long, arduous, and often painful rituals that primitive societies use to induct adolescents into the ranks of mature adults. Many who have gone through a first audit will agree that it was "long, arduous, and painful," and add "costly and frustrating" to boot.

Federal agencies undergoing the rite should take some comfort that many large private corporations found their first audits to be quite difficult, and sometimes needed several tries before achieving a clean opinion. There are two reasons for this that apply to all organizations. During their initial audit, many financial managers are unfamiliar with the annual financial statement development and audit processes, which is why we discuss them at length in here and in Chapter 6. While learning, financial managers must develop an audit infrastructure, such as financial and other information systems designed to produce auditable data. We reviewed the general requirements for such systems in Chapter 4 and will discuss their specific applications to financial statements and audits here and in Chapter 6. Also, federal auditors are relatively new at financial audits, and the rules and practices for the audits are still evolving. When auditors, auditees, and audit rules are all new, the situation is, shall we say, challenging. We will begin with an overview of the audit rules.

Legislative Background for Federal Financial Statements and Audits

The situation started to change in the early 1990s with the CFO Act. The federal government had been preparing financial statements and undergoing audits on a piecemeal basis for decades before the act. Government corporations such as the Federal Deposit Insurance Corporation and Export-Import Bank have been under audit requirements from their enabling legislation and the Government Corporation Control Act (P.L. 79-248, 59 Stat. 597, as amended). Some agencies such as the Department of Veterans Affairs and the General Services Administration had their first financial statement audits conducted on an experimental basis during the 1980s. However, it took the CFO Act to specify audit requirements, establish a pilot program, and lay a framework for auditing the entire federal government.

Recognizing that preparing and auditing department-wide financial statements could present unforeseen challenges, the CFO Act initiative started out with ten pilot agencies and all revolving and trust funds within the government. The pilots proved successful, so the Government Management Reform Act of 1994 expanded audit coverage to all Executive Branch departments and most agencies.

Starting in FY 1996, agencies will prepare annual financial statements under guidance published by the Office of Management and Budget and the Federal Accounting Standards Advisory Board. The statements will be audited by the General Accounting Office, an agency's office of the inspector general (OIG), or an independent public accounting firm. For FY 1997, the Treasury Department will prepare consolidated financial statements of the entire federal government for audit by the GAO. Efforts are under way to package financial statements in a single, consistent, comprehensive accountability report that satisfies all the requirements of the new reform legislation, including performance reporting prescribed in the Government Performance and Results Act of 1993. (For more details on GPRA reporting requirements, see Chapters 2, 7, and 8).

The Federal Consolidated Financial Statements for FY 1994

According to the FY 1994 Consolidated Financial Statements (unaudited) that Coopers & Lybrand reviewed for the Treasury Department's Financial Management System, federal revenues came to $1.39 trillion and expenses to $1.5 trillion. Interest charges alone came to $200 billion. Federal assets totaled $1.36 trillion, and liabilities $5.36 trillion that year. Thus, the federal government's accumulated net position was negative, a deficit of more than $4 trillion.

Financial statements—and more important, the process of developing and auditing them—will help Congress and administrators to understand government finance, activities, and results better. These new insights into performance, budget, and spending should raise the level of political discourse concerning the strategies and operations of government organizations.

Purpose, Form, and Content of Annual Financial Statements

An annual financial statement's purpose is to present a reporting entity's financial condition and results of operations accurately and fairly. A reporting entity can be a program, revolving or trust fund, substantial commercial activity, agency, department, or even the entire federal government as a single entity. We will use the term entity in this and the next chapter to refer to reporting entities of all types.

The purpose of an audit of financial statements is to determine if they are fair and accurate. Audits are not intended to determine absolute accuracy, because many line items on a financial statement, such as depreciation and allowance for uncollectable amounts, represent estimates only. Instead, the financial statements should reflect a reasonable and fair representation of financial data compiled under prescribed accounting and reporting guidance.

Current Contents and Formats of Financial Statements
For FY 1996 and FY 1997, OMB Bulletin No. 94-01, *Form and Content of Agency Financial Statements*, provides the authoritative guidance for entities' financial reporting requirements. The bulletin prescribes four major sections of the annual financial report:

1. **Overview of the Reporting Entity:** A description of the entity, its mission, activities, accomplishments, and overall financial results and condition that includes information on whether and how the entity's mission is being accomplished and what, if anything, needs to be done to improve its program or financial performance

2. **Principal Statements and Related Footnotes**: These statements are the equivalent of private sector balance sheets that show assets and liabilities, and income statements that reflect revenues and expenses. Also, they are an attempt to link budgets to financial results. Footnotes are required explanatory disclosures that provide greater detail than the principal statements. The statements include:
   - **Statement of Financial Position,** disclosing the entity's assets, liabilities, and net position
   - **Statement of Operations (and Changes in Net Position),** disclosing the results of the entity's operations for the reporting period, including

changes in the entity's net position from the end of the previous reporting period

- **Statement of Cash Flows,** disclosing the entity's gross cash receipts and disbursements with an explanation of the changes in cash or cash equivalents for the reporting period
- **Statement of Budgetary Resources and Actual Expenses,** providing, by program, a comparison of the entity's current fiscal year transactions and expenses reported on its statement of operations, accompanied by a reconciliation of these expenses to related amounts presented in budget execution reports.

3. **Consolidating/Combining Statements:** Where feasible and appropriate, entities should present consolidating/combining statements that present, by major programs, activities, or funds, the information presented in the principal statements, if the consolidating/combining statements will substantially improve the presentation and disclosure of the entity's financial position and results.

4. **Supplemental financial and management information:** Other financial and management information that supports information presented in the Overview of the Reporting Entity, that was not considered appropriate for inclusion in the footnotes to the Principal Statements, or that would otherwise enhance understanding of the financial condition and operations of the reporting entity. When the new form and content bulletin becomes effective, the content of the annual financial report will change. In addition to preparing an Overview of the Reporting Entity and Principal Statement, agencies will begin preparing Required Supplemental Stewardship Information (RSSI) and Required Supplemental Information (RSI). RSSI includes required disclosures of special classifications of assets, investments, and management responsibility.

RSI includes segment or disaggregated data that are reported in total on some of the principal statements. As always, CFO and agency management are encouraged to provide other information that will help users understand the financial activity of the agency.

Comparison of Private and Public Sector Financial Statements

To an extent, federal financial statements and their formats recognize the inherent differences between private sector and government reporting, but are still heavily modeled after their commercial counterparts. For example, the current federal Statement of Operations format presents the classic income, revenues, and financing sources at the top of the statement and subtracts expenses to arrive at a net income or excess/shortage of financing sources over expenses. In the private sector, this formula is used to determine a corporation's profit for the year and provides a basis for earnings-per-share computations, concepts which are less relevant in the federal environment.

Similarly, because most federal entities are appropriations-driven, their expenses are tied closely to their funding levels, so one would expect most of these entities nearly to "break even" on their income statement, not show a profit or loss. Some differences will occur because of capital expenditures that would not appear on the income statement and timing differences between recognizing transactions under budgetary and proprietary accounting. As the federal government gains experience in financial reporting, an approach has been evolving that is more appropriate to the unique characteristics of public sector entities. Proposed changes are discussed next.

Future Contents and Formats

FASAB is developing accounting standards more suited to federal financial operations and performance measurement requirements, so the nature and appearance of federal financial statements are changing. In June 1995, FASAB released the *Entity and Display* pronouncement, which laid out recommended new financial statements, and on October 24, 1996, OMB released Bulletin 97-01, *Form and Content Bulletin*, which spelled out the new financial statement formats. These new formats are effective for FY 1998 financial statements, which means that CFOs must be able to capture data elements required for the new statements and formats by October 1, 1997. This gives agencies a very short time to modify financial management and reporting practices in order to meet these new requirements—a formidable challenge for many organizations.

Under the new guidance, the Balance Sheet will remain similar in format and content, but other statements will be modified or replaced. In addition to the Balance Sheet, agencies will prepare a Statement of Net Cost, Statement of Changes in Net Position, Statement of Budgetary Resources, Statement of Financing, and for some agencies, a Statement of Custodial Activity.

The **Statement of Net Costs** would replace the current Statement of Operations; program expenses are listed first and are offset by exchange revenue received from those programs. The resulting figure is the net cost of the program that must be financed by appropriations or other sources. This presentation is far more realistic and useful for those federal entities that receive most of their funding through appropriations and deliver services with no expectation of generating "net income."

The **Statement of Changes in Net Position** is similar to a component of the current Statement of Operations and Changes in Net Position and reports net changes in an agency's "equity." This new report itemizes appropriations used, transfers-in, imputed financing, and other activity that causes changes to an agency's net position.

The **Statement of Budgetary Resources** contains budgetary accounting amounts that should be available from the agency's budget execution reports. The statement shows budgetary resources and their status. In this statement, there is no attempt to tie budgetary and financial accounting.

The **Statement of Financing** reconciles total obligations incurred for budgetary purposes to the financial accounting net cost of operations. Of the new requirements, this statement may present the greatest challenge to CFOs. While the statement sets forth the format and lists the reconciling items, it is fundamentally different from earlier reports and will require significant study of its nature and purpose.

The **Statement of Custodial Activity** highlights activities of entities such as the IRS and Customs Service, which collect duties, fees, or revenues on behalf of the entire government. Because these agencies act as agents of the government, their revenue amounts are not presented in the context of their operational financial statements. Most agencies will not use this statement.

Stewardship reporting. In addition to the principal statements described above, the new Form and Content Bulletin requires agencies to report on stewardship activity for assets and investments. This is a new reporting concept promulgated by FASAB in 1996. The FASAB Stewardship Reporting pronouncement recognizes that certain assets and investments made by federal agencies may be most effectively presented in a separate statement along with nonfinancial data and disclosures such as quantity counts and usage condition classifications. The nature and extent of required stewardship reporting will vary by agency.

Federal GAAP
Before the CFO Act, agencies used a hybrid of GAO Title 2 *(Policy and Procedures Manual for Guidance of Federal Agencies)* and GAAP as a basis for compiling data. The result was inconsistent practices among agencies. Also, this system had little enforcement strength except in dealing with the most serious violations of common accounting practices and accepted estimating techniques. In 1993, the National Performance Review's first major report contained a mandate from the Executive Office to FASAB to develop a cohesive, coherent, and comprehensive set of accounting standards for the entire federal government. Since then, the

Board has issued standards and concept statements covering topics such as property, plant, and equipment; revenue recognition; and stewardship reporting.

Until all standards are developed and implemented, OMB has established a hierarchy of accounting authority for the federal government, which is shown in Figure 5-1. The hierarchy recognizes that applying federal accounting concepts and theory is more important than private sector practices and accordingly places GAAP and other standards at a level below prevalent agency practices.

Figure 5-1

Federal Hierarchy of Authority for Audited Financial Statements

1. Individual standards agreed to and published by the OMB, Comptroller General, and Secretary of the Treasury.
2. Form and content requirements included in OMB Bulletin 93-02, dated October 22, 1992, and subsequent issues
3. Accounting standards contained in agency accounting policy, procedures manuals, or related guidance as of March 29, 1991, so long as they are prevalent (agency) practices
4. Accounting principles published by authoritative standard-setting bodies and other authoritative sources (1) in the absence of other guidance in the first three parts of this hierarchy, and (2) if the use of such accounting standards improves the meaningfulness of the financial statements.

Source: OMB Bulletin No. 94-01, *Form and Content of Agency Financial Statements.*

Prevalent agency practices are traditional accounting procedures that have been generally accepted by the federal financial and audit communities, but have not yet been addressed in formal guidance. For example, the practice of not reporting depreciation has been a prevalent agency practice applied to early CFO Act financial statements. The practice will likely change when the FASAB pronouncement on property, plant, and equipment becomes authoritative and sets formal reporting guidelines for depreciation. However, that federal accounting policy recognizes prevalent agency practices does not imply that it is proper to continue existing accounting treatments if they are deficient or inconsistent with the rest of the government. Instead, the intent of recognizing such " practices" is that certain reporting practices may be universally applied but remain unaddressed by existing FASAB, OMB, or GAO policy guidance.

With a comprehensive set of standards in place for the future, for financial statements starting in FY 1998 OMB has revised the authoritative accounting guidance hierarchy in its Bulletin 97-01:

1. Individual standards agreed to by OMB, GAO, and Treasury
2. Interpretations issued by OMB on FASAB standards
3. Requirements contained in OMB form and content bulletins
4. Accounting principles published by other standard-setting bodies.

Prevalent agency practices is notably missing from this new hierarchy. As federal standards evolve, agencies will have less latitude in accounting practices. The intent here is not to stifle individual agency reporting needs. Instead, FASAB and OMB are building a consistent, uniform framework for law and policy makers to use in measuring accountability and making decisions.

Getting in Shape for the Audit

As federal entities and auditors gain more experience in preparing financial statements and conducting audits, the angst and the time frame for completing them are diminishing. Initially under the CFO Act, audits could be completed within nine months following the end of a fiscal year; now, the deadline is five months. Many private corporations create financial statements quarterly and have the goal of completing an audit 30 days after closing their books for the year. This indicates that their financial statement and audit processes are effective, efficient, and relatively painless.

Achieving this state of preparedness requires preparation for both federal entities and their auditors.

Preparing: The Entity Side

An audit's planning phase should begin well in advance of the audit because both the CFO and auditors have significant tasks to complete before the audit starts. Some of the tasks for the reporting entity include establishing relations with senior auditor representatives; assembling an audit committee and an audit team; identifying data needs and their sources; developing an action plan; creating and coordinating auditor liaison and support; and preparing interim draft statements to identify potential problems. Here, we review the tasks as they normally are carried out to prepare financial statements and to work with auditors. In Chapter 7, we discuss some of the tasks done in a pre-audit that are useful for identifying improvement opportunities in financial management processes. Chapter 6 discusses the roles of the different individuals and organizations involved in the financial statement and audit processes. Here, we will outline how a CFO might organize two key groups: the audit committee and the audit team.

Establish relations with senior managers of the audit organization. From the very start of the audit process, a CFO must establish a direct, working relationship with the appropriate level of the auditor organization. This is not the field auditors' level, but instead is higher up in the organization. Problems occur when field auditors' understanding of the audit scope and an entity's financial condition differs from that of other members of the audit organization who may interpret the field auditors' findings. Because the federal audit process is still evolving, points of view can be quite different.

A CFO can prevent this problem through direct communication with senior management of the audit organization. An effective practice is to hold quarterly discussion meetings starting well before an audit. The meetings should include the agency chief, the CFO, the IG, and the audit organization's senior manager who directs the work of the field auditors. Such meetings can be managed by an audit committee.

Form audit committee. In the private sector, an audit committee is a group, appointed by a company's board of directors, that selects an external auditor and acts as a liaison between the auditor and the board. The committee handles problems related to audit procedures and differences of opinion between auditor and management. The audit committee is not found in the federal government, but a group similar to it would facilitate the audit process. A federal audit committee would report to the agency chief and would include the deputy chief, the agency CFO and IG and their counterparts in a parent department, senior representatives from GAO and OMB, and outside experts familiar with the financial audit process. Should the agency IG choose to use an independent public accounting firm to conduct the audit, then the firm's partner in charge of the audit might also serve on the committee.

The committee's role is to address critical issues related to the scope and procedures of the audit and, as in the private sector, to resolve disagreements between auditor and agency management. For example, an audit committee might study how materiality* is interpreted in audits of organizations that do the same type of work as an agency. Armed with this information, the committee will be better able to discuss materiality with auditors. Also, a top management audit committee that includes and reports directly to the agency chief underscores to everyone the importance of the audit, which motivates internal cooperation in areas such as data collection. Even though a CFO has the support of such an committee, he or she is still responsible for the financial statement development and audit processes, which includes putting together an excellent audit team.

---

*Materiality is the accounting principle that requires or allows only important financial events or items to be disclosed in accounting records such as annual financial statements. Materiality is discussed briefly later on in Chapter 5 and at length in Chapter 6.

Assemble audit team. The CFO must select, educate, and orchestrate a cohesive internal audit team to work on the financial statements and prepare for the audit. The team should include financial managers and program managers, and often representatives of the auditor, such as OIG or independent accounting firm staff. FFMIA requirements, which were discussed in Chapter 4, make it a good idea to include financial information systems managers on the team. Several team meetings and discussions with individual members may be needed to define and assign roles and responsibilities for collecting, developing, compiling, and reporting data. Doing this for the first time in a large federal agency can be a Herculean task, so the CFO needs to inspire the buy-in and full participation of many different components in an agency or department.

Identify data needs and sources. CFOs and financial managers must fully understand their entity's reporting requirements under the CFO Act. This may involve identifying the accounts that should be included in the financial statements and mapping existing data and systems to the requirements. Doing so will help identify gaps in the current system and where special data calls or new policies and procedures may be necessary to obtain needed information. Most data needed for financial statements exist outside of financial information systems, and are usually held by program managers. In Chapter 6 we discuss working with program managers to obtain the data.

Once financial managers know that the needed data are available, they must address data quality problems that result from unauditable data sources or deficient internal controls. By identifying these problems well in advance of the audit, the CFO can begin corrective and preventive actions to solve them. Developing interim draft statements, discussed below, is one way to identify data availability and quality problems.

Develop and execute action plan. The CFO should prepare and distribute a plan of the sequence of actions that must occur in order to meet the audit reporting deadline. Action items include:

- Prepare interim draft statements
- Identify key program accomplishments and performance measures
- Prepare draft of the Overview of the Reporting Entity
- Issue data calls for information needed from program or field offices
- Conduct year-end counts of inventories and fixed assets
- Perform account reconciliation
- Close year-end general ledger
- Draft narrative footnotes
- Prepare first draft of financial statements,
- Conduct variance analysis of selected accounts
- Prepare subsequent financial statement drafts
- Deliver final financial statements, footnotes, and overview to the auditors.

These actions should be coordinated with the auditors' plan of action to help ensure that they will have sufficient time to conduct the audit properly. When carrying out the actions, it is important to give agency management continual feedback on problems and issues that arise, so that management will not be surprised by the results of the audit.

Establish auditor liaison and support. A CFO should give auditors full cooperation and access to relevant financial information and personnel and should schedule frequent meetings with them to discuss issues. The CFO will want to stay in close touch with field auditor activities, not to influence the audit, but to coordinate requests for information to ensure that the responses are appropriate and correct. We have observed that, in some early federal audit preparations, auditor's questions and requests were often not forwarded to the proper person and that well-meaning auditors and entity staff inadvertently conveyed incorrect or misleading information. This confuses and complicates audit issues, and is best prevented by the CFO setting up formal lines and protocols for communication with auditors. In the future, as auditors and the CFO office gain experience in the audit process, the communication problem will not be as great. Even then, though, a CFO can keep the problem to a minimum by maintaining a formal, agreed-upon communication protocol with auditors.

Another good reason for maintaining continual communication with auditors is to take quick corrective action on potential problems discovered during interim testing and other tasks the auditors do as preliminaries to the audit. Sometimes such problems can be solved before the end of an audit, so that they will not affect the auditor's opinion.

Interim draft statements. A CFO may want to develop interim draft statements at some point during the fiscal year, typically in the ninth month (many private corporations do this quarterly, on a cumulative basis). For agencies new to the audit process, interim draft statements offer an opportunity for a dry run that will detect and correct data quality or availability problems. For example, often an accounting office will require information for financial statements that is not routinely available—for example, from their required footnote disclosure information that is gathered from program offices, which must understand the exact data needs and the intended use for that information. Interim draft statements are a reason to conduct such data calls in order to determine the quality of program office information, problems in communication and cooperation, and how the situation can be improved. Also, the statements can be used during a pre-audit like that discussed in Chapter 7.

Preparing: The Auditor Side

Auditor preparations include understanding the entity to be audited, reviewing previous years' and other related audit reports, conducting risk assessments and interim testing, and observing inventory counts.

Understanding the entity to be audited. During this get-acquainted phase, auditors collect information on an entity's organizational structure, accounting systems, location of accounting records, key financial personnel, and accounting processes that support the financial statements. Over time, auditors will become more familiar with a reporting entity, but must always update their knowledge during this phase of the audit process. To facilitate the update, a reporting entity must provide auditors with information on relevant changes to operating structures since the previous audit.

Review previous and related audit reports. Auditors should review previous reports such as those issued by GAO or the OIG to learn about issues that have surfaced in the past. This and other information collected form the basis for assessing risk; determining materiality threshold guidelines; and the nature, timing, and extent of testing in each activity cycle or line item.

Interim testing and inventory counts. Auditors will likely want to carry out interim testing focused on internal controls over financial data and some substantive tests of actual dollar amounts posted to the entity's systems and general ledger. If the results of the interim tests are satisfactory, then year-end testing can be lessened. Also, auditors should be invited to observe physical inventory counts before or at year end because they will attest to inventory as part of the audit.

FFMIA-96 requirements to audit financial systems may require auditors to include staff or consultants who are knowledgeable in this area. Specifically, such personnel should have extensive experience in financial systems auditing; this expertise also will be useful in other parts of the audit.

Showtime: The Audit Begins

Although the auditors will begin work before year end, most procedures will not occur until the entity closes its books and prepares financial statements. In the federal fiscal year (October through September), this may occur from mid-October to mid-January. The auditor will verify links between general ledger and subsidiary systems and conduct substantive tests of account balances. Based on their perception of errors or departures from accounting policy, auditors may propose for discussion with entity management any adjustments to the financial statements. In many cases, management accepts the auditor's recommendations and makes the necessary adjustments to the general ledger or financial statements. If management disagrees, the entity risks receiving a qualified or adverse opinion from the auditors (we discuss the meaning of these opinions next).

Completing the Audit and Issuing the Report

After their field work, auditors will issue an opinion on the entity's financial statements. Usually, auditors will share a draft version of the opinion with entity management to verify a mutual understanding of issues and findings. Management will discuss individual issues with the auditors to ensure that the facts are fairly represented in the opinion. Audit opinions can take one of four forms: unqualified, qualified, adverse, and disclaimer.

Unqualified Opinion or "Clean" Opinion. This is what organizations strive to achieve. An unqualified opinion means that auditors believe that the financial statements fairly present the operations and financial position of the reporting entity. Because federal financial systems and internal procedures were not originally designed to produce financial accounting information, gaining an unqualified opinion can take years.

Qualified Opinion. This is a more realistic short-term goal for many federal entities. A qualified opinion means the auditors believe that the financial statements fairly present the operations and financial position, except for certain areas for which they have material concerns. The qualified opinion generally denotes progress for the entity, but indicates the need for improving selected areas.

Adverse Opinion. This opinion states that the financial statements do not represent fairly the entity's financial position and operations. Such opinions are rare and generally indicate an irreconcilable policy difference between entity and auditors. For example, one government corporation routinely received adverse opinions in the 1980s by failing to recognize a loss reserve on its loan portfolio. This policy decision was driven by political rather than accounting considerations, but the auditor's only recourse was to issue an adverse opinion, declare the reason, and estimate the potential amount of the misstatement. Later, federal policy changes allowed the corporation to record a loan loss reserve, and it now receives unqualified opinions.

Disclaimer. Disclaimers are the most common opinions issued by auditors on initial financial statements prepared by federal entities. Here, the auditors feel that they cannot express an opinion on the statements for various reasons, most commonly because of poor data quality, lack of data, or unreliable financial systems. Often, disclaimers result from major financial or other management problems that require long-term solutions.

Materiality and Audit Opinions
An item is considered material if it is significant enough to affect decisions made because of information disclosed in financial statements, or if it requires that the statements be adjusted. As discussed at length in Chapter 6, auditors and reporting entities may hold differing views on the materiali-

Figure 5-2

Types of Audit Opinions Based on Materiality Levels and Conditions

Level of Materiality	*Conditions*			
	Departure from GAAP	*Inconsistent Application*	*Scope Limitation*	*Uncertainty*
Immaterial	Unqualified	Unqualified	Unqualified	Unqualified
Material — does not overshadow overall statements	Qualified	Qualified	Qualified Scope and Opinion	Qualified
Material — overall fairness of statements are in question	Adverse	Qualified	Disclaimer	Disclaimer

ty of an item, and this can cause controversies. Here, in Figure 5-2, we simply show the classic relationship of different types of audit opinions to the materiality level of an audited item or issue.

Other Audit Documents

Along with the opinion, auditors usually issue three other official documents based on the audit: a Report on Internal Controls, a Report on Compliance with Laws and Regulations, and a Management Letter. Sometimes these documents are controversial, especially in a government environment.

Report on Internal Controls. This identifies auditors' observations regarding how the reporting entity's control environment could contribute to waste, fraud, or abuse. Auditors present their observations without stating an opinion on them. Like their private sector counterparts, federal auditors struggle with the public's mistaken perception that their primary job during a financial statement audit is to identify fraud or other irregularities within an organization. Financial statement auditors do look for lapses in internal procedures that could permit fraudulent activity if unchecked, and include these in the Report on Internal Controls. However, in the private sector an auditor's scope is normally limited to how these lapses affect the fairness and accuracy of the statements. There is a difference between this scope and that of the special studies, investigations, and full-scale internal control reviews in which GAO and OIG auditors have in-depth experience and that perhaps are more appropriate for detecting actual fraud than financial statement audits.

That said, public perception is important, and even private sector audit standards have started placing more responsibility on financial statement auditors to help detect problems. Also, federal auditors are, as government employees or contractors, duty-bound to report actual or potential fraud, waste, and abuse. However, we do not believe the Report on Internal Controls and other audit documents are always the appropriate places to do so. We will discuss this issue more in Chapter 6.

Report on Compliance with Laws and Regulations.
As in the Report on Internal Controls, auditors will not express an opinion in this report. Instead, they will state that they made certain tests to verify compliance with selected laws and regulations as these pertain to the financial statements. If the auditors note instances of noncompliance, they will report it but will not comment on the extent or completeness of the agency's compliance efforts.

Management Letter. In the private sector, auditors will issue to company management a report called a management letter that lists conditions that may merit attention but were not significant enough to change the nature of the audit opinion. Often, the letters focus on internal control processes and procedures and provide useful information that can lead to finding ways to correct weaknesses in this area. Private sector management letters are not published along with a company's other financial statement documents and the audit opinion, but instead are shared in confidence with management and the board of directors.

In federal audits, the form and content of management letters are still evolving and may differ depending on the background of the auditing organization. For example, GAO has its roots in program audits and reviews, and the organization's management letter information reflects this. Usually, GAO issues its opinions in the form of a "blue book" that combines the formal statements prepared by the entity, the GAO audit results, and a letter detailing a variety of issues, some financial and others programmatic. The letter's findings may come from both the audit of financial statements and from earlier GAO program audits or reviews.

Inspectors general offices often issue a separate management letter that states internal control weaknesses that may or may not be so significant that they affect the audit results. OIGs, like GAO, have backgrounds in program audits and internal control issues and thus have tended to merge program and financial issues together, although, in our opinion, much less than GAO.

Independent public accounting firms' management letters for federal clients tend to resemble those in the private sector, but their content is evolving along with the federal audit process. Because these organizations have a background that is firmly rooted in financial audits, they tend to limit management letters (indeed, all documents in an audit) to financial issues and processes associated with the veracity and completeness of the financial statements themselves.

Perhaps the most important difference between private sector and federal management letters is that the federal letters are public documents (as are all the audit documents). Thus, a federal management letter can be a mixed blessing. While it identifies opportunities for improvements, agencies may find a management letter calls public attention to possible shortcomings, which is at the least embarrassing. That's life in the fish bowl of government service, where public disclosure is essential to democracy.

However, our observation is that some federal management letters (and audit opinions, for that matter) tend to blur the lines between fiscal responsibility and program effectiveness. If the lines become too blurred, federal leaders may lose sight of critical financial management problems in a blizzard of programmatic issues. The programmatic issues are important, but they might be better addressed through in-depth program audits and reviews, not through financial audits. We discuss this more in Chapter 6.

Postaudit Actions

The postaudit process involves responding to the audit opinion and management letter, producing corrective actions, and forming the foundation of the next year's audit. Postaudit work does not, however, need to wait until after an agency receives the auditor's opinion. If a CFO communicates regularly with auditors during the audit process, he or she will know well before the end of the audit nearly all the issues that could be addressed during the postaudit process. After receiving the audit opinion, CFOs need to maintain a dialogue with auditors in order to understand thoroughly their perceptions of the issues—after all, the auditors will be back next year. Also, good communication between financial managers and program managers is important during the postaudit period, because many of the issues addressed will require action in program areas.

Many federal agencies have struggled with the postaudit process because they did not prepare for it and could not immediately begin addressing the often challenging issues raised by auditors. Have no doubt: For agencies just starting out in financial management reform, preparing for the postaudit is as critical, if not more, than getting ready for the audit itself. Preparation includes developing a plan of action for the postaudit period. Some of the actions will be relatively minor and require little or no planning or resource investment; many of these can be executed by a simple rule change or executive memo. However, as simple as these actions may be, it is important to ensure that they produce the right results, and that the results will be lasting.

More significant issues, such as those shown in Figure 5-3, need to be ranked in order of priority and addressed in a formal action plan that includes milestones, responsibility assignments, and a budget. Sometimes the actions will require major changes in operations or major resource investments, in which case they might become part of the agency or the internal financial organization strategic plan (see Chapter 7).

Finally, one important action item for the postaudit plan is to develop an annual financial statement and audit plan. This plan should cover all the action items discussed throughout this chapter, and set a schedule, milestones, and budget for statement and audit processes. We believe that such a plan should set continuous improvement objectives such as annually reducing the time and resources required to complete and audit financial statements.

Figure 5-3

> ## Problems Uncovered in CFO Act
> ## Pilot Project Audits
>
> - Accounts receivable at one agency were overstated by tens of billions of dollars.
> - Thirteen billion dollars in loans at one agency had a high chance of being in default
> - An agency had an estimated $18 billion in unfunded future liabilities associated with hazardous waste disposal and cleanup at its installations.
> - One agency made an unsupported accounting adjustment of $1.1 billion in its reported cash balance to reconcile its accounts with the Treasury Department.
> - One agency audit showed more than $100 million in charges to contractors that lacked supporting documentation and thus will likely never be collected.
>
> **Source:** Office of Senator John Glenn.

Publishing the Results

Audited financial statements are typically only part of the required annual financial report that an entity develops and publishes. Good models for federal annual financial reports include those of corporations such as Ford, AT&T, and Motorola—and the U.S. Mint, the Patent and Trademark Office, and the Customs Service. These federal reports incorporate program objectives and performance measurements and document the agency leadership's perspective of the organization's operational results, future plans, and goals. As pilot agencies under the GPRA, the Department of Veterans Affairs, the Social Security Administration, NASA, the Nuclear Regulatory Commission, the Department of the Treasury, and the General Services Administration have incorporated their financial statements and reports for the Federal Managers' Financial Integrity Act, prompt payments, and debt management into a single annual accountability report. Other agencies would do well to review the pilot agencies' reports as potential models for their own.

The performance measurement information presented in the overview and supplemental information section of the annual financial statements are more than just a by-product of the process. Just as footnotes in corporate financial statements may be more revealing than the formal statements themselves, the ancillary information in federal reports may be more useful than the principal statements. Together, performance measurements and financial statements show how an agency used its budget authority and appropriated funds in furtherance of its mission. Such reports are designed to allow agencies to highlight the services or products they provide and the effects these had on the recipients. They also must provide historical information reflecting trends in inputs, outputs and outcomes. We provide several examples of federal agencies' GPRA performance reporting practices at the end of Chapter 8.

A Painful but Ultimately Healthy Experience

As of summer 1996, the federal government had gone through five rounds of CFO Act audits. As may be seen in Figure 5-4, each succeeding round has involved more reporting entities, and the percentage that achieved clean opinions has increased every year. For many of these organizations, the initial few rounds of audits found problems that go beyond simple financial reporting—lots of them, and big ones at that (Figure 5-3 shows a few). Yet, despite the weaknesses that initial audits revealed, the results of the effort have been largely positive, as measured in corrective actions that have improved financial management and thus helped make government more cost-effective.

Ultimately, the value of the financial statements and audits will be that they provided an opportunity and framework for people from several professions and organizations to work together on longstanding problems. The roles these individuals and organizations play in the audit process is the subject of our next chapter.

Figure 5-4

Audits and Audit Results, Federal Reporting Entities, FY 1991-5

	FY 1991	FY 1992	FY 1993	FY 1994	FY 1995*
Entities Audited	55	91	109	118	86
Entities with clean opinions **Number** **Percent**	19 37%	37 41%	50 46%	62 53%	56 64%
Entities with no material weaknesses **Number** **Percent**	N/A N/A	32 35%	45 41%	43 36%	48 56%

* Totals for FY 1995 were not yet complete; number is for statements received as of June 12, 1996.
Source: *Federal Financial Management Status Report and Five-Year Plan*, June 1996, OMB and federal CFO Council

Chapter

6

AUDIT ABILITY: IT TAKES A TEAM

A federal fiscal stewardship team sets the tone and defines the processes of financial statement development and auditing. Members include the Congress, program managers, CFOs and financial managers, inspectors general and internal agency auditors, independent public accounting firms, the General Accounting Office, the Treasury Department, the Office of Management and Budget, and the Federal Accounting Standards Advisory Board.

- Team members play different but sometimes overlapping roles: information customers, information suppliers, developers of statements, auditors, forums, and rule makers.
- Team members are wrestling with tough issues concerning financial statement audits, such as setting appropriate levels of materiality and how programmatic information should be addressed in financial audits.
- Experiences of the Customs Service and the Army show the power of financial audits to identify and help improve both financial and programmatic processes.

The CFO Act is not about getting clean audit opinions *per se,* which is a measure of discipline and control. The act is about managing the costs of government by providing cost-effective control and the right information at the right time to influence decision making and oversight. It is about taking financial management out of the back room and making it an important component of the corporate culture of an organization.

–Senior federal financial executive,
Coopers & Lybrand focus group,
April 1996

This quotation echoes former Comptroller General Charles Bowsher's belief that when the federal government produces an auditable, consolidated set of financial statements on all its operations, this will be the biggest step forward in public sector financial management in the last forty years. Even more, said Bowsher in testimony before the Senate Committee on Governmental Relations, audited financial statements, in conjunction with GPRA, will prompt a cultural change in federal agencies that will transform them into results-oriented entities.

Achieving this level of fiscal maturity and cost-effective culture will depend on cooperative action among the organizations and professions that together form the federal fiscal stewardship team. Agency CFOs and financial managers are key players on this team, so it is important that they understand their and the other members' roles and responsibilities related to the financial audit process. At this time, members of the team are engaged in expanding and refining their common understanding of the audit process. This evolutionary development has resulted in healthy debate over several key ideas, such as materiality and balancing program versus purely financial issues in audits. CFOs and financial managers can and should be active participants in the debate and they have excellent forums for voicing their opinions.

Such debate should not focus only on the financial statement and audit processes. As stated in Chapter 5, achieving a clean audit opinion is a basic requirement for fiscal responsibility. While it is an important requirement, discussions among the team members should center on how these processes can lead to other improvements in financial management.

The Federal Fiscal Stewardship Team

Key members of the team include:
- The Congress
- Program managers
- CFOs and their financial management teams
- The federal CFO Council
- Inspectors general and agency internal auditors
- Independent public accounting firms
- The General Accounting Office
- The Federal Accounting Standards Advisory Board
- The Office of Management and Budget
- The Department of the Treasury

Together, this team sets the tone of and defines the processes for federal financial statements and financial auditing. The team members are still refining and growing into their work scope, roles, and responsibilities, and it will be several years before their maturation is complete. We can divide the members into six overlapping groups: information customers, information suppliers, developers of statements, auditors, forums, and rule makers.

The Congress: Rule Maker and Key External Customer

Congress promulgated the laws requiring financial statements and audit reports and is an agency's key external customer for them. One intent of the CFO Act and GMRA is to supply Congress with information on an agency's fiscal condition and the soundness of its financial management. This is the foundation of a truth-in-budgeting movement that will better inform budget decisions.

Two congressional committees are most concerned with agency financial management: the Senate Committee on Governmental Affairs and the House Committee on Government Reform and Oversight. They hold hearings that provide forums for both federal and private organizations to present their views in this area. The leaders and staffs of these committees have been the legislative standard bearers and champions for fundamental financial reform, including the financial statement and audit initiative.

However, the pivotal congressional role will likely be played in the House and Senate Budget Committees. Actions there will answer the nagging question of whether Congress will actually use financial statement and audit report data to make decisions about budgets. Maybe, maybe not. According to a senior federal financial executive at a focus group we sponsored in April 1996, "There is the challenge that truth in budgeting will not be what decision makers in Congress really want when they eventually get accurate financial performance information."

Congressional budget decision making is, in the end, a political process driven by the need to satisfy the thousands of interest groups that vie for their piece of the federal budget pie. Relatively few groups lobby for the basic, nitty-gritty, in-the-weeds financial reforms that make it possible to develop sound financial statements. Thus, the driving force for financial reform comes largely from within the Congress. As with other types of internal reforms, this requires congressional leadership on both sides of the aisle to promote actively the reforms to their colleagues, to the point of leaders exercising their disciplinary powers.

There is more to be gained from such discipline than other options. For example, bills have been introduced on Capitol Hill that would penalize the budgets of agencies that fail to obtain unqualified audit opinions or that have not made progress in doing so. As noted in Chapter 5, this is what the Texas Legislative Budget Board has done to agencies that were not making progress in developing strategic performance measures. The potential problem with such budget-based penalties is fairness: They have the potential to punish citizens for the faults of agency leaders. Congress would do better simply to use financial statements for their intended purpose: to provide accurate inputs for budget discussions. If representatives and senators do this with the same zeal as corporate boards of directors and investment analysts, then rest assured that agency leaders will be motivated to deliver on their financial reporting requirements. Agency executives who do not do this should be held directly accountable for their failure.

Program Managers: Customers and Suppliers

If program managers understand, accept, and support the financial statement and audit processes, then CFOs can expect great success not only in those areas but in most others as well. If they resist or ignore the processes, then the best a CFO can hope for is a harder-won but more limited achievement that contributes little to long-term financial management maturation.

Program managers have two roles in the financial statement development and audit processes: as customers and as suppliers of information. These are reciprocal roles: the better suppliers will be more satisfied customers, and the better customers will want to be good suppliers. This dual role is implied in the underlying purposes of federal financial statements, which are different from statements in other sectors of the economy.

According to FASAB's concept statement, Objectives of Federal Financial Reporting, financial statements in the private sector and in state and local governments have a singular objective: to provide information to external users such as stockholders and stakeholders. These statements give little consideration to the information needs of internal users like program managers, who are assumed already to have the financial data they need. As noted throughout this book and in every significant new federal financial law or set of rules or standards, frequently this is not true in the national government. Thus, federal financial statements have a dual objective: to provide for the information needs of both external and internal users or customers.

If program managers are important customers for financial statement information, then it is important not to forget them in the rush to meet legislative requirements concerning the statements and the audit process. When properly prepared and analyzed, data in the principal statements will provide the following useful information to program managers:

- An agreed-upon, well-understood, and absolute quantity of money, outputs, outcomes, or other performance data at one point in time or for a period
- Comparison with similar data for other years. Trend analysis may uncover sharp variances that reflect performance problems, historical mistakes, or systemic errors
- Comparison to data from other similar organizations in order to benchmark internal performance or to validate performance of a potential best practices benchmarking partner or to industry standards (see Chapter 9 for a discussion of benchmarking)
- Data that, combined with other performance measures, can be used to compute meaningful ratios that help reveal organizational efficiency and effectiveness and that highlight potential problem areas.

Regarding ratios, government entities that provide goods or services to other organizations are increasingly being required to operate as would a business, and may in fact be competing with private companies or with each other. Some, such as industrial and revolving fund operations, already have several years' experience in using key financial ratios to manage and improve elements of their business. Such entities include military depots and supply operations. They and organizations such as the General Services Administration and many federal research and development (R&D) groups "sell" their services to agencies and do face competition. Even agencies that seem to have no competitors in their main business areas have internal units that do or should face competition, including basic internal support components like personnel, payroll, and information systems services.

Program managers in all such agencies and internal organizations are finding uses for the financial ratios applied by their counterparts in the private sector, including:

- Quick ratio (cash plus accounts receivable to current liabilities)
- Current ratio (current assets to current liabilities)
- Current liabilities to inventory
- Return on equity
- Average collection period (accounts receivable times 365 to annual sales or deliveries)
- Sales to inventory (annual net sales to inventory)
- Assets to sales (assets to annual net sales)
- Operating profit margin (net profit to annual net sales) and return on assets (net profit to total assets) (in some government entities, ideally this may be zero because they aim at breaking even each year).

Today, most program managers do not know the value they can derive from the analysis of annual financial statements. Financial managers must therefore assist in educating their program manager customers and counterparts about the data and the methods for their analysis, and take care that the required data are part of the statements or otherwise made available.

Unless program manager needs receive attention, the federal government could end up making the same accounting mistake as the private sector. This problem, which started in the 1920s and 1930s, was to emphasize external reporting but not financial information that internal managers could use to plan, control, and improve their operations. As a result, accounting lost its relevance to operations decisions. Interest in making accounting useful to operations started reviving in the last decade, when executives finally remembered that cost-effective product cost and operations decisions have a positive influence on the numbers in annual financial statements. We discuss this more in Chapter 10, under managerial cost accounting and activity-based costing.

Program managers as suppliers. Federal agencies, like all businesses, need to have good suppliers. We noted in Chapter 5 that up to three-fourths of the information needed for federal financial statements often resides outside the office of the CFO, mostly with program managers. A key initial challenge for financial managers is to motivate their program manager suppliers to respond promptly to special data calls for financial statement information. A good example of this is the experience of one of our clients, an organization that manages a large dollar value of equipment and property in the defense community. During a financial statement audit, at first the organization's top logistics managers did not understand why auditors were citing them for problems that seemed to be strictly financial issues better handled by its finance group. A financial manager explained that valuation information on property, plant, and equipment resided in the logistics managers' databases, not in financial systems, which made the logistics managers key players in developing financial statements. This understanding formed the basis for initial discussions about an ongoing partnership between financial and logistics managers, which led to improvements in stewardship reporting.

Also, CFOs must remember that auditors often require extremely detailed information, especially documentation of data that support the numbers in financial statements. Frequently, data integrity depends on the skills and actions of clerical and technical personnel throughout an agency. The CFO must ensure that, if necessary, these personnel receive additional training on CFO Act data requirements, with emphasis on following appropriate internal control procedures related to data integrity.

Over the long term, special data calls and data integrity problems will become less frequent and arduous because financial and program managers will team up to develop information systems that record routinely the basic financial, accounting, and performance data needed for program decisions. Such systems are the main reason that many organizations require only a few weeks to prepare financial statements and have them audited. The ability to do this reflects a far higher level of financial management maturity than a mad scramble for data once a year.

Most agencies will need parallel financial systems for budgets, external reporting, and internal use. Such systems should ideally be co-developed and draw from common data sources. In this way, an agency will be better able to determine the link between program decisions and financial results.

The Agency CFO and Financial Management Staff: Suppliers and Developers

These professionals provide the financial management skills and processes for their agency. Typically, the CFO "owns" the financial statement development process, including preparing the statements, working with auditors, and taking action on financial management, internal controls, and performance measurement system findings of audit opinions and related reports.

In addition, the CFO must champion the use by the rest of his or her agency of financial statement information and audit results. As with other types of change management, this begins with educating top executives on this information and obtaining their commitment to use it for agency decisions.

The Federal CFO Council: Forum

Established by the CFO Act, the council meets periodically "to advise and coordinate the activities of the agencies of its members on such matters as consolidation and modernization of financial systems, improved quality of financial information, financial data and information standards, internal controls, legislation affecting financial operations and organizations, and any other financial management matter." The council is chaired by the Deputy Director for Management of OMB, and includes the Controller of the OMB Office of Federal Financial Management, the Fiscal Assistant Secretary of Treasury; and the appointed CFOs of the 24 agencies recognized in the GMRA. Because the council exercises significant policy influence on all facets of annual financial statements and audits, it is a key forum for audit issues, and also conducts related seminars and publishes policy papers on topics of interest to CFOs.

Inspectors General and Internal Agency Auditors: Auditors

IGs are responsible for a wide range of audit and investigative activities. We will limit discussion to their audit responsibilities associated with the annual financial statements, internal controls, and compliance with related laws and regulations, as set forth in the CFO Act. Specifically, IGs are charged with conducting or managing their agencies' annual financial statement audit. The CFO Act permits them to conduct an audit with their internal staff or retain the services of an independent public accounting firm.

Most IGs and their staffs have experience in program or operational audits, not financial audits. Many IGs believe—and not without reason—that their customary core workload of program audits is significantly underfunded. They view financial audits as competing for program audit resources needed to assure basic program integrity. Other IGs, perhaps more forward-looking, see that financial audit work can and should be integral to the information gathering that is already part of program audits. Given the mixture of financial and program information within federal financial statements and their related documents, the latter is arguably the more progressive view.

However, this same mixture has fostered often heated debate between IGs and CFOs. Traditionally, IG offices are investigators who focus on waste, fraud, and abuse. To a certain extent, this tradition has carried over to the annual financial statement audit process. Also, many IGs (and the GAO) tend to look for and report programmatic problems discovered in a financial audit. CFOs have argued that including such problems in an audit report can be out of scope and make it difficult to obtain a clean audit opinion on otherwise fair representations of agency finances. This dispute should be resolved as the federal audit process matures, but it will take much discussion and teamwork over the next several years. As of the writing of this book, the President's Council on Integrity and Efficiency (PCIE), made up of appointed federal IGs, and the CFO Council have begun engaging in such discussions.

Despite disagreements between CFOs and IGs, the CFO Act, GPRA, and GMRA have created closer relations among both groups. This relationship is evolving in ways similar to that of public accounting firms and their corporate clients, which we discuss next.

Independent Public Accounting Firms: Auditors

Usually, IGs retain independent certified public accountants (CPAs) to conduct agency audits for one or more of three reasons. Some IG offices lack a sufficient number of trained staff for annual financial audits, and so need outside assistance for their first few audits. Also, some IGs may not want to invest ever-scarcer resources in hiring, training, and maintaining internally the full staffing capability to conduct a once-a-year audit. For them, an independent CPA firm is a more cost-effective alternative, because the firm's CPAs do audits full-time and are required by their licenses to stay current with the latest developments in public accountancy. Finally, some IGs elect to follow the tradition of private corporations.

By law, CPAs are the only auditors used by the approximately 10,000 publicly owned corporations in the United States whose debt or stock securities are traded on stock exchanges or over the counter. Many corporations and their CPA firms develop long-term relationships, so that the auditors become familiar with a client company's operations, industry, and financial management approach. Because of their size and complexity, most major corporations have their audits done by large accounting firms capable of fielding an appropriately sized auditor team. When a corporation has holdings in several industry areas, the auditor team includes CPAs familiar with them. Also, most large CPA firms provide their clients with additional services such as pre-audit assistance, internal control assessments, and improvements to financial information systems and processes, which enables the firms to help their clients correct problems uncovered in audits.

The General Accounting Office and the Comptroller General: Auditor and Rule Maker

The GMRA requires that that the Comptroller General, who heads GAO, be responsible for auditing the consolidated financial statement for the entire federal government, which will be done for the first time for FY 1997. At the discretion of the Comptroller General, GAO may review financial statement audits done by an IG or an external auditor, or may actually conduct an audit. Also, GAO works with OMB, Treasury, and agency CFOs and IGs on task forces that address accounting and auditing issues. GAO provides support for the work of FASAB and, along with OMB and Treasury, is responsible for approving the accounting standards FASAB recommends.

Much like IGs, early in its CFO Act auditor role GAO needed to build an organizational structure to handle large-scale audits such as those required by the act. This included adding new and retraining existing staff in the financial statement audit process. GAO has been actively helping agencies prepare for their first audits, especially the CFO Act pilot agencies. Mostly, the GAO has audited large and complex organizations, such as the Customs Service and Army, and then taken on an oversight role; we discuss these two agencies' audit experiences later in this chapter. Sometimes, GAO teams with IG staff to undertake different aspects of an agency audit. In a few cases, such as the IRS, GAO has continued its auditor role over several years.

The Federal Accounting Standards Advisory Board: Forum and Rule Maker

FASAB's mission is to recommend accounting standards for the federal government after considering the financial and budgetary information needs of congressional oversight groups, executive agencies, and other users. FASAB was established in 1990 by the secretary of the Treasury, the director of OMB, and the Comptroller General, who are authorized to approve its recommendations. The board includes representatives from each of those organizations and other federal agencies, and three representatives who are not from the federal government.

As of the writing of this book, FASAB has developed pronouncements related to accounting standards in such areas as cash, accounts receivable, accounts payable, direct loans and loan guarantees, inventory and related property, managerial cost accounting, liabilities, property, plant and equipment, revenues, and other financing sources and stewardship assets. Two pronouncements relate directly to the presentation of financial statements: *Objectives of Federal Financial Reporting* and *Entity and Display,* the latter of which was discussed in Chapter 5.

Some have erroneously compared FASAB to the Financial Accounting Standards Board (FASB) and the Government Accounting Standards Board (GASB), which develop standards primarily for external financial reports for, respectively, the private sector and state and local governments. FASAB has a broader role, which is to serve financial information users who are both internal and external to an audited federal entity, for reasons we discussed earlier in this chapter under Program Managers. FASAB recommendations reflect the unique characteristics and objectives of the federal government. For example, FASAB concluded that federal agencies should report separately revenues received as a result of an exchange transaction and those received through the government's exercise of its sovereign power. Also, because the nature of the work of federal agencies is extremely varied, FASAB tries to maintain some flexibility in its recommendations for standards.

To develop recommendations, FASAB forms committees that include federal financial executives and outside experts in accountancy and financial management. A committee develops a draft recommendation that is circulated for comment to the appropriate financial and other executives in the federal government. Thus, at the developmental stage of rule making, FASAB is the central forum for resolving issues and controversies about government-wide accounting standards.

The Office of Management and Budget: Rule Maker and Developer

OMB is the President's primary "agent" for fiscal matters and is specifically authorized by the CFO Act to issue the rules of the federal financial statement and audit initiative. Through its circulars and other pronouncements, OMB has established the form and content of agency financial statements, the universe of reporting entities, and basic principles for conducting audits. This rule making is not done solely within the walls of OMB, but instead comes after expert, agency, and public consultation and comment on the rules and consensus among OMB, the Treasury, and GAO. For example, if the three organizations approve a FASAB recommendation, OMB will issue it as a Statement of Federal Financial Accounting Standards (SFFAS), which is considered GAAP for Federal agencies. OMB provides technical assistance to agencies in interpreting SFFASs, unless it decides that the explanation should be developed along with Treasury and GAO. After further consultation, OMB may then issue an Interpretation of Federal Financial Accounting Standards.

Also, the OMB consolidates agency CFOs' annual five-year financial management plans and annual reports and submits to Congress a government-wide five-year financial management plan and a financial management status report. The plan and report address government-wide issues related to financial statement development and auditing.

The Department of the Treasury: Developer and Rule Maker

Treasury CFO George Muñoz says that his department's Financial Management Service (FMS) is the "final accountant" for the federal government. This is because FMS will prepare the government-wide consolidated financial statements. Treasury is working closely with both the CFO Council and the President's Council on Integrity and Efficiency to develop plans for that audit. Also, as mentioned earlier, Treasury is one of the organizations that approves FASAB accounting standards, participates on the CFO Council, and is active in formulating audit policies.

Other Organizations That Influence the Audit Process
Other organizations also influence this process, especially in its more controversial areas. For example, the Joint Financial Management Improvement Program, the Association of Government Accountants, the American Society of Military Comptrollers, and the National Association of Public Administration provide forums for discussing issues and sharing best practices in preparing and auditing financial statements. Their work and opinions inform the decisions of the team members, and provide a forward look at what the process may eventually become once all issues and controversies are resolved.

Issues and Controversies

Earlier, we said that there were differences in opinion among CFOs, IGs, GAO, and independent accounting firms over the appropriate inclusion of nonfinancial program information in financial statement audits. Related to this issue is the appropriate level of materiality for federal audits. Also, there is debate over which organizations are the most cost-effective auditors for federal agencies. Such controversies are to be expected because the federal audit process is still new.

Materiality: I Know It When I See It
According to the chapter on field work standards for financial audits in the GAO's Government Auditing Standards (also known as the Yellow Book):

> **[4.8]** Auditors' consideration of materiality is a matter of professional judgment and is influenced by their perception of the needs of a reasonable person who will rely on the financial statements. Materiality judgments are made in light of surrounding circumstances and necessarily involve both quantitative and qualitative considerations.

As the term "professional judgment" indicates, it is up to the auditor to make a determination of materiality, and no one disagrees with this authority. The current controversy surrounding materiality concerns whether auditors are being too conservative in this area by setting materiality levels unreasonably low.

In the private sector, past practices in judging materiality are giving way to a movement toward more disclosure rather than less. One reason is the increased litigation directed at companies and their CPA firms for allegedly failing to disclose all material weaknesses during an audit. As a result, CPAs are becoming more conservative in their approach to materiality. The downside of this conservatism is two-fold. First, it has increased the already voluminous pages of notes typically attached to a financial statement, which confuses some readers. Second, lower materiality thresholds require more audit work and tend to drive up the cost and time needed for an audit.

Thus, if federal auditors simply followed the trend of private auditors, they would become more conservative about materiality. However, our experience is that many IGs and GAO auditors are even more cautious, for reasons given in the following Yellow Book paragraph (the key terms are highlighted):

> **[4.9]** In an audit of the financial statements of a government entity..., *auditors may set lower materiality levels than in audits in the private sector* because of the public accountability of the auditee, the various legal and regulatory requirements, and the visibility and sensitivity of government programs, activities, and functions.

Implied in the paragraph is that government audits should be held to a higher standard than private sector audits. GAO is the agent of the Congress, so the office's standards have considerable weight in determining how best to comply with a congressional mandate such as the CFO Act. However, we think it fair to ask if paragraph 4.9 can sometimes be interpreted in ways that go well beyond the general purpose of annual financial statements and of Congress's intended uses of them. This question can be addressed by looking at how the size of budgets can affect materiality judgments, and how such judgments can make it difficult to set improvement priorities.

Size of budgets and materiality. The budgets of most federal agencies dwarf those of private companies. Even a relatively small discrepancy in the disclosures of an agency's financial statement can result in failing to fairly account for millions of dollars. This argues for materiality thresholds established by absolute dollar amounts, rather than a simplistic rule of thumb such as 3 percent of total budget.

On the other hand, many federal CFOs feel that lower thresholds misconstrue the financial condition of their organizations. CFO John Hamre of the Defense Department told us that there were discrepancies amounting to half a billion dollars arising from one military payment center. However, he says that the discrepancies appear far more significant than they actually are because of the order of magnitude of the volumes of transactions the center handles—it disburses between $20 million and $40 million every hour. Hamre pointed out that, computed as a percentage of the total money involved, the proportion of true discrepancies is actually smaller than in most private sector organizations. "We've been able to reconcile most of the half billion dollars that were thought to be lost," he added.

With a total budget of more than $1 trillion a year, and several agencies with budgets approaching or passing $100 billion, the federal government has to think carefully about its policy toward materiality. A $1 million discrepancy is significant by itself, but still is only 1/1000 of $1 billion. If the purpose of a federal financial statement is to provide reasonable assurance about the financial condition of an agency, a better balance must be struck between admittedly large amounts of money that are relatively small in comparison to an agency's overall record of fiscal stewardship.

First things first. Experienced financial auditors are excellent detectives. In the course of a normal audit they will discover most material discrepancies that affect the

fairness of representations in a financial statement.
However, the cost of an audit that discovers nearly all such
discrepancies would be enormous, and would still miss
some of them. Also, the extra time needed would delay and
thus decrease the value of audit results to inform congressional decisions.

Finally, one of the chief aims of CFO Act audits is to
guide agencies in fixing quickly their most serious financial
management problems. Unfortunately, even relatively minor
federal financial issues, once raised in public, require corrective action and resources that would be better used on
truly serious problems. In the future, once major discrepancies are solved, it would be reasonable to expect that federal
audit policy will require lower thresholds of materiality. But
for now, first things first.

Program Versus Finance Audits

The Yellow Book also sets forth the difference between program and financial audits, but indicates that there may be an
overlap of the two types in some circumstances. During the
initial CFO Act pilot audits, federal auditors frequently
appeared to combine program and finance issues. One reason is that IGs and the GAO have traditionally carried out
program audits, and their work in this regard has oriented
them toward program performance. This means their audits
tend to have a scope broader than simply financial reporting
issues, and is one reason that relatively few CFO Act pilot
agencies received clean audit opinions from IGs and the
GAO.

We believe that federal financial audits will always
focus on a mix of both programmatic and financial issues.
Achieving the right balance of the two is the challenge. In
the meantime, IGs, GAO, and independent CPA auditors
need to reflect on what the mixture means to their dual roles
as auditors and partners in improving agency financial management.

**Federal financial auditors: partners or program crit-
ics?** In state governments, some audits by IGs and oversight
agencies have gone beyond strictly financial examination

into the more political arena of program evaluation. Some have said this represents a "power grab" by state legislatures that compels government auditors to second guess the decisions of agency administrators. It is true that legislators hold the purse strings and would be remiss in their responsibility if they did not make every effort to ensure that funds are being spent in ways that deliver the right results. However, this can strain the relationship between agencies and their auditors. If the IG community and the GAO have a "gotcha" orientation, it will be much more difficult for them to become partners in program improvement.

A partnership based on a healthy mix of financial and program focus can certainly be beneficial to agencies. According to Hamre "The message here is that, in today's world, finance can't solve the problems that are created in other communities without working with the other communities in order to fix them. And the problem at DoD is that rarely can you fix your own problem. You have to get someone else to fix it, and he doesn't really have a feel for the problem." In our opinion, it takes a blending of financial and programmatic skills to formulate the right solutions, as we have seen in the Customs Service and the Army.

Case Study—Customs Service: Find the Goods! Where Are the Goods?

When it comes to collecting revenues, the Customs Service is second only to the IRS. Initial financial audits at Customs revealed several severe problems, not all of which were strictly related to financial reporting. The problems included that the agency did not:

- Adequately ensure that all goods imported into the United States were properly identified and that the related duties, taxes, and fees on imports, reported to be more than $21 billion for fiscal year 1993, were properly assessed and collected
- Have adequate controls to detect and prevent excessive or duplicate refund payments
- Provide for adequate accountability over tons of illegal drugs and millions of dollars of cash and property seized or used in its enforcement efforts

---

- Have adequate controls over the use and reporting of its operating funds.

The audit prompted the Commissioner of Customs to make a strong commitment to resolve these problems and recognize the necessity for sustained efforts by Customs' management to improve financial performance. Acting on this commitment, Customs developed and tested nationwide a new program to reliably measure the trade community's compliance with trade laws. This program is expected to achieve better compliance with trade laws and has resulted in tighter controls to ensure that the government receives all of the revenues to which it is entitled. It also helped Customs ensure that it is making the best use of limited inspection and audit resources.

In addition, as a result of the audit report findings, Customs developed and applied methodologies for reporting more accurately its collective accounts receivable. It also reorganized its debt collection unit, formalized its collection procedures, and aggressively pursued collection of old receivables. This effort resulted in additional collections of more than $35 million. And the bottom line for Customs is that for the FY 1995 audit report just issued, it received an unqualified opinion for the first time in its history. Commitment and focus can pay off.

Case Study—The U.S. Army: Frustration and Progress

As a component of DoD, the Army has a mission orientation characterized by combat, readiness, and minimizing casualties. This precludes, to a certain extent, application of the same type of performance analysis and requirements that can be used elsewhere. For example, Treasury CFO George Muñoz points out that GSA (a property manager) and the Pension Benefit Guaranty Corporation (an insurer) have an operational orientation. Such agencies can, like commercial enterprises, recoup certain costs, making it easier to apply financial control, accounting procedures, and performance measurement standards to them.

Under Fire

Problems revealed by the Army's pilot audit were on the same scale as those of the Customs Service. Yet, as the Assistant Secretary of the Army for Financial Management and Comptroller, Helen T. McCoy, stated in congressional testimony on November 15, 1995 regarding the audit: "The single greatest benefit the Army has derived from its experience as a CFO Act pilot is our recognition and acknowledgment of the difference between systemic and management problems—between problems which require DoD-wide efforts and will take years to resolve, and those which we in the Army can and must take immediate responsibility for." She noted also that rectifying the deficiencies had prompted the Army to "[engineer] a breakdown in the traditional stovepipe barriers between functional and financial managers and [prompt them to work] together to fix our problems and to improve every aspect of stewardship."

The Army started preparing agency-wide audited financial statements as a pilot under the CFO Act for FY 1991. The GAO did the audit for fiscal years 1991 and 1992 and the U.S. Army Audit Agency for fiscal years 1993-95. Neither auditor has been able to express an opinion on the fairness of the Army's financial statements. Both noted that the major problem precluding a qualified or unqualified opinion was that the accounting systems that support the statements did not have an integrated general ledger and did not produce account-oriented transaction files. Without a complete general ledger, the Army used systems designed to manage and physically account for Army assets to derive the value of those assets. The management systems, however, did not interface with the Army's accounting systems, nor meet requirements for generating reliable, auditable financial information.

McCoy noted that, whereas the audits for fiscal years 1992 through 1994 acknowledged significant progress from previous years' reporting, the Army's systems still fell far short of producing the information necessary to support the reliability of financial statement data, and thus she admitted that auditors would likely be unable to express an opinion for some time to come.

Nonetheless, she added, the requirements of the CFO Act prompted the Army to begin working with the DoD Comptroller, the Defense Finance and Accounting Service, and the other military departments to bring about the necessary comprehensive reforms of financial management systems and processes. "Although it will take years to achieve the streamlined and reliable processes that are its goal, the Army has achieved a great deal of progress," she stated, noting also that, although the state of its accounting systems has been the single greatest factor cited in the audit opinions, other negative findings proved to be within the Army's ability to resolve.

"Audits of the first Army financial statements, and the associated hearings and media reports, were often—and in some cases, justifiably—harsh in their criticism of the Army as a steward of public resources," said

McCoy. "The Army responded by getting back to the basics, by bringing together key financial and program management personnel to resolve problems one by one. It initiated a number of disciplined efforts to improve our management practices, ensure fiscal responsibility, and promote sound stewardship—actions that will not end even when we do have integrated functional and financial management systems."

Fire and Maneuver

McCoy reviewed the benefits of the audit process to Army, saying, "The Army has formed strong partnerships with functional proponents throughout the organization to resolve internal problems with how we safeguard and account for the assets and has been very aggressive in our efforts to find new and improved ways of doing business with the tools and resources that are available." Specific improvements included the following:

- Management control processes were decentralized and made more flexible. Commanders and managers were empowered and given a sense of ownership and control. Courses were offered, and educational materials such as briefing documents and videotapes were disseminated to facilitate implementation of these changes.
- Enhancements have been made to systems interface capabilities and process reengineering efforts.
- An Army Joint Reconciliation program has been established in which financial skills of accounting and budget personnel are combined with the expertise of acquisition specialists, logisticians, auditors, and legal staffs in creating horizontal teams to analyze problem disbursements—payments that do not match obligations. This led to reductions in the value of unmatched disbursements from $750 million to $368 million.

The Army audits also prompted improvements in the areas of acquisition and financial review, requisition and accounting, military pay, and personnel systems.

As McCoy noted, the impact of the audit process on the Army was far-ranging: "The statements and audits are the means to an end—and that end is the integration of financial and functional information, not only in systems and data, but in all aspects of our day-to-day management." Ernest Gregory, Deputy Assistant Secretary of the Army for Financial Operations, adds: "This view of the world is reflected in everything we are doing with our functional partners."

Chapter

7

STRATEGIC THINKING, ACTION PLANNING

Law and necessity require that CFOs and their financial organizations participate in agency strategic planning and develop strategies for improving financial management processes.

- The Government Performance and Results Act of 1993 mandates that most federal agencies prepare strategic plans, performance plans, and performance reports.
- OMB Circular A-11, Preparation and Submission of Budget Estimates, requires agency CFOs to prepare financial management plans as part of their budget submissions.
- As a valued partner on the agency-wide strategy team, the CFO must first and foremost play the role of providing ideas for strategic solutions to both operational and financial challenges. Also, the CFO plays a critical role in securing financing for strategic initiatives.
- The office of the CFO can support the agency-wide strategic planning process through research and analysis of financial aspects of strategies. Outside headquarters, other financial managers assist their operations and support colleagues in preparing deployment plans that implement strategic initiatives.
- CFOs and their financial teams should be proactive in providing strategic planning services to other parts of their agencies.

A strategy is the pattern or plan that integrates an organization's major goals, policies, and action sequences into a cohesive whole. A well-formulated strategy helps to marshal and allocate an organization's resources into a unique and viable posture based on its relative internal competencies and shortcomings; anticipated changes in the environment; and contingent moves by intelligent opponents.

–James Brian Quinn, *The Strategy Process*

Strategy is what an organization does to sustain and cultivate its ability to provide value to customers in the future. Strategy is a continuing process of decisions and actions that starts with understanding what needs to be done and ends with rewarding those who do it. Finally, strategy is an iterative process that, constantly repeated, allows organization to reposition themselves to meet new challenges.

Strategic planning is the part of the strategy process that determines the direction in which an organization needs to go in the future. *Strategic implementation* allocates resources to activities required to gain the goals, then ensures that these activities are executed according to plan and produce the desired results. These activities should be aimed at changing the core business processes that produce products and services for external customers. Indeed, strategy cannot be successful unless processes change, because today no organization can conduct business as usual and hope to survive the ever-changing business environment.

Becoming a Powerful Voice in the Strategy Process

CFOs and other top financial executives have two sets of strategic responsibilities. The first is to be a partner with other executives in the agency-wide strategy process. This responsibility is part of the CFO's Strategist and Visionary role discussed in Chapter 3. The second is to develop a financial management strategy that is aligned with the agency's other strategic goals and processes. This internal strategic plan guides the CFO office in achieving the Team Leader organizational role discussed in Chapter 3.

Thus, as a member of an agency's top executive team, a CFO makes strategy, while his or her office supports the strategic planning process. This is not a subtle difference in semantics. It underscores that the CFO is, first and foremost, a senior leader in his or her organization who has been invited by agency need and legislative mandate to take part in strategy formulation. Like other senior leaders, the CFO must be an informed, intelligent voice at strategy discussions, speaking not simply from the financial perspective, but also from a profound understanding of an agency's business.

To become a powerful voice in strategy development, a CFO must carry to the planning table creative solutions to issues in programs and core business processes. Finance-related solutions to operations problems may include electronic commerce, developing fee schedules that recover full costs, performance-based pay, outsourcing, acquisition reform, and activity-based management (see Chapter 10), to name a few. A CFO must devote some of the resources of his or her office to researching such solutions well in advance of planning sessions. This does not trespass on the turf of program managers. Rather, searching for solutions in partnership with program managers fosters ongoing cooperation. Also, operations executives will likely be grateful for the CFO's assistance in exploring the costs, benefits, and risks of solutions—all solutions, not just those that are finance-based. Offered proactively and productively, such assistance usually provides opportunities for CFOs to be a powerful influence on the form and substance of a solution.

For agencies, the rewards for a strategic combination of financial and operational knowledge and skills are obvious. For the individual financial professional, the reward could be advancement to the top of the agency; this has certainly been the case in the private sector, where many of today's CEOs started out in finance.

Federal Mandate for Strategic Planning

Most federal departments and many agencies have engaged in some form of strategic business planning over the past few years. This practice has been codified by the Government Performance and Results Act of 1993, which requires most agencies with budgets of more than $20 million to develop long-term goals and strategic plans and annual performance objectives based on the goals, and to report to Congress each year on goal attainment.

The CFO Act requires most agency CFOs to prepare and revise annually an agency plan to implement the five-year financial management plan prepared by the Director of the Office of Management and Budget. Though the agency financial plan is not, strictly speaking, a strategic plan, OMB directives concerning it include many of the elements of the GPRA's agency-wide plan. Thus, CFOs may wish to consider developing their agency financial plans using the basic concepts of strategic planning, and coordinate them with GPRA-required strategic plans.

GPRA Requirements for Strategic Planning
To comply with GPRA, an agency's strategic plan should:
- Cover a five-year period, be delivered to OMB and Congress by the end of FY 1997, and be updated at least every three years thereafter
- Be developed in consultation with Congress and other interested or affected parties
- Define and describe an agency's major missions
- Include strategic, general, and longer-range goals related to missions
- State the agency's current performance in goal areas
- Describe systems, resources, and processes related to achieving the goals
- Identify key factors external to the agency and beyond that could affect achievement of its goals
- Describe how program evaluations are used in establishing goals and objectives and provide a schedule of future program evaluations.

Congress intends to monitor strategy implementation through annual performance plans and reports. Performance plans are to be prepared for each program activity in an agency, and should be related to an agency's strategic plan.

The performance plans are to be given to OMB and Congress starting in FY 1999. Each plan must establish performance goals based on the general goals of the agency strategic plan; describe resources needed to achieve the performance goals; set performance indicators to progress toward goals; and compare actual program results with performance goals.

Performance reports are to describe the performance goals in an agency's plan and compare actual to planned performance; give reasons for not achieving goals; and describe actions the agency will take to meet them. This report is to cover performance in the previous fiscal year, starting with FY 2000, and the three preceding fiscal years starting with FY 2002. It is due by March 31 after the end of the applicable fiscal year. An agency may include all program performance information required by the GPRA in the annual financial statement mandated by the CFO Act if the statement is submitted to Congress before March 31 of the applicable fiscal year.

OMB Circular A-11 Requirements for Financial Plans

This circular, entitled Preparation and Submission of Budget Estimates, directs agencies to provide the following information related to financial management as an integral part of their budget justification materials:

- A statement of the CFO's vision for financial management
- Goals and strategies for implementing financial management improvements
- A discussion of the current financial management systems structure and plans for moving to the targeted systems structure (this section of the financial plan may fulfill the requirement in OMB Circular No. A-127, *Financial Management Systems*, that agencies prepare an annual plan for the systems)
- A discussion of impediments to the submission of required annual audited financial statements.

These five-year plans require the same type of coordinated strategic approach outlined in this chapter for GPRA strategic planning.

Setting the Stage for Strategic Planning

Agency leaders who jump into strategic planning without preparation end up with worthless plans. Preplanning increases the chances for success and starts with assessment of an agency's internal and external environment and internal capabilities, which reveals the organization's current strategic position. Also, assessments provide the hard facts that should drive workable strategy and the direction that nonstrategic components of the agency will take.

Agency-Wide Preplanning Assessments

Strategic assessments can include customer surveys; cultural surveys of the work force; economic, demographic, and political analyses; industry trends; projections and scenarios; external benchmarks of performance; and other methods. During the strategic planning process, participants review and discuss assessment results and other factors that affect their operations. Then, they identify an agency's key strengths, weaknesses, opportunities, and problems in successfully addressing issues raised by the assessment.

Role of the CFO during agency-wide assessment. The CFO office has a large, unique tool kit for addressing many of the questions raised during agency-wide assessment. This tool kit includes the ability to calculate current costs of providing a service or serving a specific customer group, then compare them this with benchmark costs in industry or other organizations. Also, financial professionals can determine the cost implications of demographic and economic trends to construct scenarios of a likely new agency environment. Some organizations use a business case study approach to assessment, which can benefit from the analytical skills of financial professionals, as we discuss later.

Preplanning Assessments Within the CFO Office

Just as organization-wide assessment prepares an agency for strategy development, a strategic assessment of financial processes allows the CFO office to determine its own position relative to agency requirements. Several assessment methods can provide a quick look at the office's capabilities: internal customer surveys, analysis of recent audits, benchmarking, and maturity analysis.

Internal customer surveys. An internal financial organization's primary customers should be program and other nonfinancial managers within the same agency. Even though they are important, Congress, OMB, and oversight organizations may be classified as secondary customers or stakeholders. As noted in Chapter 3, surveys and focus groups are good ways to learn how the financial organization's internal customers rate its services. Figure 3-4 in Chapter 3 shows example questions for a financial organization's survey.

Audit results and pre-audits. Audits reveal deficiencies and material weaknesses that can be corrected with both tactical and strategic actions, and the management letter accompanying an audit report may offer specific organizational, process, or control improvement recommendations. However, a financial organization need not wait until an audit is complete to correct deficiencies. Pre-audits can help avoid this embarrassment and provide information for improving audits in subsequent years The box at the end of this chapter outlines a pre-audit methodology that is useful for preplanning assessment.

Benchmarks. Chapter 9 discusses benchmarking in detail, with emphasis on best practices for financial processes. During the assessment, a CFO office would do well to benchmark the quality, cost, or cycle time of its major financial processes, using the competitive or industry benchmarking approaches described in Chapter 9. While a comprehensive benchmarking project may require months, assessment benchmarking efforts are less detailed and can be completed in a few weeks. For example, a quick comparison of a CFO office's processes to best practices in other financial organizations does not require the extensive internal and external process analysis required to adapt and adopt external practices. However, a quick look can provide insights into the direction that improvements should take.

Maturity analysis. Maturity analysis uses instruments such as the QuikGrid matrix shown in Figure 3-3 in Chapter 3 to gauge the maturity of a financial organization. Maturity analysis highlights areas in which an organization needs to improve in order to reach world-class service standards. Questions based on the elements of the QuikGrid help determine an organization's position on the matrix. Maturity analyses do not require much time or money and are useful for periodically assessing improvement progress.

These and other assessment tools offer CFOs a well-rounded picture of their financial organizations and the services they provide within an agency. They also help the CFO understand his or her position relative to other senior executives. For example, what if an internal customer survey indicates that the financial information a CFO office provides to other parts of an agency is only marginally useful? How, then, can a CFO expect to be treated as an equal at the strategic planning table? Fortunately, such assessments also show what the CFO and financial organization need to do to gain respect and thus achieve equal partnership in agency leadership and strategy development.

Why Most Strategy Is Not Really Strategy

In most organizations, "strategic" planning is an annual or semi-annual ritual of setting incremental goals. This is really tactical planning, involving no substantial change in processes. Tactical planning is not a leadership function, because most managers could do the work involved, with a sign-off by executives. However, such planning is a recipe for disaster for federal agencies that need quantum leap improvements in order to survive, much less meet their missions.

True strategy is based on challenging the underlying assumptions of an organization, and of its competitors and customers. It embodies the principles of the National Performance Review, which is to reinvent the way that government provides services to citizens. Such strategy aims at achieving innovations that are different in form and function from business as usual. It is revolutionary rather than evolutionary and may even reposition an agency in the "market." For example, an agency may choose to shift its approach from providing services directly to customers to creating links between its customers and other providers of the same type of service.

Tactical planning is relatively easy, taking only a few days of the year from the schedule of busy executives. Strategy is demanding, requiring major investments of senior leaders' and many other people's time and energy. Indeed, true strategy does not follow an annual or semi-annual calendar. Instead, is an ongoing, iterative process designed to align an organization with where its customers and competitive environment will be in the future.

In tactical planning, the federal CFO and other financial executives are largely relegated to the role of ferreting out incrementally better ways to squeeze a few more pennies of value out of a budget dollar. In strategy, they have the opportunity to help transform their agencies. This begins with understanding the strategic planning process.

Strategic Planning for Agencies and for Internal Financial Organizations

Strategic planning is a component of the strategy process, the part that establishes directions and goals. Several good frameworks exist for the strategic planning process. Most are cycles that begin with clarifying agency missions and end with measuring the achievement of goals and objectives, then loop back to the start of the cycle. A brief outline of one such planning cycle is shown in Figure 7-1. This planning cycle can be used by a team of top executives, including the CFO, to develop agency-wide strategies. An internal financial organization can use the cycle to develop its own objectives, which should be aimed at aligning

Figure 7-1

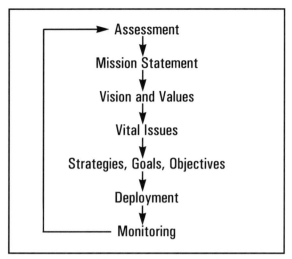

financial processes with agency strategy during the Plan Deployment.

Assessment offers agency executives a view of the strengths, weaknesses, opportunities, and constraints that form the agency environment; this analysis is sometimes called an environmental scan. Other key elements of strategic planning include a mission statement, vision, values, vital issues and key accomplishments, and strategies, goals, and objectives.

Mission Statement

This short statement defines an agency's reason for being, or its purpose, services, products, and customers. Mission statements set the basic priorities for strategic planning, for both an entire agency and its components, including the financial organization.

The CFO office mission statement. An agency CFO office also benefits from having a clear mission statement. The statement may include providing accurate and timely financial information for cost-effective decision making, exercising sound stewardship of public funds, developing internal controls that add value to operations processes, and creating leading-edge financial transaction processes.

Figure 7-2

Federal Financial Management Vision Statement

Enabling government to work better and cost less requires program and financial managers—working in partnership using modern management techniques and integrated financial management systems—to ensure the integrity of information, make decisions, and measure performance to achieve desirable outcomes and real cost effectiveness.

We envision an environment where:

Program and financial managers work in partnership to achieve the full integration of financial (finance, budget, and cost), program, and oversight information and processes.

Financial management policies and practices enhance effectiveness and efficiency of governmental programs; measuring performance is a critical element in making decisions.

Financial management emphasizes customer service based on customer needs.

Integrated financial management systems, with adequate internal review and controls, provide information that is timely, accurate, and analyzed for options in ways that specifically help achieve program objectives. Government-wide systems are shared among agencies, and accountability is assured.

Quantitative standards, collecting performance data on a timely basis, and comparing the results against appropriate standards are an integral part of the assessment and planning processes used by agency management, Congress, the Executive Branch, and the public.

Agencies assure Congress and the public that assets are being safeguarded, financial results are reported accurately and timely, and performance is measured accurately.

Financial management processes are streamlined, effective, and allow for the highest operational standards.

Financial managers are recognized as leaders in their profession, creative in finding solutions to management issues, and valued members of any management team.

Financial management goals are backed by recruitment, training, performance, and reward structures.

Program managers embrace their responsibility for managing financial resources with support from the financial management communities.

Source: *Federal Financial Management Status Report and Five Year Plan*, June 1996.

Vision

A vision is a description of the desired outcome of the strategic plan—an agency's to-be state at some point in the future once all goals are achieved. The vision serves as a target, so all agency strategy should in some way contribute to realizing it. In his or her role as Strategist and Visionary, a CFO can make a major contribution to agency strategy by influencing other executives to develop a clear, comprehensive, and specific vision of the future.

The CFO's vision statement. When developing a strategic plan for the financial organization, a CFO must work with other financial executives to develop a vision that serves as a target for improvement. Figure 3-2 in Chapter 3 shows the vision of the Johnson & Johnson Finance Group. This was not the first vision statement the group developed. Instead, it is the result of years of work at defining those vital few areas where the group can and must be a Team Leader for the entire Johnson & Johnson organization.

Another guide for developing a financial organization's vision is the federal CFO Council's vision statement shown in Figure 7-2, which OMB Circular A-11 directs agency CFOs to use as a basis for their visions. This helps ensure that an agency's financial management strategies are aligned with government-wide strategies.

Values
Values are the principles and standards that define how an agency wants to operate. They describe how leaders intend to guide and manage the agency and the behaviors expected from everyone in the organization.

Vital Issues and Key Accomplishments
These are the vital few strategic issues that represent the most critical challenges to fulfilling a mission and reaching a vision. They are also called critical success factors (CSFs). Execution of the strategic plan means addressing and improving the CSFs. To identify CSFs, strategic planners list all issues that arise during preplanning assessment, then collapse them into common categories. They rank categories by importance to achieving the vision and rate how well they are doing on each. The categories with highest importance scores but lowest performance scores often become the CSFs. Then, participants develop and reach consensus on "mini-visions" of the to-be state for each CSF,

set five to ten years in the future, which we call key accomplishments.

Strategies, Goals, and Objectives

Strategy. A strategy is a narrative description of how an organization will move from the as-is to the to-be state described in a key accomplishment. Forming strategy is the heart of the strategic planning process, and also the most exciting and fulfilling. This is a good time to examine the strategies of best-in-class organizations that have met similar challenges, to call on the creativity of experts from inside and outside the agency, and to "think outside the box" to develop totally new solutions. Then, alternative solutions must be carefully analyzed to determine their potential costs, benefits, and risks. This is a task in which the CFO office can provide excellent service to the agency.

Goals and objectives. A CSF may have several goals associated with it, and one goal may be linked to several CSFs. A goal is a three- to five-year milestone of the strategy. Under the GPRA, these will be performance goals with measurable results. Objectives are one- to two-year milestones that support long-term goals. In both cases, the responsibility for achievement must be assigned to an executive or senior manager. As discussed in Chapter 8, performance measures must be developed for goals and objectives. The measures are a way to judge progress, define improvement requirements, and communicate success.

Strategy, capital resources, and the role of the CFO office. Capital resources are the life blood of strategy, and goals and objectives should dictate where to invest these resources. If achieving a strategy requires no investment of capital dollars, one must question whether it is indeed strategy. Here, the CFO office can become an essential contributor to strategy. For example, financial professionals can help build strong business cases for major changes in capital resource allocation. These cases can be carried forward into the budgetary process. Business case analysis is a good tool

Figure 7-3

Goals and Strategies for Implementing Government-Wide Financial Management

GOAL: **Provide leadership to promote the efficient management of government resources and assets**

- Improve accountability by ensuring that management control is a day-to-day process.
- Create a culture that demands quality financial management by marketing the vision at all levels.
- Create an atmosphere that provides incentives, eliminates impediments, and encourages responsible risk taking.
- Build a partnership to ensure the functioning together of information resource management, program management, financial management, and budgeting.
- Attract, retain, and develop highly qualified financial professionals who are valued members of the management team.

GOAL: **Provide quality financial services to customers based on their needs**

- Change the view of financial management from solely control to service.
- Establish customer orientation within organizations through a partnership between financial and program managers.
- Fully identify customer needs by involving customers.
- Commit to achieving high standards of customer financial services through continuous improvement.
- Help customers restructure their work processes in order to achieve their service objectives more efficiently.

GOAL: **Provide complete and useful financial information on federal government operations that fully supports financial and performance reporting**

- Establish standards and definitions.
- Create a system for integrating performance measures, cost information, and financial reporting.
- Establish integrated government financial management systems that minimize data entry and human intervention.

- Provide cost-effective reporting, analysis, and advice that are interactive, timely, reliable, and user-friendly and that fully satisfy user needs.

GOAL: **Establish a government-wide framework to provide sound financial policies and services and to facilitate effective communication**

- Improve the integration between the budget and management functions within the government.
- Re-examine functions and improve the coordination among OMB, Treasury, and the General Accounting Office.
- Improve and expand collaboration, cross-servicing, and user-friendly outreach within and among government organizations.
- Strengthen the partnership between the Executive Branch and Congress to improve financial management.

Source: *Federal Financial Management Status Report & Five-Year Plan*, June 1996.

---

for both the agency-wide plan and the internal CFO organization.

CFO office goals and objectives. OMB Circular A-11 requires that, in their financial management plans, agencies discuss how they will achieve the goals and strategies for implementing government-wide financial management improvements associated with the CFO Council's vision. This discussion should focus on those goals and strategies that agencies determine to be priorities, and should include examples of ongoing and proposed initiatives. Figure 7-3 presents a set of government-wide financial management goals developed by the federal CFO Council and the OMB that can be a starting point for discussions about internal financial goals and objectives.

Plan Deployment

All strategic plans, no matter how good, are of little value unless they are deployed throughout an organization. Thus, agencies must create a structure and system for communicating goals, objectives, and strategies to all managers and employees. There are alternative structures, but the best provide for both horizontal and vertical deployment.

Horizontal deployment. Strategy can be horizontally deployed through CSF or vital issue teams headed by an executive champion who is responsible for goal attainment in his or her issue area. Members of these cross-functional teams are recruited from the core business processes involved in a CSF area, and should include financial managers if they can contribute to the teams.

To align strategic planning with GPRA requirements for performance plans and reports, major agency programs or program areas can be treated as core business processes. Both usually start at that point of operations where customers first come into contact with an agency and end when they receive products and services. Other types of core business processes may not be directly related to customers, but are critical to agency survival or community safety. For example, maintaining safety in a nuclear facility is a core business process.

Vertical deployment. Vertically, the plan is deployed by having component managers prepare supporting plans for how they will help achieve strategic objectives. These plans may include contributions to cross-functional teams or work done solely within a component. Teams of component managers monitor progress toward their work units' objectives and update plans for improvement.

Communication as deployment. Other horizontal and vertical deployments are done through communication with employees and suppliers by briefing these groups, through written media, and by continually underscoring the importance of the plan. If an organization has natural work groups or self-managed teams, they are directed to focus most of their improvement efforts on strategic goals and objectives.

CFO office role in plan deployment. To the extent that it addresses agency goals, a CFO's five-year financial management plan may satisfy the need for vertical deployment in the CFO office. Also, financial managers can provide invaluable assistance to other managers by working with them to ensure that deployment plans have the financial rigor necessary for cost-effective innovation. Beyond this, financial professionals have the challenge of helping to "drill down" financial performance measurements and internal controls into operations processes. This is the information that operations managers need to manage costs, anticipate problems, and monitor progress toward strategic objectives. Finally, there is nothing to preclude even an entry-level accountant or financial analyst from researching potential solutions to help nonfinancial groups achieve their plan objectives.

Plan Monitoring

Executives establish a system for monitoring plan implementation, to include regular reports on progress, evaluation of results, and achievement of performance goals. This should be a continual monitoring system, not limited to an annual report such as that required by the GPRA. We discuss this more in Chapter 8.

Updating Strategic and Deployment Plans

We believe that an agency must revisit its strategic plan periodically to ensure that it is up to date and on track. The GPRA requires that this be done every three years. However, we recommend updates whenever there are major changes in an agency's mission, environment, customer requirements, or funding. Internal financial organizations should revise their deployment plans annually, to ensure that they are aligned to an agency's one- to two-year objectives for achieving long-term goals.

The CFO's Critical Role in Strategic Planning

In Chapter 3 and in this chapter we emphasized that the Strategist and Visionary role is critical to a CFO's ability to influence agency strategy. Achieving the Team Leader role requires that the entire financial organization provide strong support for the strategic planning process—because strategic planning will not be effective unless an agency's leaders understand its current and future financial environment and issues and the fiscal reality and implications of different strategies. Without such financial information, strategic plans are unrealistic and will drive an agency in the wrong direction.

More important, plans that have no real financial foundation are simply ignored. For example, we visited one intelligence agency at which financial managers were not involved in the strategic planning process. Indeed, the entire planning process was done by a single division of the agency, so that strategy was created in a vacuum. When we asked about the strategic plan, one senior financial manager told us that the only way it could have value would be if the agency declassified the document—so it could be used as a door stop!

Sometimes financial managers are not aware of the critical role they can play in strategic planning. In another agency with which we worked, the CFO's initial reaction to an invitation to participate in strategy sessions was that "they" wanted him there to answer questions about the budget. After all, the previous departmental secretary had consigned CFOs to that role. To the CFO's surprise (and to the benefit of the agency), the new secretary gave the CFO and his office a prominent role in the planning and performance measurement development process. Since then, the CFO's role has quite naturally expanded into plan deployment and monitoring.

CFOs cannot wait to be invited to the strategy table— law and necessity require their participation. However, CFOs and their financial teams must be proactive in making their insights and services available to strategic planners. In the rest of this book, we will discuss tools and methods that are useful for strategy development and implementation, as well as for daily use in financial management.

Pre-Audits

A pre-audit helps to identify causes of financial management problems that auditors uncover during the course of an audit. Some conditions identified in this way can be solved quickly, so correcting them is tactical action. Solutions to others require long-term investments or major restructuring of staff and structure, which puts them in the category of strategy.

Pre-audits include some normal audit planning preparation activities such as those discussed in Chapter 5, using tools and techniques that will help identify the causes of problems encountered. They are done by a team of internal financial and functional professionals or external consultants. Usually, pre-audits begin months before an agency prepares for an actual audit. When used for the first time as an assessment tool for planning financial management strategy, they may be done up to a year in advance.

Based on a review of the general ledger, a pre-audit team groups accounts into logical components or activity cycles. The groups may include cash; revenue and receivables; advances and prepayments; purchases and payables; electronic data processing; and financial reporting. Team members do a high-level walk-through of each account area, creating maps of the major process flows. The maps identify manual and automated operations and major internal controls, and are accompanied by descriptions of process inputs, outputs, and internal operation and special requirements such as legislative or regulatory mandates. Also, the team verifies that internal controls are in place and working properly. The team interviews process operators and customers to ascertain their views on the effectiveness and efficiency of the processes and their outputs. In some cases, the team may measure the cycle time of a process to determine if it is too long to ensure that users receive timely information.

By component, the team prepares a list of issues discovered through the assessment and determines the risk of not addressing each issue. Examples of issues may include:

- Lack of written standard operating procedures, which has a risk of increased human errors
- No formal procedures for identifying and estimating the amount and likelihood of contingent liabilities and commitments, which implies that they may not be appropriately disclosed in financial statement.

Risks may be quantified in dollars and classified by degree or type of risk. A classification scheme we often use in pre-audits is as follows: high, in that the issue may affect the audit opinion; medium, for potential reportable conditions; low, for potential management letter issues; and efficiency, which is an internal efficiency issue that may not affect the audit opinion but is still an opportunity for improvement. The team ranks the issues in order of risk severity. Usually, a severe risk has a high dollar amount assigned to process failure and would result in less desirable audit opinions—the two tend to go together. Top-ranked items become priorities for corrective action.

First-time pre-audits used for preplanning assessment help to identify data gaps, or the difference between data elements that are currently available and the data that are needed for financial statements. Of course, the first place to look for the needed data would be in existing financial systems. Our experience is that most of it will not be in those systems, so the team will need to look in nonfinancial systems and conduct special data calls.

Part of a CFO's strategy for financial management should be to develop a cost-effective way to obtain such data while maintaining the highest degree of data integrity and internal controls. Often, this will drive changes to business processes. To determine the need to make major changes to obtain the data, the CFO office may use risk analyses similar to those applied to judging the need for internal controls. For example, OMB form and content guidance requires a breakdown of an agency's operating leases, including payouts for the next five years. Some agencies will have few or no such leases and thus do not need a complex system to track related data. In these cases, the CFO weighs the benefits of fully complying with requirements against the cost of doing so for potentially insignificant or immaterial amounts of money, and uses more appropriate and cost-effective alternatives.

Finally, CFOs who elect to do pre-audits should think long and hard about how this method can lead to improvements throughout an agency, not just in the ability to obtain a clean audit opinion. Indeed, nearly every form of strategic assessment for internal financial organizations touches almost every part of an agency, just as do most financial processes. As discussed in Chapter 5, most of the data needed for financial statements reside in nonfinancial information systems. If pre-audits can identify ways to improve those systems, then program managers will gain better information for their daily decisions— one of the main benefits addressed in the next chapter on performance measurement.

Chapter

8

PERFORMANCE MEASUREMENT: STARTING WHERE YOU ARE, GETTING TO WHERE YOU WANT TO GO

Financial managers can lead their agencies in developing a useful, forward-looking, and insightful approach to performance measurement and analysis that links strategy to tactics and problems to solutions.

- This approach is essential for *performance-based governance*, a system in which agencies are given flexibility in programming and budgets in return for a higher level of accountability. The CFO Act and the GPRA apply this system to the federal government.
- Although some agencies have difficult-to-measure missions, all agencies have some functions that can be easily measured.
- Three models offer insights into a sound measurement approach that includes a mixture of measures useful to different groups in an agency: the balanced score card, the value tree, and the hierarchy of measures.
- A common database of internal and external measures enhances successful performance measurement.

Lessons learned from GPRA pilot agencies highlight best practices in preparing reports on performance to OMB and Congress.

You've got to be able to see right through the bureaucracy to what is really happening—not just on the financial side but also on the results side. In both respects you need to have a clear notion of what you should be getting, so you have a means of comparison and access to financial information is made easy.

— John Mercer, Majority Counsel,
U.S. Senate Committee on
Government Affairs

In their role as Information Manager, CFOs are in touch with all operations, understand financial issues, have quantitative skills, and can provide an objective perspective on performance. Can they add value to their agencies by providing their colleagues with a better set of agency-wide performance measures than are currently used? The answer is "Of course!" How, then, can the CFO office move an agency from score keeping and purely financial and retro-spective information, to forward-looking and insightful measurement and analysis?

That is one of the greatest opportunities and toughest challenges facing federal financial managers. Department of Transportation CFO Louise Frankel Stoll explains why: "The Government Performance and Results Act has really been a boon. We are now able to ask people: How do you know you have succeeded? But what we are discovering is that most of them don't know. It is very hard to get people to think about what success means." The managers are not to blame for this. Some work in programs with hard-to-define results, but most simply have never been asked to provide definitive information on program outcomes. They have "grown up," professionally speaking, in an environ-ment that measures inputs (full-time-equivalents and budget dollars) and outputs (number of transactions or obligations and expenditures.) They work with management systems designed for tactics and that are not explicitly linked to strategy. Instead of trying to make this linkage, executives create separate strategic measurement systems with their own databases.

All these problems make it difficult for federal agencies to develop measurement approaches that:

- Focus on customer and stakeholder requirements for excellence
- Predict the future, not just report on the past
- Are useful for making decisions about process improvement
- Reflect how a program or process operates and how it connects to strategic goals
- Share the same measurement database, which includes data on processes, customer expectations, benchmarks, and other important information.

By meeting these criteria, an agency can achieve the main goal of measuring performance: Stakeholders and internal personnel actually use the measures to make appropriate decisions about operations, funding, and improvement.

In this chapter, we will explore how public organizations in the United States and other countries develop and use performance measures to enable leaders and citizens to make sound decisions about agency results and funding. This is called performance-based governance or results-oriented public service. Also, we will discuss how agencies use performance measures to provide managers with the information they need to control and improve operations. This is simply good management.

Federal Mandates for Performance Measurement

The CFO Act
The CFO Act includes among the functions of federal CFOs the development and reporting of cost information and the systematic measurement of performance. OMB guidance in this area comes from the document *Form and Content of Agency Financial Statements.* which states that performance measures should be included in the "Overview of the Reporting Equity" section of financial statements to enable people to use the statements to assess both financial and program performance. Wherever possible, financial data

Figure 8-1

Key Performance Measurement Terms

Term	Description	Examples
Input	Resource used to perform work or provide services	Hours of labor Dollars spent
Output	Amount of work accomplished or service provided	Number of buildings inspected Hours of training provided
Outcome or results	Impact, quality, or value of the work or service (Note: sometimes also called effectiveness measure)	Percent reduction in accidents rates Increase in competency due to training
Satisfaction	Customer assessment of the product or service provided (Note: Customer satisfaction can also be viewed as a type of "outcome")	Satisfaction with inspection services Satisfaction with the training provided
Efficiency	Ratio of effectiveness work to the resources required to produce it	Amount of rework required to correct errors Ratio of resources used in non-value-added versus value-added activities (see Chapter 10, value analysis)
Productivity	Economic output per unit of labor; a measure of the amount and quality of finished products or services against the amount of resources required to provide them	Units produced per labor hour Revenue per employee
Trend analysis	Analysis of statistical data collected over a period long enough to reveal patterns that can be used for forecasting future scenarios	Changes in customer population Changes in costs of materials

should be related to other measures of performance on a program-by-program basis. The CFO Act further provides for the incorporation of both financial and performance measures in the "Overview of the Reporting Equity" and "Supplemental Information" sections of an agency annual financial report.

Government Performance and Results Act

The GPRA is the primary law requiring most agencies to measure and report to Congress on their performance. Congress passed this act because it felt that federal managers could not improve efficiency and effectiveness without clearly defined goals and adequate program performance and results information. According to the GPRA, this insufficiency seriously handicaps congressional policy making, spending decisions, and program oversight. GPRA, which is the cornerstone of performance-based governance in the federal sector, is intended to do the following:

- Improve agency accountability with a focus on results, service quality, and customer satisfaction
- Initiate program performance reform
- Provide information about program results
- Improve congressional decision making
- Improve internal management of the federal government.

GPRA requirements for performance goals. As we discussed at the start of Chapter 7, GPRA requires agencies to develop long-term goals and strategic plans. It mandates that agencies set specific annual performance goals or targets based on the strategic plan goals and to report annually on performance compared to the targets.

The act says that performance goals should be stated in an objective, quantifiable, and measurable form, using indicators that measure or assess relevant outputs, service levels, and outcomes of each program activity. The performance plan for the measures must describe how the measures are verified and validated. If an agency cannot state a performance goal in an objective and quantifiable form, it may use an alternative form that describes what the organization would be doing if it were minimally effective versus if it were successful.

GPRA and performance-based governance. Through a series of pilot projects, GPRA tests the fundamental concepts of performance-based governance. The pilot agencies were to receive temporary waivers of administrative procedures and controls. These controls included congressional specification of personnel staffing levels, limitations on compensation or remuneration, and prohibitions or restrictions on funding transfers among certain budget line items.

In return, the pilot agencies agreed to "specific individual or organization accountability to achieve a performance goal." We understand, though, that few waivers were actually granted, which may indicate a reluctance by Congress to relinquish control of agency administrative matters. At the end of this chapter we present brief reports on some of these pilot initiatives.

Training. The GPRA provides that the Office of Personnel Management, in consultation with GAO and OMB, will develop a strategic planning and performance measurement training component for managers. Unrelated to this mandated training is Congress's plans to train itself. It was announced at an October 1996 CFO Council seminar on performance measurement that, with the backing of Representative Newt Gingrich, the National Academy of Public Administration plans to provide training to members of Congress and their staffs on interpreting GPRA-related reports from agencies.

GPRA is, in theory, a revolutionary experiment in federal management. The act's success depends on its ability to stimulate discussion of program goals and progress, beginning at the staff level and reaching all the way to the corridors of Congress and ultimately to the public. In the later stages of implementation, GPRA performance measurement has the potential of permeating the federal culture with results-oriented values.

CFO Act + GPRA = Transparent Government

Most elected officials, much less average citizens, find it difficult to penetrate the complex details of government operations. John Mercer's quotation at the start of this chapter echoes the belief that that government should be transparent. Combined, the CFO Act (with its required financial management information) and the GPRA (with its goals and performance measures) can provide that type of transparency.

OMB Controller Ed DeSeve agrees, saying that connecting finance with mission performance can turn rhetoric into analysis when considering funding alternatives. "There is a quantum of performance that is going to be attained by Program A and a quantum of performance that is going to be obtained by Program B. The two quantums may be very different. One may be education for children; the other may be safety from international terrorism. Two very different things; they each cost $100 million. You may never make the trade-off between those two programs. That's not necessarily the issue. The issue is: Do I know enough about each program so I can allocate $100 million to it and be comfortable that I'm going to get a result—that I have some sense of what can and should be achieved?"

DeSeve's question "Do I know enough to be comfortable?" is the key one asked by legislators when they make budget decisions. Finding the answer is why governments adopt performance-based governance.

Customer Service Standards

Complementing the GPRA is Executive Order 12862, *Setting Customer Service Standards*, which requires agencies to be customer-driven and the level of their service to be the "best in the business." This order requires agencies to do the following:

- Identify their customers, survey them to determine their perceptions of customer service, and report on the results
- Develop and post the agency's service standards
- Measure performance against them.

The order grew out of the National Performance Review, which set customer service as one of the four guideposts for reinventing the federal government. More than 150 agencies have set more than 1,500 customer service standards, such as quicker tax refunds and making product safety information available 24 hours a day. These standards are available from the NPR (*see* Appendix A).

Four National Models for Performance-Based Governance

GPRA principles of performance-based governance have been used in the United States and overseas, and the results have largely been positive. David Osborne and Ted Gaebler, in their book *Reinventing Government* and also a recent GAO study, reported on the experience of four countries in using performance-based governance: Australia, Canada, the United Kingdom, and New Zealand. All four faced serious economic problems resulting in part from high levels of spending and out-of-control budget deficits that started during the 1980s. Most of their agencies had no accountability, much less good systems for measuring results. Also, many internal constraints inhibited performance measurement, the most serious of which were the cultures of the government agencies.

Measurement Central to the New Approach
To change this, agencies were required to define their missions and come up with annual objectives linked to those missions. In addition, the countries used performance information to measure results of operations in terms of quantity, quality, efficiency, and cost of outputs.

The United Kingdom and Canada measured the quality of services provided directly to the public, and all four countries established performance agreements between different levels of management. All agencies in the four countries have prepared performance reports for their respective parliaments and the public.

Greater Autonomy in Return for Accountability
The parliaments, in turn, gave the agencies more flexibility over resources and incentives, eliminating detailed control of operating expenditures and staffing levels and providing more authority for agencies to manage resources within overall budget ceilings. They also created incentives by implementing market-type mechanisms, such as competition, requiring agencies to charge for their services, and funding operations with the collected revenues. Canada has given departments the authority to reallocate resources across line items and to carry over some of their capital funds from one year to the next. New Zealand has eliminated many regulations, giving managers greater freedom to manage. Australia required its agencies to cut their spending

by 3.75 percent over three years, but gave them greater spending flexibility and the right to keep any money saved beyond the 3.75 percent. In exchange, Australian agencies are subject to more rigorous performance measurement.

State and Local Measurement Initiatives

State and local initiatives also provide insights on concepts of and problems with performance-based governance. We provide two examples: Texas and the City of Indianapolis, Indiana.

Texas Outcome Measures

Federal managers who wonder about the effect of the GPRA on government management would do well to examine the model offered by the State of Texas. In 1991, the Texas Legislative Budget Board (LBB) directed state agencies to adopt an outcome-based focus for program management that integrates results-oriented performance measures in the state's strategic planning and budgeting system shown in Figure 8-2. Before 1991, the state's budget formulation approach focused on agency work load or efforts and used input and output measures.

A good example of measurement in this model was reported in the Coopers & Lybrand book *Improvement-Driven Government.* At the Texas Commission for the Blind, one five-year strategic goal is to help blind or visually impaired people to live as independently as possible with their capabilities. An objective of the goal is to increase by two-thirds the number of visually handicapped people who achieve their personal independent living goals. One strategy to reach the objective is to provide services that equip blind high schoolers to make the transition from school to working. In turn, the objective's performance measures the numbers and types of students served (output measures), service outcomes, and efficiency measures such as the cost per student served.

Statewide automated measurement system. In 1995, the agencies used about 10,000 measures, and the LBB labeled 3,000 as key measures. Key measures are considered budget drivers, generally have an external focus, strongly relate to an agency's funding, and tie closely to the statewide strategic plan.

Figure 8-2

Texas State Government Strategic Planning and Budgeting

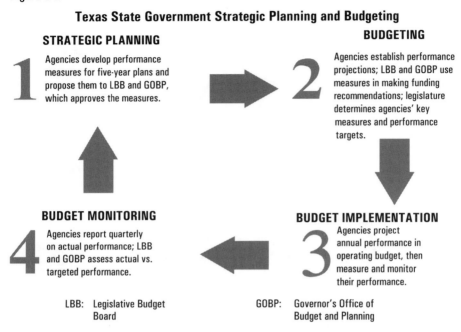

STRATEGIC PLANNING

1 Agencies develop performance measures for five-year plans and propose them to LBB and GOBP, which approves the measures.

BUDGETING

2 Agencies establish performance projections; LBB and GOBP use measures in making funding recommendations; legislature determines agencies' key measures and performance targets.

BUDGET MONITORING

4 Agencies report quarterly on actual performance; LBB and GOBP assess actual vs. targeted performance.

BUDGET IMPLEMENTATION

3 Agencies project annual performance in operating budget, then measure and monitor their performance.

LBB: Legislative Budget Board

GOBP: Governor's Office of Budget and Planning

Source: *Guide to Performance Measurement for State Agencies, Universities, and Health-Related Institutions, 1995 Edition,* Texas State Auditor's Office

State agencies, universities, and health-related institutions report on key measures quarterly, mostly by entering the data directly into the Automated Budget and Evaluation System of Texas (ABEST II). The ABEST II database includes each measure's definition, classification (input, output, outcome, efficiency, cumulative and non-cumulative), targeted and actual performance, and an explanation of any variance greater than 5 percent between targeted and actual performance. Thus, agency executives, the LBB, the Governor's Office of Budget and Planning (GOBP), and other oversight groups have timely access to performance indicators that all agree are important. Also, having the measures available quarterly helps to identify negative trends that might otherwise go unnoticed until the end of the fiscal year.

How legislators use the data. Performance targets may be suggested by agencies, but the state legislature sets the targets. Targets for key measures are displayed in the state's general appropriation act with the corresponding appropriation. Agencies are held responsible for not meeting their performance targets, and the LBB has reduced several agency budgets for this failure.

Also, legislators consider an agency's previous year and projected performance when making funding decisions. Besides wanting to know why agencies do not meet targets, the Texas House Appropriations Committee takes them to task for poor documentation of performance measures and reported data.

Auditing performance measures. The State Auditor's Office helps prevent the problem of poor measures by auditing and certifying that agency performance measures are reliable, valid, free from bias, and verifiable. Also, the auditors determine if measurement systems have internal controls that will ensure their continued reliability. In a performance measurement audit, auditors review or "test" a statistical sample of documents supporting key measures reported by agencies to ABEST II. A "certified" or clean audit opinion for a performance measure means that:

- Original source documents were accessed manually or on-line by computer
- All items tested were materially correct within sampling constraints
- Calculations were performed correctly by the agency and in conformance with calculation definitions
- The numbers as calculated were the numbers appearing in ABEST II reports.

Texas's strategic planning and budgeting system shows how a comprehensive approach to performance measurement can provide the information that legislators and top executive branch officials need for effective decisions, about both budgets and the quality of agency management. This is a good example of the type of performance-based budgeting system envisioned by the GPRA. Another example is the approach used by the City of Indianapolis.

Activity-Based Budgeting in Indianapolis

The Coopers & Lybrand book *Activity-Based Management in Government* reports how the City of Indianapolis uses performance-based budgeting for its street, alley, and bridge repair and maintenance department. The department's 1994 budget was developed using activity-based costing (*see* Chapter 10), which enabled the city to show the quantity and unit cost of proposed services. Examples include how many linear feet of deteriorated curbs would be repaired or replaced (1,500 feet, at $23.50 per foot) and that the city would make and install 14,000 road signs averaging $30.24 each.

Citizens love performance-based budgeting. As part of the budget review process, the document was presented for comment to neighborhood groups and reporters, all of whom were favorably impressed. One reason was that it was a budget anyone could understand. Using the data provided, stakeholders could make comparisons with outside vendors of the same services. Equally important, the budget was a performance promise to citizens regarding costs, and also a promise to increase productivity and efficiency. It included performance goals, such as "Crews will improve response time by 25 to 50 percent," and targeted cost reductions. Goals were backed up by details of how the city planned to accomplish them.

"We call it our popular budget," an Indianapolis financial officer told the book's authors. "Before 1994, we gave citizens a line-item budget. We would spend hours explaining it, but many would still not understand. With the popular budget, what you see is what you get, plain and simple. Citizens tell us they love it, and our managers understand and apply the budget to control and improve their operations. We still prepare line-item budgets required by statute, but we use an activity-based budget."

Motivation for performance. We add that activity-based budgeting in Indianapolis is, in a very real sense, part of an extreme approach to performance-based governance, going beyond the budget reductions handed out by the Texas Legislative Budget Board. Indianapolis Mayor Stephen Goldsmith makes his maintenance districts compete with private contractors for the business of maintaining city streets and bridges. He says "Activity-based costing has to come in front of competition because we can't even get our own folks into a bid mentality until we know how much it costs to provide a service." Once they got into that mental set, though, city employees became hard-nosed business people, and they have won most of their competitions. Indianapolis won, too, since the cost of road repairs dropped by as much as 60 percent.

Lessons Learned from Experiences in Performance-Based Governance

According to GAO, in the four national government experiences:

- Long-term investments in information systems were critical.
- Staff needed training in measuring performance, interpreting results, and operating in a more commercial environment.
- Central management must play an active role in providing guiding and training program managers to implement results-oriented management reforms, strategic planning, performance measurement, and budget flexibility.

Our observations of the Texas and Indianapolis examples include the following:

- The best measures show whether organizations are achieving their strategic goals and objectives.
- Both internal managers and outsiders who review the measures must agree that they are useful.
- Strong incentives are critical to any performance measurement system, or no one will be motivated to

increase performance. However, reducing an agency's budget because it fails to provide adequate performance measures is potentially unfair to the agency's beneficiaries. Agency management is responsible for measurement, so incentives—negative or positive—should be directed at them.

We recommend that agencies conduct more detailed reviews of the past and future progress of these and other performance-based governance organizations; there is ample journal literature on them. Also, the performance plans reports and performance measurement manuals of Texas and some of the foreign governments can be found through the Internet at their Web sites, along with related white papers and other information. Articles and reports on the progress of federal PBOs have just started to be published; the National Performance Review has some of this information, and can supply contacts at the pilot agencies. We summarize their experiences in reporting performance to OMB and Congress at the end of this chapter. Knowledge of the PBOs' overall experiences will help to address some of the tough issues surrounding how to measure government services, and how even to define what some agencies do.

Problems in Defining Agency Performance

All agencies can develop meaningful performance measures for their main missions, but it can be difficult for some. For example, CFO Jay Brixey of the Federal Bureau of Investigation wants to see his agency take the lead in law enforcement performance measures, and has made great progress. But the Bureau is struggling with some unique challenges. One of the things the FBI does quite well, for instance, is surveillance. But surveillance requires a long-term commitment, and its success is often difficult to measure. Many investigations of organized crime and terrorist activities can take years and cost millions of dollars. As difficult as it is to measure the costs of such long investigations, attaching a value to them is even more forbidding. How, then, should such costly investigations be accounted for in a performance report for the entire Bureau?

Other agencies have similar problems in measurement. Any honest scientist will admit that most experiments have negative or inconclusive outcomes, but will make the very true point that such results are still valuable. Basic researchers in the United States, most of whom are supported by the federal government, have no real idea of the potential pay back for positive outcomes. The mission of the Department of Defense is to help maintain peace, but how can the value of peace be measured?

This is why the GPRA allows agencies to state and measure some performance goals in ways that are not as precise or quantifiable as others. The principle behind this is that indirect measures of performance are acceptable so long as their underlying logic is clear and they are useful for making decisions.

Even though some of an agency's performance goals cannot be framed in an objective, quantifiable, and measurable statement, many can be and must be. Agencies whose missions are virtually impossible to measure directly have many other areas of performance that interest the Congress and Executive Office, such as basic support and operations processes and fiscal stewardship. Such agencies would do well to become excellent in measuring these areas, because doing so will increase the comfort of lawmakers with the less measurable areas.

Three Measurement Frameworks

An agency is a complex organism in a complex environment, so single measures of performance viewed in isolation may cause more harm than good. Outside stakeholders and top management need a mixture of measures to understand agency health and prospects, but for the mixture to make sense it must be linked to a logical framework. Managers and employees need a different measurement mixture that is linked to higher level measures. Three measurement frameworks help to create this linkage: 1) the balanced scorecard, 2) the value tree, and 3) the hierarchy of measures. The key to the success of each is a common database of measures used by everyone in an agency.

The Balanced Scorecard

Many business leaders use only on a few financial measures to judge the health of their companies. The problem is, they have no way to measure what causes the financial numbers to go up or down. Robert Kaplan and David Norton created the balanced scorecard concept in order to provide four sets of key measures to help business leaders see the big picture of their companies, including how well they are preparing for the future.

Three of the sets—financial, customer-oriented, and internal operations measures—are always used. Organizations choose a fourth set that fits their industry, environment, or interests. Ideally, each set has both retro-spective and prospective measures, so that decision makers focus on the future, not just the past. Similar measurement concepts include the corporate dashboard, which, like an airplane's instrument panel, has many different measures of organizational health, direction, and progress.

Figure 8-3

The Balanced Scorecard Applied to an R&D Agency

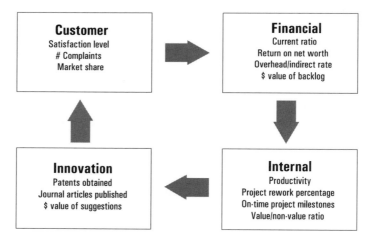

Figure 8-3 is an example of a balanced scorecard for an agency that provides research and development services to other agencies. The arrows between the boxes remind users of the scorecard that each of the four sets is related to the others. For this agency, customer measures include levels of customer agency satisfaction, numbers of customer complaints, and the percentage of their R&D business that customers give the R&D agency. Financial measures include the agency's overhead or indirect rate charged to customers for their projects, because the agency wants to lower this rate by making more direct charges. Internal measures include those for productivity and efficiency, including a ratio of resources devoted to value added and non-value-added activities discussed in Chapter 10 under value analysis. Because the agency's business is R&D, it is concerned with maintaining its capabilities for innovation. Innovation is a hard concept to measure directly, so here it is quantified indirectly by the number of patents professional staff obtain and the number of articles they publish in peer-reviewed journals. The agency wants innovation from all staff, not just R&D professionals, so it also measures the dollar value of employee ideas accepted through a suggestion program.

There can be balanced scorecards for an entire agency, for each of its components down to the division or office level, and for major programs. Because agency leaders are most concerned with strategy, many of their measures are linked to performance goals of a strategic plan. Managers' scorecards may be a mixture of strategic and nonstrategic measures, many of which can be developed using the value tree model discussed next.

The Value Tree
Stakeholder value should drive the selection of strategic performance measures. Stakeholders include customers, Congress, employees, suppliers, and the communities in which agencies operate; an agency's products and services should be perceived as valuable by them. The value tree is a good model and tool for selecting measures of what stakeholders value most. Figure 8-4 is a value tree for an agency that provides support services to other agencies.

As shown in the top row of the figure, this agency has five sets of stakeholders; the value tree in the figure focuses

Figure 8-4   **Value Tree**

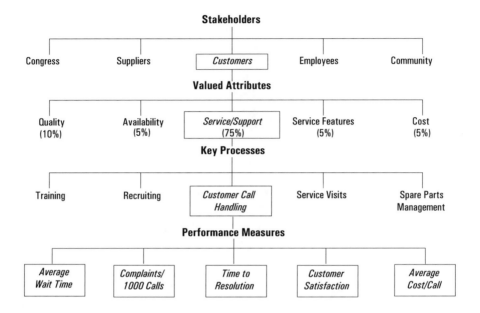

on customers. The second row shows the attributes of the agency's services, which include quality, cost, features, availability, and support. A survey of customers showed that, of these features, they valued support the most. The third row shows the key processes of customer support, one of which handles phone calls requesting support services. Discussions with customers indicated that they were dissatisfied with this process, so that improving it became a strategic concern.

The fourth row shows five performance measures selected for the customer call handling process. They include three measures of efficiency and productivity: 1) average time customers waited on hold; 2) average time between answering a call and resolving a problem; and 3) average cost per call. Also, there are two measures of effectiveness: 1) the rate of customer complaints about call handling and 2) the percentage of customers satisfied with the outcomes of their calls. Like the balanced scorecard, the five measures present a balanced picture of call handling.

The Hierarchy of Measures

Strategic plans aim to change how employees work in order that performance goals can be met. Employees work best when they have guidance for and feedback on their work. Good feedback comes from a system of performance measurement that shows people at all levels of an agency how well they are helping to meet those goals.

Such systems are, in one sense, a hierarchy of measures. Strategic goals guide the selection of measurement indicators that executives use to gauge agency-wide performance. These indicators guide the choice of lower-level indicators of process performance that, singly or combined, provide the data needed for the higher-level measures.

Figure 8-5

Strategic Framework of Measuring Performance

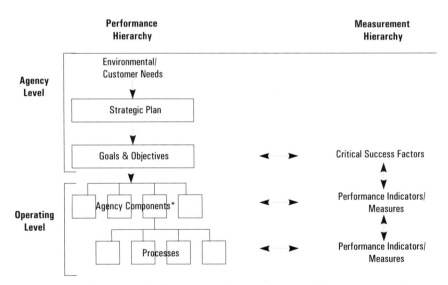

*Depending on an organization's structure and management approach, its programs, core business processes, or products and services may be measured at this level instead of component units.

Because of this linkage, an executive who is alerted to a potential problem by a strategic measure can quickly trace its potential causes down to the process level. Conversely, an employee or supervisor who is alerted to a problem by a process-level measure understands how this might affect the strategic goals of the agency. Creating such a measurement system is part of the strategic planning process, as shown in Figure 8-5.

Common Data Sources and Databases Are Critical

A hierarchical system of measures does not mean that an agency's measurement system should be designed solely around the information needs of executives and external stakeholders such as Congress. Indeed, it is a grave mistake to do this. Managers will be angry because they must spend too much time away from their main jobs in order to produce numbers for "the bosses." Even worse, it will lead managers to develop their own internal measurement systems, which will become isolated database islands in a data archipelago like that discussed in Chapter 4.

Instead, a measurement system should be designed to produce different views of performance based on the same data. Most of the data sources should be from within processes, so a best practice in performance measurement is to build data collection into process operations. Ideally, much of the data is captured automatically at the source through use of information technology.

Activity-based costing and a common measurement database. In Chapter 10, we discuss how ABC creates a common database of financial and nonfinancial performance measures that are linked to all processes in an agency. An ABC database contains definitions of all processes, including their cost drivers; it can produce reports on agency components, processes, types of activities (e.g., inspection, rework), and unit costs of products and services. As discussed in the Indianapolis example earlier in this chapter, ABC also can produce budgetary documents; these can be configured as activity-based budgets or line-item budgets.

Other measures in the common database. The measurement database should contain information on customer expectations and levels of satisfaction; external benchmarks for key processes; and environmental, demographic, and economic data needed for trend analysis. These data enable managers and employees to see how their processes are performing compared to customer perceptions, best practices, and future scenarios.

Modeling and Trend Analysis Are Essential to All Measurement Approaches

Given the pressure on federal agencies to conform to GPRA requirements, some may be tempted to focus their measurement initiatives on score keeping, or recording historic levels of performance. However, any manager will tell you that it is more important to know what is going to happen tomorrow than what happened yesterday.

A measurement system can meet this information need in two ways. First, its common database should include demographic, economic, and other external data such as that discussed above, which will help managers to forecast future demands on agency processes. Second, the system should be capable of providing this information along with data on current process performance in a format useful for simulation modeling. Such modeling tests alternative assumptions and process configurations to determine how best to address both current and future demands. Financial modeling can be done on ordinary spreadsheet software. Process modeling is easier to do using specialized software that permits process mapping and the combined use of financial and nonfinancial performance data. Most agencies can use relatively inexpensive personal computer process modeling software.

Change Management and Performance Measures

Implementing new performance measures will change the way that people work by giving them objective information on how to control and improve operations—but only if agency personnel understand, accept, and use the new measures. Ensuring that they do is a change management responsibility for executives and managers (see Chapter 10 for more on change management). Tasks in this area include the following:

- Communicate to personnel about the new measurement system through briefings, discussions, and publications.
- Involve people in developing measures, especially at the process level.
- Train personnel in skills needed to collect, analyze, and use the measures.
- Insist that people back up their reports, proposals, and budgets with measurement data.
- Ensure that top management uses measurement data for their decisions.
- Tie peoples' salary increases, promotions, and bonuses to the performance measures of their processes.

Again, the best way to ensure that people use performance measures is to make the measures useful in their daily work. This also is true for the performance reports that the GPRA requires be delivered to OMB and the Congress, which we discuss next.

Reporting Performance Results

GAO selected 13 GPRA pilot agencies and their projects for review, discovering several best practices that enhance the value of performance reports.

Show the linkage between annual performance information and the agency's strategic goals and mission. The Forest Service provided such a linkage in its report by describing how each of 22 programs related to one or more of the agency's four broad strategic goals. The agency's Reforestation and Stand Improvement Program had a performance goal of "to annually reforest an area equal to the area annually deforested by timber harvest, fire, insects, disease and adverse weather." The report explained that the program and performance goal related to the strategic goal of "ensuring environmentally acceptable commodity production." This was because the program re-established disturbed areas, enhanced and maintained site productivity, and planted stock with desired genetic characteristics. This made it easier to understand the program's performance goal, which was related to the broader strategic goal.

Include cost information. Linking the cost of programs to performance, especially in measures such as unit cost per output or outcome, can be important information for congressional decision makers. The Social Security Administration conducts hundreds of thousands of hearings a year, but those numbers have limited meaning for cost-effective decisions without knowing the cost of a hearing. SSA's report included the unit cost of processing a hearing and showed changes in that cost since FY 1990, which enabled reviewers to compare this information to other similar hearings.

Provide baseline and trend data. The SSA provided a baseline (FY 1990) and trend data (FY 1990-4) for its hearings. Besides lending context to an organization's performance, trend data show whether goals are realistic, given the history of an agency or program. The Forest Service's Wildlife, Fish, and Rare Plants Management Program showed that it met 82 percent of its performance goal of improving the number of acres of habitats for threatened, endangered, and sensitive species. This performance suggests that the program was not as successful as hoped. However, trend data for FY 1990-4 showed that FY 1994 performance exceeded that of three of the previous four years, was more than double 1990 performance, and continued an overall upward trend in habitat improvement.

Explain the results. Performance reports should explain and describe the reasons for any unmet goals and plans, and set forth schedules for achieving those goals. The U.S. Mint has a goal of surpassing the previous year's sales of coins and medal sales. In FY 1994, sales fell well below this goal. The agency offered several explanations in its report, including that the U.S. commemorative coin market was saturated, lack of enthusiasm among core customers, and sluggish market conditions for bullion products. Then, the Mint described the actions it would take to address the shortfall.

Include other relevant information. Reports should include the reasons for any changes made to performance goals and measures during the year, explanations for how to interpret performance results, and any limitations in the data themselves. The Coast Guard's report explained that oil and chemical spills of 1 million or more gallons are rare. Lumping that volume in with data on other smaller spills would cause major fluctuations from year to year and have an extreme influence on statistical trends. So, the report continued, the Coast Guard does not use the large spills in its trend analysis, establishing performance goals, or measuring performance. Instead, it reports them separately using stacked bar charts to illustrate the number of large spills.

Validate and verify. GPRA requires agency reports to describe how their data are verified and validated. The National Highway Traffic Safety Administration included an appendix to its performance report that discussed the sources and, in some cases, the limitations of performance data.

Make reports easy to use. Pilot reports were most effective when written for lay audiences and when they included visual aids, defined technical terms, avoided jargon, and had reference items like glossaries or indexes. The Forest Service used bar graphs in its presentation, which offered a clear, easy-to-understand framework for the user—the ultimate measure of performance measurement reporting.

Bridging the Gap Between Strategy and Action

CFOs are in the best position to help their agencies use performance measures to bridge the gap—some might even call it a chasm—between strategic planning and the day-to-day actions and decisions of workers and managers. That bridge is made of performance measures that report at every level of an organization how well it is meeting critical goals and objectives. CFOs take part in the strategic planning process, and so can insist that the process include a powerful approach to performance measurement. CFOs are involved in creating new information systems designed to report both financial and performance facts; melding these facts into useful information for both strategic and daily decisions is the primary challenge. Applying the information to performance improvement is the next logical step, as we show in Chapters 9 and 10.

And be certain of this: CFOs do not have to be invited to take part in developing an agency's performance measurement system. They have a mandate to do so from the new reform legislation. Perhaps the CFOs' most productive response to that mandate is to underscore to other agency leaders that performance measurement is a step-by-step process. Leaving out a step—or not meeting the information needs of everyone in the organization—will eventually cause the bridge to crumble and fall.

Chapter

9

FINANCIAL MANAGEMENT BENCHMARKING AND BEST PRACTICES

Few things hold more promise for an agency than discovering that another organization does something better. It is often easier to borrow a good idea than to recreate it from scratch—and the process of looking outside an agency's walls for ideas always is healthy.

- In best practices benchmarking, an agency compares its key processes with those of outside organizations, then adopts the ones that best apply.
- Success in benchmarking comes from choosing the right processes and following a comprehensive methodology than begins with measuring internal performance and ends with adapting external processes to an agency's needs and work environment.
- Financial managers can be important members of agency benchmarking teams, especially in quantifying financial and other performance of internal processes and making "apples-to-apples" comparisons of performance and costs with external processes.
- A wealth of information on best practices in financial management is available; we present highlights of best practices in information management, accounts receivable and payable, billing, travel and expense reporting, purchasing, and controls and compliance.

We can't be afraid of comparison. We have to be prepared to look at ourselves and say, "OK, we are not where we ought to be and not nearly as good as we should be, but it is also not all that way." There is a balance.

–CFO Dennis Fischer, General Services Administration

B est practices benchmarking is a method in which an agency or company compares its key processes with the practices of leading organizations, and then adopts the practices of the very best. Benchmarking is not the same as a comparison study. Every agency has conducted (or been subjected to) studies that compared its services with those of organizations that do the same thing. The studies are seldom used because 1) no one was committed to acting on the results, 2) a "not invented here" attitude exists, 3) the comparison was invalid, or 4) all of the above. Best practices benchmarking is designed to overcome these problems. Used correctly, it will deliver the information an agency needs to take its place in the ranks of world-class organizations.

Financial managers can play two important roles in this form of process improvement. First, as members of agency benchmarking teams they can provide their operations colleagues with financial analysis skills that are essential for making sound comparisons between internal and outside processes. Second, as owners of an agency's financial processes, they can use benchmarking to find ways to improve them. Many do just that: In Coopers & Lybrand's 1995 CFO Act survey, two-thirds of the senior financial managers reported that they routinely sought or used innovations and best practices of other agencies.

When "Good Enough for Government" Means World-Class

Private companies have long used benchmarking to discover, adopt, and adapt the best practices of outside organizations. Within the federal government, too, more and more agencies have successfully used benchmarking to attain the highest levels of performance.

According to the National Performance Review, when the Social Security Administration wanted to improve its phone service processes, the agency benchmarked industry leaders such as American Express, AT&T, Citibank, and the Saturn Corporation. SSA found that the companies were delighted to share their procedures, to the point of becoming partners in improvement. This enabled SSA to improve its 800 number phone service so much that today it is rated by independent researchers as one of the world's best telephone response processes.

When *Business Travel News* sought the best business travel management operations in the country, it came up with four "Master Tacticians": Hewlett Packard, Bankers Trust, Texas Instruments, and the National Security Agency (NSA). Yet, not too long ago the agency's travel process moved like a slow boat to China. NSA was taking 79 days to process paperwork for the average business trip, at an administrative cost of more than $8 million a year. There had to be a better way.

NSA travel staff benchmarked their processes with private sector organizations like AlliedSignal, Apple Computer, The Aerospace Corporation, and IBM, learning their best practices in travel management. The resulting process improvements cut the time NSA travelers spent filling out forms by 74 percent and paperwork processing time by 93 percent, and drove down total processing costs by 75 percent.

In the processes just described, SSA and NSA are not ranked as "the best in government," but simply as the best. This is why, for example, at its 1996 Annual Professional Development Conference, the Association of Government Accountants devoted an entire afternoon to sharing best practices from a host of federal and state agencies. The NPR makes it a point to publicize agency best practices, as do the journals of public sector professionals. Agencies that win the President's Award for Quality and Productivity and the Quality Improvement Prototype award readily share how they did it with others.

Background to Benchmarking

In benchmarking, an organization compares its internal functions and activities to those of best-in-class organizations with similar processes. A best-in-class organization is an industry leader because its operations deliver extra value to customers. The reason is that these processes are the highest in quality, efficiency, or cost-effectiveness—and usually all three—in an industry or functional area. With a little research at the library, on the Internet, or through a professional or industry association, anyone can find best-in-class organizations. So, why not stop reading right now and just go do it? Thus far, benchmarking seems like a fairly simple proposition: find a best-in-class organization and imitate it.

But benchmarking involves much more than simply comparing processes with world leaders. In working with many organizations to benchmark financial and other processes, we find that often they do not initially understand what a careful, meticulous, step-by-step process this has to be in order for it to succeed. A highly successful process in one organization may not be a best practice in another. The process may even be inappropriate, proving counterproductive or disastrous if emulated. Even when appropriate, most processes cannot be transferred from one organization to another without some modification. And there are some operations in an agency that should not be benchmarked, for reasons we will discuss.

Processes Appropriate for Benchmarking

Successful benchmarking focuses on processes, so first an agency has to be sure that what it wants to benchmark is in fact a process. Then, there are several criteria for selecting candidates for benchmarking from among several processes.

Is it a process? Unless an operation is a process it probably cannot be benchmarked. Processes have these elements: identifiable suppliers who provide inputs to a process; a transformation component that includes people, equipment, methods, materials, and environment; and customers who receive outputs. Boundaries separate one process from others at the points where the process gains control over inputs and loses control over outputs. Figure 9-1 shows how process elements relate to one another. Some examples of financial processes include compiling month-end or year-end financial statements, developing an agency's annual budget, and generating financial status reports.

Defining an operation as a process helps people under-stand it, which is the first step in benchmarking. The improvements that are derived from benchmarking come from understanding how the elements of an internal process differ from those in a best-in-class process. These differ-ences are most commonly described in process terms, which is the lingua franca of benchmarking and other improvements methods such as total quality management, reengineering, and activity-based costing.

Figure 9-1

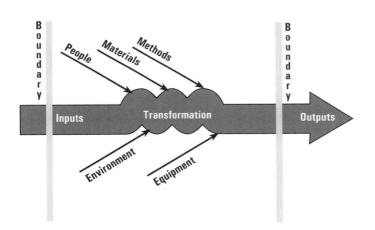

How much improvement does the process need? If a process need improve by only 10 percent or less in order to meet requirements, or if it is only that far from being world-class, then a full-scale benchmarking project may not be appropriate. Other process improvement methods such as those used in total quality management will be less costly and time-consuming. Even so, a less formal and extensive search for best practices can help improvement team members discover optimal solutions.

Is the process important enough to warrant the cost of a full-scale benchmarking project? Most strategic processes are good candidates for benchmarking because they are critical to the success of an agency's mission. Nonstrategic processes whose cost, quality, or cycle-time problems are causing major "pain" within an agency also should be considered. For example, how much time does an agency spend each year to develop future budgets? In many cases, it is an inefficient process, and reducing budget cycle time alone could save millions of dollars. This is not to say that other nonstrategic or less painful processes should not be benchmarked; we only mean "First things first."

Have other methods failed to produce the desired results? The 1995 GAO report *Best Practices Methodology: A New Approach for Improving Government Operations* suggests that agencies should consider benchmarking for operations in which they have been trying to develop a best-in-class practice but have had limited success. Somewhere, somehow, an organization has probably encountered and overcome the problems that are stalling progress—so try benchmarking it!

Do industry trends suggest the availability of new best practices? A review of current industry trends may show that a process is rapidly falling behind world-class standards. Fortunately, the same review also will reveal opportunities for benchmarking.

Take commercial-off-the-shelf software, for example. Within the federal government, some agencies have had great success in applying COTS solutions to financial management processes. Financial managers can learn from their peers which COTS packages are best-in-class and also the best practices for implementing them.

Types of Benchmarking

While many benchmarking hybrids can be very effective, there are only two basic approaches—an internal look that compares processes within an agency and an external look at other organizations.

Internal Benchmarking

Here, an agency benchmarking team compares the performance of similar processes in different offices. Having identified the best-in-class office in the process being benchmarked, the team studies the practices of that office (these are the best practices), then helps the other offices to adopt and adapt them. This type of comparison reduces the chances of taking a process out of context and making wrong assumptions about it. Also, such internal assessments are cost-effective and can usually be completed promptly. Finally, an internal best practice may be more likely to be accepted as valid by other offices.

We recommend that agencies or their components with little or no benchmarking experience start with a strictly internal approach. This will achieve some easy wins and prepare the agency for external benchmarking. However, internal benchmarking has its limits, unless the internal best practice it discovers is already world-class. If not, and if the process is critical to an agency's mission or survival, then external benchmarking may be best.

External Benchmarking

There are three subtypes of external benchmarking: 1) competitive, 2) industry, and 3) best-in-class. Each has its advantages and disadvantages, depending on an agency's performance improvement needs.

Competitive benchmarking means looking at the products or services of direct competitors. The increasing practice of outsourcing, franchising, and otherwise contracting out for government services means that many agency functions face stiff competition, especially financial transaction operations and information processing. It is therefore wise to compare performance levels and features of internal products or processes with those of competitors.

Industry benchmarking means looking for best practices among competitors and noncompetitors in the same field. Here, an agency may benchmark the practices of other government agencies or of private companies that do essentially the same work. For example, when an Air Force base wanted to improve some of its aircraft servicing processes, it benchmarked them against commercial airlines.

Competitive or industry benchmarking's advantage is that it shows the minimum level of performance a process must achieve in order to stay even with industry standards. However, competitors do not share their secrets with rivals, so learning their best practices is difficult. Still, chances are that the practices are already fairly well known. Trade journals, conference speakers, vendors, consultants, and informal contacts usually talk about them. Finally, meeting competitor or industry standards is not beating them, so an agency will discover few true innovations this way. Becoming the leader often requires a higher level of benchmarking

This higher level is called best-in-class benchmarking. Here, an agency looks beyond its industry, as when the Air Force benchmarked its contract invoice process against that of the Ford Motor Company and achieved significant improvement in cost and cycle time. However, the most challenging form of best-in-class benchmarking—and the one with the highest potential payoff—looks for external processes with similar operations but different outputs from an internal process. For example, when a commercial airline wanted its aircraft servicing process to perform beyond industry standards, it benchmarked a race car pit crew. Both aircraft and race car servicing processes have similar characteristics: checking and replenishing, regularly scheduled tasks such as refueling, fixing unanticipated problems, people with different skills, and a critical need for speed in completing the job. Interestingly, cleaning and setting up tightly scheduled operating rooms are also similar, which is why one hospital also benchmarked these processes against a pit crew's. In this way, best-in-class benchmarking can stimulate the type of outside-the-box thinking that delivers true innovations in an industry.

While each form of benchmarking is slightly different from the others, all share the same basic methodology. Benchmarking is a process and, as such, follows a logical sequence of steps that we discuss next.

A Process for Best Practices Benchmarking

When looking at public and private organizations (and it is wise to look at both), financial managers need a comprehensive, detailed benchmarking methodology, which would take too long to describe in this chapter. The C&L book *Benchmarking: A Manager's Guide* (1995, 110 pages, see Appendix A) is a proven, step-by-step guide to the entire benchmarking procedure, from defining the scope of the project through institutionalizing the improved process. Its authors, our colleagues, have trained and coached many government benchmarking teams. This chapter highlights key points of the methodology as it is used for best practices benchmarking. However, most of the basic procedures we describe can be used in other types of benchmarking. Figure 9-2 below shows the benchmarking as a cycle, used repeatedly to improve first one process and then another.

Benchmarking Process   Figure 9-2

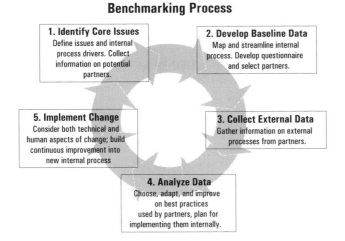

1. Identify Core Issues
Define issues and internal process drivers. Collect information on potential partners.

2. Develop Baseline Data
Map and streamline internal process. Develop questionnaire and select partners.

5. Implement Change
Consider both technical and human aspects of change; build continuous improvement into new internal process

3. Collect External Data
Gather information on external processes from partners.

4. Analyze Data
Choose, adapt, and improve on best practices used by partners, plan for implementing them internally.

Step 1: Identify the Core Issues

An agency team starts the benchmarking process by identifying unmet customer requirements, a performance gap, a problem area, or a strategic goal that cannot be met unless its associated processes are greatly improved. The team defines the problem or issue in measurable terms and identifies the internal processes associated with it.

Next, the team does a preliminary analysis of the internal processes to determine if they are good candidates for benchmarking, using criteria we discussed earlier. During this analysis, the team looks at the factors that drive process performance. As discussed in Chapter 10 under Activity-Based Costing, drivers cause process performance to vary along different dimensions. Cost drivers affect cost; volume drivers, the amount of output produced; and quality drivers, the characteristics of the output. Processes with higher error rates cost more and produce lower quality; thus, errors are cost and quality drivers.

Finally, the team uses its preliminary analysis to develop a list of external organizations that are potential benchmarking partners. The term partner is used because a benchmarking project is ideally an exchange of information between two or more organizations, each of which benefits from the transaction. Thus, an agency's benchmarking partner may wish to know about some of the agency's processes. Together, the selected performance measures, process drivers, and external organizations serve as inputs for the actions in Step 2.

In their search for partners, financial managers can attend forums and conferences where their peers discuss and promote benchmarking. These include meetings sponsored by groups such as the federal CFO Council, the Association of Government Accountants, and the American Society of Military Comptrollers.

Step 2: Develop the Baseline Data

Using the outputs developed in Step 1, processes selected for benchmarking are examined in greater detail using process flow charts and refinements of performance indicators. Working with process operators, the team determines the root causes of the variation in key process drivers. Another joint task for team and operators is to conduct a value analysis of the processes (see Chapter 10). If the amount of non-value-added work is significant, estimate the level of performance a process would deliver if such work were eliminated or greatly reduced. The estimate becomes the baseline level of performance against which external processes are compared. This way, the team will focus on searching for truly innovative external processes, instead of being side-tracked by those that do pretty much the same thing as internal operations, but with less non-value-added work.

Now, the team develops a benchmarking questionnaire to guide the selection of benchmarking partners, measure their processes, and discover their best practices. The questionnaire, the primary data-gathering tool, should focus on vital information needs only, with relevant, direct questions presented in a succinct manner.

The final activity in this step is to select from the list of potential organizations those to target for benchmarking. Select organizations that exhibit most of the same process drivers identified in the internal process review. This helps ensure apples-to-apples comparisons.

Step 3. Collect External Data

The team contacts and screens potential benchmarking partners. An efficient data collection approach uses a combination of telephone introductions and mailed or faxed questionnaires that are followed up with telephone clarifications or selected visits. This can be done with several partners at once.

Partners need to be informed of several things: what is being benchmarked; who on their side should be involved and the time it will take; that they will be guaranteed the level of confidentiality they demand; and, finally, "what's in it for them." Government agencies have a slight advantage in obtaining private sector partners, perhaps because of corporate America's patriotism, but also because the agencies do not compete with most companies. Still, it helps tremendously if an agency has a few excellent processes in which a partner has a real interest; this opens doors and encourages a healthy partnership.

Step 4. Analyze Data

Analysis of questionnaire information should help the team generate a list of ideas on process improvement and a plan for implementing them. Most of the ideas will be adaptations of the benchmarked processes to the agency's needs and work environment. However, exposure to outside processes usually stimulates ideas for improving even the best of practices, so the team's goal should be to push the envelope and strive for an internal process that is an even better practice. Limited resources may mean addressing critical problems now and others later, so a phased implementation may be needed.

Two areas of apples-to-apples cost comparisons need to be given attention. When comparing internal and external processes, financial managers should ensure that the full costs of each be captured and understood. As discussed in Chapter 10 under ABC, traditional cost accounting can distort actual costs because of how it allocates overhead or indirect expenses. ABC, on the other hand, traces all indirect costs to a process, which makes ABC ideal for accurate financial comparisons during benchmarking. Also, an agency needs to factor out of the comparison any inherent advantages or disadvantages it has when compared to a potential benchmarking partner. For example, federal agencies benefit from tax-exempt status, which can make some of their processes less costly than those of private companies. On the other hand, an agency's requirement to hold public hearings may slow down and increase the cost of a process that moves quickly and inexpensively in the private sector.

Finally, the team develops an implementation for transitioning from the existing internal process to an improved best practices process. This plan should follow an agency's normal planning process, with new emphasis on change management and continuous improvement.

Step 5: Implement Change

This step executes the implementation plan. Many organizations have problems at this stage because it means change, and people resist change. We recommend that the implementation plan include a change management component to overcome this problem (see Chapter 10). Following implementation, the team measures performance of the processes that have been benchmarked in order to confirm their success.

Because the world does not stand still, today's best practice can quickly become tomorrow's obsolete process. To stave this off, an agency needs to build procedures into the new process that will ensure that it continual improves over time.

Benchmarking Shows What to Do and How to Do It

Our experience is that agencies must look for more than just technical innovations. Just as important to success is how organizations with best practices developed and introduced them. Also, agencies that use best practices benchmarking the right way are in for a pleasant surprise. They may start out searching for solutions to narrowly defined problems, but by staying open to new ideas and concepts they often discover more comprehensive best practices that add major new sources of value to customers.

For example, a large state agency asked Coopers & Lybrand to assist its financial organization in benchmarking best practices in four functional areas: 1) purchasing, 2) accounts payable, 3) accounts receivable, and 4) time and attendance. Besides finding technical innovations, our client wanted to validate strategic decisions about centralizing and investing in technology for some of the functions by looking at the results of these changes in other places. Also, the agency had experienced problems with employee resistance in earlier reengineering efforts, so leaders wanted to know how other organizations had successfully overcome that problem.

We recommended that the agency's benchmarking partners should: 1) have a reputation for excellence in at least one of the four functional areas, 2) use information technology to support an area, and 3) have recently reengineered, centralized, decentralized, or otherwise reorganized one or more of the areas. A search identified thirteen benchmarking partners, but only two were agencies in other states with the same mission as the client agency. The others: seven Fortune 500 companies, one entire state government, a federal agency with a totally unrelated mission, a quasigovernmental corporation, and a nonprofit association.

By studying its benchmarking partners, the agency identified dozens of best practices that could be adopted and adapted to the four functions. But by staying open to new ideas, it also discovered an excellent new organizational concept for a comprehensive, centralized financial operation. As important, agency leaders benefited from the hard-won experience of benchmarking partners in introducing major change to their organizations. For example, in the accounts payable and receivable functions, the agency learned these best practices and lessons in implementing them:

- A centralized customer service or financial services center can provide excellent assistance to both internal and external customers and suppliers, not only for accounts receivable and payable, but also for many other financial services, some of which the client agency had not been offering.
- Organize the center around cradle-to-grave processes that deliver discrete products and services to customers.
- Develop solutions teams in the center to work directly with customers on their problems.
- Marketing is the most important skill of the centers' management teams, who must sell the new services throughout the organization.

- The center concept means higher education requirements for employees because they must be more
analytical than clerical.
- Plan for employees' resistance to increase in
responsibilities but no increase in staff (training
alleviates such concerns).
- It is difficult to make both organizational and computer system changes at the same time; employees
need time for training and to become comfortable
with the new operation.

As a result, the agency is now developing far-reaching
changes to its financial services operations that will provide
more value to internal and external customers—and thus
give the agency an edge over less customer-oriented competitors.

Best Practices in Financial Management

In the September 1995 issue of *CFO* magazine, Stephen
Barr and Mary C. Driscoll polled consultants respected for
their work in financial process reengineering and came up
with best practices in several core financial processes: 1)
information management, 2) accounts receivable and
payable, 3) billing, 4) time and expense (T&E) expense
reporting, 5) purchasing, and 6) controls and compliance.
We include summaries of these practices here with examples of their use in the federal government.

Information Management Best Practices
- Create a single, unified set of definitions for all primary business data—avoid Tower of Babel systems
that speak different, incompatible languages.
- Use general ledger-based systems as they were
intended—general ledgers should be confined to
external reporting; they should not provide input to
operating decisions or be burdened with irrelevant
management data.
- Insist on single entry of all data at the source of
transaction—data should be captured and structured

so to have both a transaction use and an information use; this will help eliminate the rekeying of data.

- Capture transaction data at every meaningful level—and not, as is often the case, at only a summary level that does not provide enough basis for decision-making.

Example: U.S. Department of Veterans Affairs (VA)—eliminating the flood of paper. VA needed to reengineer its payments processes, so it combined electronic processing and electronic commerce systems, practically eliminating document handling and reducing the number of steps needed to validate invoices and issue checks. The agency outsourced parts of the payment process and realized significant savings.

Implementation has proceeded rapidly. In FY 1995, the VA payment center in Austin, Texas, handled 11 million pieces of paper. In FY 1996, the number fell to 7.7 million, and in FY 1997 is expected to decline to 1.3 million. Invoices and supporting documentation come through the facility's mail room, where they go through a high-speed scanner. They are then routed through a network of personal computers equipped with Windows™ software that can post transaction activity on accounting and recordkeeping programs. Operators have the ability to communicate with the field directly while they are checking with vendors or others if necessary. The entire receipt/payment cycle is on VA's electronic data interchange (EDI) that receives invoices as well as purchase orders.

The system is linked with that of a private bank that directs payment to the vendors. VA issues one check to the bank daily that covers 60,000 individual payments. The efficiency of the system allows the bank to offer VA a substantial discount on the cost of short-term credit, 64 basis points plus another basis point for downloading reports electronically and another for paying daily.

Accounts Receivable and Payable

Best Practices, Receivables

- Transform credit and collections into a customer service-oriented function—removing problems may mean making preemptive customer contacts to discuss payment issues. Closely monitor customer satisfaction and alert marketing people to any overlooked issues.

- Prioritize accounts and discriminate among key clients—organize your customers by value rather than by alphabet or geography, and don't feel that all customers require equal amounts of attention. Have senior people deal with critical accounts.

- Generate process metrics that offer meaningful data—various metrics are relevant at different levels of the organization. Reporting should reflect the different uses of data.

- Implement an effective dispute management process—accounts receivable staff should be trained to analyze and document the causes for short or late payments and identify any patterns in pricing or billing discrepancies at the source.

- Set days sales outstanding (DSO)—although a company's theoretically best DSO may never be reached, at least it sets a relevant stretch goal.

Best Practices, Payables

- Process all accounts payable through a single system—accounts payable activities that are disbursed throughout the organization are inefficient.

- Assume receipt for transactions less than $1,000—it ends up being less expensive to pay these bills without review than to spend money scrupulously matching invoices with receipts.

- Use on-line purchase order requisition and electronic purchase order generation—an automated process will allow you to keep track of all purchase orders without having to generate actual ones that will only add to the paper trail.

- Allow automatic payment for standard, recurring items—there are several ways to do this: You can pay upon receipt of materials or merchandise at agreed-upon prices; use production data as a proxy for invoices; or work with key suppliers to combine invoices for recurring items.
- Eliminate manual check generation and signatures.

Example: Consolidation of accounting functions at the Department of Energy (DOE). DOE developed its consolidation initiative—which intends to consolidate into three service centers all the accounting functions now done in nineteen field offices—in order to encourage the streamlining of operations through the department's Strategic Alignment Initiative; to support the NPR recommendations; and to leverage new technology. Working groups consolidate functions in four areas:

1. **Systems**—responsible for all software, hardware, and telecommunications necessary to assure success. Telecommunication is now in place, and the process of moving databases to the three service centers that began in April 1996 will be completed by August 1996.
2. **Travel**—responsible for installing a paperless travel system that will be operational by December 1996. Achievements include implementation of travel management software, mandatory use of an agency credit card for airline tickets and cash advances; and reimbursements by EFT or third-party checks.
3. **Invoice Payment**—responsible for consolidating all payments through the maximum use of electronic commerce and the minimum movement of paper.
4. **Accounting Operations**—responsible for policy, procedures, and identification of system changes necessary for the transition of all other accounting functions.

The department has identified several keys to the success of this project: effective team building; open and frequent communication; detailed planning; a phased approach; and process reengineering. Projected savings are estimated at $17 million over five years.[1]

Billing Best Practices

- Provide customers with a single point of contact for inquiries—one possible approach is to position the billing-error-prevention process at the point of contact with the customer.
- Develop a seamless interface among order entry, billing, and credit. Salespeople enter the order data directly in the system that then automatically verifies product data and runs a credit check before an invoice is released.
- Whenever possible, avoid sending out invoices— consider pay upon receipt agreements.
- Use summary statements for high volumes of transactions.
- Design clear and concise invoices—although a standardized invoice maximizes efficiency, you should work with customers to determine the best invoice format, media, and timing that will best reduce the number of bills and unnecessary paper transactions.
- Consolidate invoice printing and distribution to take advantage of bulk-mail discounts.

Example: The Department of Defense EDI strategy. An EDI project of unprecedented scope has been underway at the DoD Information Systems Agency. The goal of this project was to channel 300,000 DoD suppliers into the business mainstream through an EDI test facility, the first of its kind in any federal agency. DoD wanted to present a single face to trading partners, no matter which service or agency they might trade with. DoD's acquisition reform made sense considering that 70 percent of all federal purchases were made nationally.

In an initial study, DoD found that with a manual process they could test about twenty suppliers a month. At that rate, even with 100 people testing full-time, it would be into the next century before all 300,000 suppliers could be tested and able to transact business electronically with the government. In addition, the EDI industry figured that the average testing cycle cost a prohibitively high $2,000 to $3,000 per trading partner.

The new EDI approach allows DoD to test and approve more than 7,000 vendor trading partners per month. Michael E. Green of the DoD EC/EDI Program Office commented on how revolutionary this new approach truly is: "A successful certification consists of three consecutive tests, without error, within seven tries. When the certification test is passed, you can logically do business with any part of DoD because we're all using the same data elements and segments. We anticipate that DoD will use myriad transactions as EDI expands to other business areas—automation is critical! This program will become the basis for every federal agency to implement EDI with their suppliers."

The new approach uses software tools to do precise standards compliance checks and interactively flag errors and warnings for data not in compliance with the user's specifications. For DoD suppliers, this provides "an immediate visual identification of the error location."

During early brainstorming sessions about the test facility, DoD came up with a distributable vendor kit. A full-compliance self-test software integrated with EDI implementation guidelines, the kit allows suppliers to test themselves formally with DoD after performing their own self-tests. Using a file format for implementation guidelines known as standard exchange format (SEF), DoD distributes its specifications electronically over the Internet. Several other federal agencies have expressed an interest in the unique self-test approach DoD is using for compliance testing, communications with networks, and centralized contractor registration.

With military bases closing around the country, this new technology is a boon for small suppliers who have built their business around base purchases and who will now have the opportunity to sell products nationally. As Green stated, "Like corporate America, we are trying to reduce labor costs, but at the same time, we do not want to cause undue hardship on small or medium-size business. We want to provide opportunity, not leave these suppliers behind because of technology."[2]

Time and Expense (T&E) Reporting Best Practices

T&E is a touchy area that requires particular attention. Too often, time and resources are allocated to simply generating vouchers, authorizations, and reports. In one well-known government case, the cost of handling T&E represented an exorbitant 30 percent of the actual cost of travel. The following best practices are more streamlined and cost-effective ways of T&E reporting.

- Develop, communicate, and enforce a uniform T&E policy—do not tolerate different policies in different units. It might be worthwhile to install a travel manager who oversees the agency's travel policy administration and manages contracts with vendors.
- Replace cash advances with a corporate-sponsored credit-card program, so that the employee is reimbursed for expenses through the payroll system and payments made to the credit card issuer.
- Do away with travel authorizations—have faith in the integrity of your employees. It is unlikely that they will take a business trip without first bringing it to the attention of their boss.
- Rely on statistically based audit samples and tolerances—controls should be embedded in the system for keeping track of the average cost of a hotel room in a particular geographical area, allowing any inappropriate charges to be flagged.

Example: GSA's reengineered travel program. GSA's reengineered and streamlined approach to travel will eliminate the three basic processing problems most travel programs have—the travel order, the travel advance, and the travel voucher—by doing away with the paper trail. Employees who travel check into a hotel that has an agreement with GSA for direct billing. They pay for telephone calls with a telephone card and use an American Express card for advances. Through payroll, the agency can determine the per diem for a particular area. And, with the exception of miscellaneous expenses such as cab rides, no expense reports will ever need to be filed.

The new travel process reduces the need for travel advances, allows individuals to stay at preferred properties at rates lower than the daily lodging rate, and eliminates mounds of paperwork. As important, it changes the paradigm within the agency from one of auditing every voucher to one of trusting employees to use good judgment.[3]

Purchasing Best Practices

- Use a procurement card—giving a credit card to thousands of employees requires minimal investment and can lead to major savings for organizations with a high volume of small-dollar purchases.
- Use an automated system to process small-dollar requisitions—if the purchase is with an approved vendor, the purchasing department need not be involved. This reduces processing costs and improves cycle time for routine transactions.
- Rationalize the supply chain—reduce the number of vendors, develop a certification program, and negotiate national and global supply contracts for each commodity.

Example: third-party draft at the Federal Bureau of Investigation. Changes in the FBI's accounting system happened quickly at its headquarters but didn't reach the agency's field offices until very recently. Field offices now have control over supply budgets, travel budgets, equipment budgets—everything except personnel. Before 1992, permanent advances were issued for FBI employees in a continuing travel status. Now, advances are issued through the third-party draft system, a subsystem of the accounts payable system.

Advances at the FBI involve four major sections: 1) commercial advances, 2) travel advances, 3) advances for employee transfers, and 4) confidential advances. Third-party drafts are currently processed at 62 FBI draft sites and are used instead of imprest funds. They are negotiable instruments that do not require cash disbursements from the U.S. Treasury when issued. Funds are initially provided by a commercial bank when the holder cashes in the draft. The bank is reimbursed by Treasury only after presenting the drafts to the FBI for payment.

The third-party draft system has been highly successful at the FBI. An uncomplicated and well-monitored reimbursement and reconciliation process allows the system to run smoothly. For the Bureau's CFO Jay Brixey, the third-party draft is "the best thing we've done since we got our new accounting system." Brixey explained that, under the old system, if the field office made a purchase, headquarters didn't find out about it until the bill came in, even an investigative expense, such as an agency paying an informant. Although agents had to produce vouchers monthly, sometimes headquarters wouldn't see them for two months. "We were running six to eight weeks behind the actual expenditures," Brixey said. "When you neared year-end, you'd have to do projections based on historical knowledge or anything you could pull together. Now with the third-party draft, we get this information instantaneously. So, not only do we give the field office more authority, we get more control."

Controls and Compliance Best Practices

- Perform back-end reviews on highest-risk conditions—instead of full reviews, perform audits based on statistical samples and build in proper reporting tools.
- Build front-end controls into automated processes—embedded tolerances can simplify and reduce the costs of a variety of processes.
- Track and justify the cost of controls—the cost of checking travel expense receipts, for instance, far exceeds the dollar amount found in most discrepancies.

In addition to Barr and Driscoll's list of controls and compliance best practices above, please see the discussion of internal controls in Chapter 10.

Example: The Department of the Interior's new approach to internal controls. Interior is currently putting in place for its management control program a new model for ensuring the integrity, accountability, and effectiveness of its operation. The performance-based model is flexible and highly supportive of the department's strategic goals. Throughout the process, which involved downsizing and reengineering, Interior sought a new, integrated, and less resource-intensive method for fulfilling its management control responsibilities under the Financial Managers Financial Integrity Act.

An administrative program was selected for pilot testing of this new performance-based monitoring system that links requirements for meeting the objectives of FMFIA, OMB Circular A-123, GPRA, and the CFO Act. It is a continuous, real-time monitoring and assessment methodology that is more proactive in identifying and correcting material deficiencies. The approach also provides a meaningful assurance report that will highlight best practices for management. Interior anticipates that the new model of internal controls and compliance will result in substantial cost savings.[4]

An old African proverb say's that it is other people's experience that makes the older man wiser than the younger man. Just so, organizations grow wiser when they use benchmarking to capitalize on the experience of others—an easier, less costly way to find solutions than most internal efforts In the long term, the greatest benefit of benchmarking is to replace all-too-common "we're unique" and "not invented here" attitudes with a philosophy of searching for best practices, no matter where they may be.

Chapter

10

NEW TOOLS FOR NEW ROLES

Financial managers are using a new set of management and financial methods to fulfill their new roles:

- Activity-based costing is a set of management information and accounting methods used to identify, describe, assign costs to, and otherwise report on the operations in an organization.
- Value analysis is a method for identifying activities that do not add value to products and services so that agencies can eliminate or reduce the resources consumed by these activities.
- The current best practice in management and internal controls, developed by five leading accounting and finance organizations, directs attention to the cultural aspects of controls as well as the more traditional technical aspects.
- Business process redesign or reengineering is a set of methods used to gain radical improvements in processes, as measured by cost, cycle time, service, and quality.
- Change management is the process of aligning the human, organizational and cultural elements of an agency with new ways of doing business.

The decision that achieves organization objectives must be 1) technologically sound and 2) carried out by people. If we lose sight of the second requirement or if we assume naively that people can be made to carry out whatever decisions are technically sound, we run the risk of decreasing rather than increasing the effectiveness of the organization.

–Management pioneer Douglas McGregor

America's Western frontier was conquered by pioneers with muzzle-loading rifles and axes. As government financial managers enter accounting's final frontier, some will be equipped only with the management equivalent of such primitive tools. Tools like outmoded cost accounting methods that distort true costs. Ineffective and costly internal controls appended to operations as afterthoughts. Improvement methods that at best deliver suboptimal results or at worst do not deliver at all. Approaches to change that leave personnel angry and unable to meet new challenges. Many of those accounting pioneers will "leave their bones beside the trail."

Others will have modern management tools that are proven in government and industry. These tools include activity-based costing, which gives managers the information they need for cost-effective decisions. Internal controls that are built into processes and organizational culture. Improvement methods like business process redesign that produce rapid yet sustainable performance increases. Effective management of all four dimensions of change: technical, organizational, human, and cultural. Financial managers with these types of tools will survive, thrive, and be true stewards of public funds.

In this chapter, we provide an overview of several modern accounting and management tools that will be useful to government financial professionals who want to take on the new roles described throughout this book. The tools are especially important for the partnership role, in which financial and operations managers team up to make business decisions and improve operations. Two themes common to employing the tools are technical process improvement and changing the behavior of individuals, groups, and organizations—the point captured in the opening quotation by Douglas McGregor.

[F]ive standards set forth the fundamental elements of managerial cost accounting: (1) accumulating and reporting costs of activities on a regular basis for management information purposes, (2) establishing responsibility segments to match costs with outputs, (3) determining full costs of government goods and services, (4) recognizing the costs of goods and services provided among federal entities, and (5) using appropriate costing methodologies to accumulate and assign costs to outputs.
     —*Managerial Cost Accounting Concepts and Standards for the Federal Government*, Statement of Recommended Accounting Standards #4, Office of Management and Budget

Managerial Cost Accounting and Activity-Based Costing

If government is the last frontier of the accounting profession, then managerial cost accounting is its greatest challenge. Few agencies have accurate cost information, and few federal managers use sound managerial accounting methods, which makes it difficult to make cost-effective decisions. They and Congress know what agencies spend, because that information is in budgets. However, it is very difficult to determine what a government-produced product or service actually costs, because federal accounting systems are not designed to provide accurate cost data.

If the systems could do this, budget discussions would focus more on the quality, type, and volume of services and goods that agency executives and Congress could "buy" from managers, instead of on what the managers wanted to spend. This is the key concept of performance-based budgeting and the performance-based organizations discussed in Chapter 8. The City of Indianapolis activity-based budget for street maintenance, shown in that chapter, is a good example of performance-based budgeting: It gives the full unit cost and quantity of different services that will be delivered. Some federal agencies have core services that cannot be quantified in this approach—but all agencies have some products and services that can. (For the rest of this chapter, we will refer to agency outputs as services.)

Background on Activity-Based Costing

Private companies' problems have been somewhat similar to those of governments in this area. Most use an outmoded system of cost accounting that allocates overhead or indirect costs evenly to all products with a formula such as a multiplier of direct labor costs. Overhead includes administration, quality control, security, planning, facilities, maintenance, and many aspects of financial management. Such formulas can distort cost information because different products consume different amounts of overhead. This was no great problem 50 years ago, when overhead rates were low, but now they often exceed direct costs. For example, 50 years ago companies and agencies did not have large information systems. In the Information Age, every organization of any size has at least one, which adds significantly to overhead costs.

Activity-based costing solved this accounting problem by directly tracing instead of allocating overhead costs to the processes that make specific products. With tracing, some companies discovered that their so-called profitable products in fact lost money for every unit sold. This led some to raise prices, reduce costs, and in some cases abandon certain products.

Many companies discovered more powerful applications for ABC than simply figuring out product costs. They used it to generate financial and operations information for improving processes and determining the appropriate budget and staffing for operations, as we discuss next.

ABC's Many Users and Uses

ABC has been called a cost accounting method, but this definition is too narrow. It is a set of management information and accounting methods used to identify, describe, assign costs to, and otherwise report on the operations in an organization. Users of ABC include corporations like GE, John Deere, Johnson & Johnson, and American Express and municipal governments such as Phoenix, Arizona, and

Indianapolis, Indiana. Federal users include the Internal Revenue Service, the Department of the Treasury, the Defense Mapping Agency, the Air Force, the Navy's shipyards, the Postal Service, the Department of Energy, the Army, and the Immigration and Naturalization Service.

The Federal Accounting Standards Advisory Board recognizes four types of managerial cost accounting: 1) job order costing, 2) process costing, 3) standard costing, and 3) ABC. The board noted in particular that ABC "has gained broad acceptance by manufacturing and service industries as an effective managerial tool. Federal entities are encouraged to study its potential within their own operations." Other board recommendations, including those on full costing, reimbursable activities and intergovernmental transfers, will require approaches like ABC to be successful and useful.

Today, our program managers more often view financial information as a way to get a larger budget for their programs. Even in this environment of declining budgets, they will focus on incremental resource initiatives, rather than on what's driving those costs. We haven't given them the information nor the incentive to change that practice—but we're working on it!

—Senior federal financial executive at C&L
focus group, April 1996

Figure 10-1 shows two views of a purchasing department's budget. At the top of the figure is the traditional view of the budget, which is line-item funding and full-time-equivalent staffing. Line items do not offer useful explanations of where the department's money goes. They cannot be easily matched to specific services or outputs such as the unit cost of processing or updating a purchase order. Without unit costs, the department cannot determine if it is cost-effective, benchmark its costs against those of other organizations, or determine whether an improvement project actually saved money.

Figure 10-1

Two Views of Purchasing Department Budget

Line-Item Budget View

Salaries	$742,538
Computer	91,500
Telecommunications	30,880
Supplies	34,115
Facilities	81,373
Total	$980,407
Full-time equivalents (FTEs)	18.6

ABC View

Activity	Volume	Output	FTEs	Total Cost	Unit Cost	Labor Cost	Computer	Telecommunication	Supplies	Facilities
Process new purchase orders (p.o.)	70,000	Completed p.o.'s	7.8	$407,167	$5.82	$303,333	$35,000	$17,500	$14,000	$37,333
Update p.o. files	210,000	Updated p.o.'s	5.8	322,000	1.53	227,500	52,500	10,500	10,500	21,000
Answer audit queries	50	Queries answered	0.7	33,533	670.67	30,333	0	0	0	3,200
Design training courses	3	Courses designed	0.1	8,287	2,762.22	5,547	0	0	2,100	640
Conduct training courses	270	Days of training	0.2	12,900	47.78	6,825	0	0	6,075	0
Supervise p.o. operations	16	Employees supervised	2.0	120,160	7,510.00	104,000	2,000	1,440	720	12,000
Other administrative/ clerical work		No unit measure	2.0	76,360		65,000	2,000	1,440	720	7,200
TOTAL			18.6	$980,407		$742,538	$91,500	$30,880	$34,115	$81,373

Source: *Activity-Based Management in Government.*

The bottom half of Figure 10-1 is an ABC view of the same department with almost all costs traced to individual processes that produce specific outputs. With this view, managers can see the unit cost of outputs, including their component costs. Such information allows managers to:

- Compare their unit costs to those of other organizations
- Carry out economically sound make/buy analysis
- Adjust their budget and staffing level to reflect anticipated changes in work volume
- Identify priorities for cost reductions
- Measure the savings of process improvements.

Most of all, ABC helps to give managers what quality pioneer W. Edwards Deming called *profound knowledge* of their operations. They will understand what causes costs to vary, and knowledge of these causes will enable them to make cost-effective decisions. This knowledge accumulates during the process of developing ABC information.

Developing ABC Information

ABC is based on two cost concepts. The *cost assignment concept* is that activities consume resources, and cost objects consume activities. Cost objects are products, services, customers, and other items. ABC's primary purpose is to produce cost reports on cost objects. The process concept is that cost drivers affect resource consumption, which in turn affects performance. Cost drivers are the root causes of variation in the amount of resources an activity consumes. Such drivers include problems in a process that cause errors and rework; different types of customers that may demand more resources from a process; and so on. Reducing the cost of a process could mean automating it, but more often the job can be done by identifying and correcting problems that drive up costs.

Data collection for ABC is a two-stage procedure. First, an agency maps out its processes down to an appropriate level, which is usually the activity level shown in Figure 10-2 below. Second, costs are traced to processes using data obtained from existing financial ledger accounts and data

Figure 10-2

The ABC Process Hierarchy

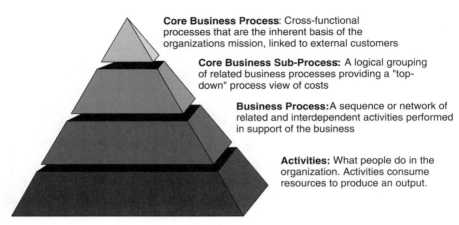

Core Business Process: Cross-functional processes that are the inherent basis of the organizations mission, linked to external customers

Core Business Sub-Process: A logical grouping of related business processes providing a "top-down" process view of costs

Business Process: A sequence or network of related and interdependent activities performed in support of the business

Activities: What people do in the organization. Activities consume resources to produce an output.

systems and other methods such as labor surveys. Having collected cost data and associated them with activities (the lowest level of operation shown in Figure 10-2 and of most interest to employees and line supervisors), cost reports can produce this information by activity. Cost reports for managers and executives can aggregate the data into costs for higher-level processes that are composed of the activities. Thus, everyone in this hierarchy shares the same data sources. Executives can associate problems with processes and activities down the hierarchy, and employees in activities can understand their contribution to the big picture.

Activities can be aggregated hierarchically, as shown in Figure 10-2, and also in different arrangements to produce many types of cost reports, such as those shown in Figure 10-3. For example:

- As shown in Figure 10-1, all activities in a work unit can be aggregated to show its actual expenses.
- The full cost of services can be determined, because ABC identifies all cost elements flowing into their production.

- All overhead or indirect costs in an organization can be aggregated, including those that occur outside of administrative and support offices.

Figure 10-3

**ABC Allows Financial and Performance Information
to Be Viewed by Process or By Organization**

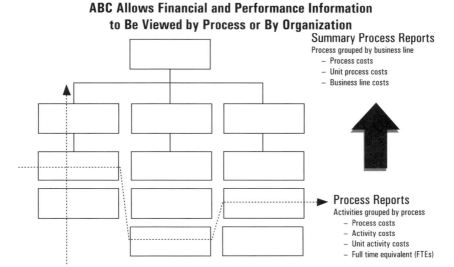

Summary Process Reports
Process grouped by business line
– Process costs
– Unit process costs
– Business line costs

Process Reports
Activities grouped by process
– Process costs
– Activity costs
– Unit activity costs
– Full time equivalent (FTEs)

Organizational Reports
Activities grouped by functional area
– Activity costs
– Unit activity costs
– Full time equivalent (FTEs)

A cost report on a cross-functional process can reveal surpassing information that would otherwise be hidden, even by a department activity budget such as that shown in Figure 10-1. While the total cost of operations in the purchasing department may be $700,000, the actual cost of processing purchase orders may greatly exceed that amount. This is because the purchase process begins and ends outside the purchasing department. Other departments spend resources preparing purchase orders, and accounts payable offices spend time responding to vendors' invoices. ABC can capture all these costs, add them to the relevant costs of the purchasing department, and produce a total cost of the purchase order process. This may reveal that there are twice as many FTEs devoted to the purchase order process outside the purchasing department, which should stimulate serious thoughts about finding a less expensive way of buying.

To be effective, ABC information should be generated from the same financial systems used to track an agency's budget and expense data. ABC does not need to replace existing systems; instead, ABC complements them by providing a process view of cost data. This lets management generate results-oriented reports on the agency's financial condition and operating performance through the integration of available budget, accounting, and program data—a key goal of the CFO Act, GMRA, and GPRA.

Activity-based management

Recently, some organizations have made major modifications in their management approach to create what is called activity-based management. The business practices of activity-based management include:

- Using ABC as the managerial cost accounting system
- Building management structure around core business processes instead of functions, offices, or other organizational components
- Applying activity-based budgeting along with more traditional budgeting (few private companies use only activity-based budgeting)
- "Sizing" capacity to match work load, based on the system of volume drivers discussed earlier
- Usually, following quality management principles and practices.

Of these practices, the most important is that process or activity owners manage the operations of an organization. Sometimes, these are line managers in charge of products, programs, customer groups, or business processes. At other times, they are the heads of the departments most concerned with a particular process, even though parts of that process fall outside their boundaries. A good example of this management structure is the Navy's shipyards, where the manager of a single ship undergoing maintenance or refitting has the clear and unchallenged authority to command resources from functions and departments.

Roles for Financial Professionals in ABC

ABC or any other sound managerial cost accounting approach should be integrated in an agency's financial framework. This does not always happen, however, especially when program managers see ABC primarily as a tool for one-time cost studies or for streamlining and restructuring operations. While these are legitimate applications, the true value of ABC comes from daily use by all managers.

To ensure acceptance of ABC as a key management tool, CFOs and financial managers can be the catalysts, advocates, architects, teachers, internal consultants, and caretakers of this accounting approach. By assuming those roles, financial managers will forge an enduring partnership with their colleagues in other parts of an agency.

Value Analysis

Downsizing and streamlining are government-wide challenges that are poorly addressed by outmoded management methods such as reductions in force (RIFs) and employee buy-outs, which eliminate workers but not their work. Value analysis is a better approach because it identifies unneeded activities, enabling fewer workers to work better, faster, and at less cost.

Downsizing Does Not Necessarily Mean Less Work

Since the beginning of the Clinton's Administration in 1993, the federal government has shed more than 250,000 positions—11 percent—making the Executive Branch the smallest since John F. Kennedy was President more than thirty years ago. However, many agencies say they are being stretched too thin. One reason is that their workforce was downsized without a corresponding decrease in workloads, according to an August 1996 report by the General Accounting Office. As a result, many agencies are experiencing work backlogs, production and service shortfalls, and increased overtime. Also, voluntary buy-outs offered to federal workers as part of downsizing induced experienced personnel to quit or retire early from critical operations, causing skill imbalances and an exodus of corporate memory and competence. More workforce reductions are inevitable so the situation will only get worse unless agencies can reduce workloads through more efficient and effective work practices.

> ABC encourages management to evaluate the efficiency and cost-effectiveness of activities. Some ABC systems rank activities by the degree to which they add value to the organization or its outputs. Managers use such value rankings to focus their cost reduction programs.
> — *Managerial Cost Accounting Concepts and Standards for the Federal Government*, Office of Management and Budget

CFO offices have not been immune to this problem. In our 1995 survey of federal CFO offices, only one-third reported that they had received additional funding for CFO Act implementation, despite the increased workload this entails. One-third said that downsizing inhibited their ability to meet the requirements of the new financial legislation. Three out of five reported the same problem due to the National Performance Review's emphasis on streamlining administrative functions.

Value analysis has an objective of identifying resources devoted to activities that do not add value to services so that agencies can eliminate or reduce the resources going to them. Usually, these resources are labor-intensive, so that reducing them can result in increased employee productivity. But value analysis is not simply about reducing workload. It also is a tool for identifying process problems that, if solved, will improve performance as measured in cost, quality, cycle time, and better customer service.

```
┌─────────────────────────────────────────────────┐   Figure 10-4
│            Value Analysis Classifications         │
│                                                   │
│ Value-added criteria                              │
│   ● Work that is absolutely essential to providing a service the │
│     customer needs                                │
│   ● Work that changes the fit, form, or function of the final out- │
│     put delivered to customers                    │
│   ● Any work that increases the net worth of the output (quality, │
│     value) as perceived by the customer           │
│   ● Work that customers believe is valuable and for which they │
│     would be willing to pay                       │
│ Non-value-added criteria                          │
│   ● Any work or other resource used beyond what is absolutely │
│     essential to delivering the service the customer needs │
│   ● Work that can be eliminated with no deterioration of perfor- │
│     mance of value-added work                     │
│   ● Any work that does not transform inputs into outputs, such │
│     as supervision, reviewing work, inspection, and rework │
│   ● Any work that can be eliminated if a previous task or activity │
│     is done right the first time                  │
└─────────────────────────────────────────────────┘
```

Value Analysis Concept and Criteria

Value analysis is often misunderstood, so we will be clear about its most basic concept: Customers determine what adds value to the products and services they buy. Value-added activities transform work-in-process in ways that customers perceive as beneficial, but non-value-added activities do not (and sometime do not make any transformation at all). Figure 10-4 shows a widely accepted set of classification criteria for value analysis. An agency should be firm about using written and understood criteria for value classification, because many managers will insist that all the activities in their operations be value-added.

Non-Value-Added Work in Financial Operations

Sometimes activities that don't add value are necessary. For example, as part of our work with a federal facility, we found many repeated inspections of nuclear systems. Technically, inspection is a non-value-added activity, but for nuclear products and services it makes common sense, and customers are willing to pay for it. However, the facility also had a payroll process in which payroll documents were being inspected manually twice before their release. When asked why, a financial manager said that multiple inspections were the norm in a nuclear facility. That was not common sense, and we think that customers would say, "The payroll process should deliver error-free documents the first time. Computers make it possible to automate payroll inspection. Why should we pay for the facility's costly manual operations, inefficiency, and mistakes?"

Mandated non-value-added work. Financial professionals spend a significant portion of their time documenting events and preparing reports. To the extent that these activities contribute to the value of agency products and services, they are classified as value-added. However, many reports do not add value, and some may not even be required by customers or outside stakeholders such as Congress. Thus, financial managers should review the law or regulation that appears to require a report or a special activity that does not add value to agency services to customers. NPR's Elaine Kamarck told us about the importance of this review: "We asked the agencies in 1993 to take a 50 percent cut in internal regulations. Some people said, 'Oh, we can't do that, it's the law.' So I said okay, let's see the law. Guess what? It is very rarely the law. The law is usually written with very broad aims. Sometimes the problem is a formal regulation in the Federal Register, but we in the Executive Branch can fix those, and we have a project to do this. But sometimes the problem is neither law nor formal regulation. It is the internal, bureaucratic regulations within the agency, and we are encouraging the Cabinet Secretaries and the members of the President's Management Council to get rid of them."

In our own value analysis work with federal agencies, we often find that many unnecessary or overly strict internal regulations are on the books for the wrong reasons. Agency managers may have been too conservative in interpreting a law, or decided to manage a low-level risk with an internal rule that costs more to administer than the problems it prevents. At some point in the past, a crisis arose that was "solved" by an internal rule, but that rule is no longer needed. Someone in authority wanted to be "in the loop" in a decision and wrote this into a regulation. A rule requiring paper documentation may have been needed in the past for a manual process, but now the process is automated and no longer needs a paper trail. Spending authority levels may not have been raised to keep them current with inflation, buying technology, and best practices, which creates extra work. The list can go on, so suffice it to say that there are more potentially wrong reasons to have an internal regulation than right ones. This is why all such rules should be subject to periodic challenges.

Financial managers at the Department of Energy have been systematically reviewing their directives system to identify "self-inflicted" regulations. In one instance, rewriting regulations for DOE's capital asset management program saved $10 million a year.

Non-value-added tasks in value-added processes. Even when a financial process is value-added, it may still contain non-value added tasks that can be eliminated without harming services. Start out by asking the customers of the process what they expect from it. With these expectations in mind, look at each task in the process and ask, "Would the customer pay for this task?" If the answer is no, then the task may be non-value-added. Also, examine the process for things such as unnecessary sign-offs, approvals, or paperwork; multiple reviews of the same document; rework to correct errors; materiality levels that are not in keeping with risk; expediting; or extra coordination caused by fragmented responsibility. Many of these tasks can be eliminated by fiat: Just order people to stop doing them. Others require a careful study of how to remove the root causes of problems that create the need for the tasks.

After all this analysis and improvement, some non-value-added tasks and processes will still remain. Then, the objective is to discover ways to reduce to an absolute minimum the amount of resources they need to do their work. Solutions may include technology that automates manual processes and outsourcing a process to a vendor or other agency that can do the same or a better job for less. However, the most important solution is a relentless, continuous effort to improve such processes and to prevent non-value-added tasks from creeping back into them.

Streamlining versus maximizing value added. Is removing non-value-added work from a process the same as streamlining it? Most people would say yes, but we do not think this is the right question. It is better to ask, "Has the value-added content of the process been maximized?" because this challenges an agency to find ways of adding value instead of simply removing processes with no value. For example, an internal control that is simply a postproduction inspection is non-value-added. Move the control into the process and transform it into real-time feedback to process operators. Then, they have a better way to measure process performance and so can control and improve the quality, cycle time, and cost of process outputs. This way, the control meets the value-added criterion of work that increases the net worth of output as perceived by customers.

The Magnitude of Non-Value-Added Work in Administrative and Support Processes

C&L has helped dozens of federal organizations to apply value analysis to administrative and support processes, including financial operations. It is not unusual for the agencies to discover that two-thirds of the resources flowing into these processes go for non-value-added work as defined in Figure 10-4. In a support department of one facility, the figure was 85 percent. One reason is that some of these processes are by nature necessary or truly mandated non-value-added operations. There are historic reasons for the high figures as well. Most line operations that produce an agency's main services were consciously planned and designed by experts to be efficient. Many administrative and support operations spread, grew, and multiplied without careful design, usually in response to immediate problems and issues. As a result, they are less efficient than line operations and have many redundancies and needless tasks.

What the two-thirds non-value-added figure means is that, when searching for unneeded work, look first at administrative and support processes. Most budget cutters are aware of this and are increasingly looking at such overhead functions. Thus, it behooves CFOs and financial managers to make serious efforts to reduce any unneeded work by using value analysis, best practices benchmarking, reengineering, new technology, quality management, and other methods. This is surgery with a scalpel instead of the meat ax that budget cutters might use. More important, it leads to improved performance, which makes the National Performance Review goal of "a government that does more with less" a reality, not a slogan.

Role of Financial Professionals in Value Analysis

Financial managers should use value analysis to streamline and identify areas to improve financial processes in order to reduce their non-value-added content. Freed from much of the work that produces cost but no value, financial professionals will be able to devote more time to truly necessary work—and there is certainly more than enough to go around.

When an agency applies value analysis, financial professionals should help in calculating the costs of non-value-added activities. This enables an agency to set priorities for cost reduction and focus on non-value-added activities that consume the most resources. Also, this cost information provides baseline data for measuring process improvements. Finally, a ratio of the resources devoted to value-added and non-value-added activities could become an important measure of the performance of an agency and its processes.

Management and Internal Controls

As a Big Six accounting and management consulting firm, Coopers & Lybrand is frequently asked to assist organizations in auditing and improving their management and internal controls. Our experience is that problems in this area arise not from an absence of controls, but from a control structure that has not kept pace with change. In fact, we often find that organizations have too many controls, but not the right ones. As stated earlier, many controls were added on as after thoughts to processes and most are classified as non-value-added. More seriously, often controls simply are not effective, so that major loss and scandals result. All these problems are found in both government and industry, and corporate America recently started to remedy them with a new look at the objectives and operations of controls.

The COSO Report: A New Look at Controls

In 1987, after several well-publicized financial scandals, the National Commission on Fraudulent Financial Reporting, known as the Treadway Commission, decided to address control problems in the private sector. The commission's sponsors include the American Accounting Association, the American Institute of Certified Public Accountants (AICPA), the Financial Executives Institute, the Institute of Management Accountants, and the National Accounting Association. Together, they formed a Committee of Sponsoring Organizations (COSO) to integrate and reconcile conflicting control concepts into a common framework. In 1991, COSO retained Coopers & Lybrand to study the framework. Our report, entitled *Internal Control— Integrated Framework* (commonly known as the COSO Report), is endorsed by the sponsors and widely accepted as the standard for measuring the effectiveness of an organization's control and compliance programs. The framework is consistent with the objectives of the CFO Act, GMRA, GPRA, and OMB Circular A-123, *Management Accountability and Control.*

Instead of considering controls as an isolated management tool, agencies should integrate their efforts to meet the requirements of the Federal Managers' Financial Integrity Act with other efforts to improve effectiveness and accountability. Thus, management controls should be an integral part of the entire cycle of planning, budgeting, management, accounting, and auditing...support the effectiveness and the integrity of every step of the process and provide continual feedback to management... assure that performance measures are complete and accurate...align staff and authority with the program responsibilities to be carried out, improving both effectiveness and accountability...more closely (align) budget accounts with programs and (charge) them with all significant resources used to produce the program's outputs and outcomes.

—OMB Circular No. A-123,
Management Accountability and Control

Appendix A has ordering information for the COSO Report, which is published by the AICPA. Besides a detailed explanation of the approach, the report has sample questionnaires, data collection forms, and rating sheets useful for a comprehensive audit of controls under the standards of this best practice.

Definition of controls. The COSO Report's definition of internal controls is consistent with how OMB Circular A-123 defines of management controls:

- **COSO Definition of Internal Controls:** "A process, effected by an entity's board of directors *(for government, subsitiute 'elected officials')*, management, and other personnel, designed to provide reasonable assurance regarding the achievement of objectives in the following categories: effectiveness and efficiency of operations, reliablity of financial reporting, and compliance with applicable laws and regulations."

- **OMB Definition of Managment Controls:** "The organization, policies, and procedures used by agencies to reasonably ensure that programs achieve their intended results; resources are used consistent with agency mission; programs and resources are protected from waste, fraud, and mismanagement; laws and regulations are followed; and reliable and timely information is obtained, maintained, reported, and used for decision making."

Note that the COSO definition says that controls are a process. Taking a process approach to improving controls enables the use of performance measurement and process improvement methods discussed in this book and others listed in Appendix A. Thus, we will not dwell on the way to improve controls, but instead will describe their objectives, the COSO integrated framework, and the role of financial managers in creating the framework.

Control objectives. Traditional approaches to controls take a narrow view of them, focusing mostly on the financial, security, and compliance aspects of risk reduction, and use formal policies, rules, checks and balances, and inspections. However, an organization can have the greatest controls available in these areas, yet still be at grave risk of failing to meet its mission. The broader view set forth by the COSO Report and OMB addresses this by setting operational as well as financial reporting and compliance objectives. Operational objectives relate to an agency's ability to achieve its mission and strategic goals by controlling and improving processes so that they meet customer and stakeholder requirements. Such controls aim at producing timely, useful performance measures, and thus are critical for meeting CFO Act and GPRA requirements for such measures. They also provide information on how resources are invested to meet operations and strategic goals, on changes in customer requirements, and on the external environment, best practices, technologies, and related subjects, and the capability of personnel and processes to respond to these changes. Finally, they provide assurance that the agency protects the public trust.

Components of Integrated Control   Figure 10-5

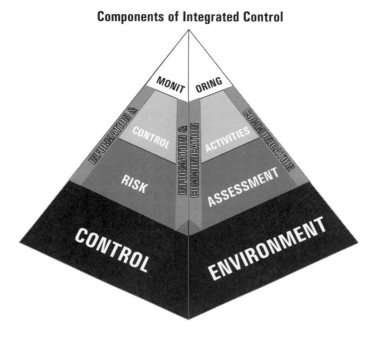

Will traditional control policies, rules, and practices be enough to meet these objectives? Of course not, which was the primary reason for the COSO study. Both the processes and the culture of an agency may need to change, and we will discuss this next when describing the integrated framework for internal controls.

The Integrated Framework

Figure 10-5 shows the framework developed by the COSO initiative. This is an integrated approach, with elements such as ethics, management philosophy, risk assessment, performance measurement, physical controls, communication, information systems, and others. Combined, the elements operate in four dimensions: technical, organizational, cultural, and human, which we discuss later in this chapter under change management.

Control environment. The framework's foundation is the control environment, which is how agency personnel behave, are organized, and are managed. In its technical dimension, this foundation has many traditional internal control principles. These include that audit and oversight groups must be independent of management, that some operations should be segregated from each other, and that opportunities to steal or conceal poor performance should be removed or minimized. However, the control environment has a cultural dimension as well. This dimension is defined not only by its official and unofficial rules, norms, beliefs, and values (we discuss the cultural dimension more under change management later in this chapter).

We have used the COSO Report approach with several client organizations that had just experienced serious, headline-making internal control problems. Our opinion is that such problems were cultural, starting with the "tone at the top" set by executives. In some cases, executives were dishonest, unethical, or incompetent. More often, executives were honest, ethical, and competent, but did not invest their time and energy to make these virtues a priority for their organizations. Either way, executives set the stage for undesirable behavior by employees.

A proactive approach to internal controls in the control environment starts with executives establishing standards of behavior for themselves and their personnel. Then, the standards must be communicated, exemplified, and enforced through executive word and deed. Also, executives must commit to ensuring the competence of their personnel, including developing human resources policies and practices that enable competence. Management's philosophy and operating style also affect the control environment. This includes the types of risks that are acceptable, attitudes toward financial reporting and performance measures, attention to internal control objectives, and how authority and responsibility are assigned.

Risk assessment. Government bureaucracies have a tendency to send dollars off to chase pennies. They tend to be overly risk averse when it comes to small problems or losses such as a few dollars in a travel expense report. This can border on the ridiculous: We found that one federal agency spent $1 million a year to mitigate the risk of losing an annual total of $30,000. Sound risk assessment should be the basis for a reasonable balance between the severity of negative consequences, probability, and cost. On the other hand, agencies often ignore the need to mitigate severe risks such as not meeting their strategic goals, failing to understand what customers want, or falling behind their competitors. We suggest that agencies put all controls through a sound risk assessment annually or whenever there are external or internal changes that may alter risk.

Control activities. Most of the resources devoted to control activities should be for mitigating the most serious risks to agency mission, strategic goals, and the core business processes that make an agency's main services. Such activities include performance measurement and management; information processing that checks and documents the accuracy, completeness, and authorization of transactions; physical controls; dividing and segregating duties to reduce risk of fraud; and management reviews of performance that are followed by improvement actions. As stated earlier, many control activities can be built into processes.

Information and communication. These components hold the integrated framework together. The objective for information systems is to deliver the right information at the right time to the right people, in sufficient detail to enable them to take appropriate action. Also, internal controls for information systems should be aimed at ensuring that these systems are tied to and enhance progress toward strategic goals. The aim of controls in communication is to ensure openness, accuracy, and effectiveness of internal and external communications channels among employees, different work units, customers, suppliers, stakeholders, regulators, and the public.

Monitoring. Both the COSO Report and OMB Circular A-123 stress the need for continuous monitoring of the effectiveness of controls. The CFO Act and other legislation require periodic audits of controls by IGs and other auditors, but audits alone are not sufficient. More important are routine management actions. These include periodic management reviews of the effectiveness of controls; ensuring that improvement projects have addressed control issues; and regular discussions about control issues with managers, employees, and suppliers.

Role of Financial Managers, Program Managers, Auditors and Inspectors General in Creating and Maintaining Effective Controls

The COSO approach to controls goes beyond the normal scope of financial managers, IGs, and auditors, and into the realm of managers in other parts of an agency—which is exactly the point of the approach. Developing an integrated framework of controls requires partnership and teamwork among the executives and managers of all components of an agency. Usually, this is done by forming a steering committee chaired by an executive (who may be the CFO) and senior managers from key operations divisions and from the CFO, IG, and human resources offices. OMB Circular A-123 suggests that an agency senior management council is the appropriate group to charter such a committee.

Financial, IG, and other managers carry out an audit for the committee, using the COSO approach. Such an internal audit can be done well in advance of an annual financial statement audit, which will prevent control deficiencies that could result in an undesirable audit opinion. Then, the committee develops goals and strategies for more effective controls, followed by action plans, implementation, and monitoring.

CFOs should find ways to make financial controls less costly, more reasonable, and more effective. Today, the best practice is to build the controls into processes as they are designed. Often, information technology enables this proactive integration by making information on standards, rules, laws, and regulations readily available to personnel; automatically flagging exceptions and negative trends in performance or spending; building decision rules into interactive software used to address issues such as eligibility for categorical programs; and providing security by restricting access to information. Most reengineering and information systems projects provide opportunities for enhancing internal controls, but often these chances are missed. We will discuss how to take advantage of them in this next section.

Business Process Redesign or Reengineering

BPR is a set of methods used to gain radical improvements in processes, as measured by cost, cycle time, service, and quality. As the words redesign and reengineer imply, BPR's approach is to virtually eliminate all parts of old, outmoded, or dysfunctional processes and replace them with newer technology and methods. Newer often means fewer, both for the number of work steps in the new process and the number of people who work in it.

BPR as an integrator

Reengineering arose from a lack of integration in information technology, process engineering, and the management of organizational change. In automating existing processes, information technologists and systems engineers did not consider that they were simply "paving the cowpaths" of meandering, redundant, and inefficient processes. On the other hand, the capabilities of information technology were not being exploited, because operations managers and process engineers did not understand them. Neither group fully grasped the effect of major change on people inside and outside the organization. Finally, top leaders in organizations did not devote sufficient time to causing this integration to happen.

As a result, billions of dollars in new technology investments were wasted because they did not return comparable benefits in higher performance. At the same time, many private companies suffered severe losses in profits and market share to competitors who had pulled ahead of them by virtue of continuous improvement and better use of technology. Governments faced similar problems, as their processes became antiquated and incapable of performing at levels that met customer expectations. Caught behind the eight

Figure 10-6

Successful Business Process Redesign Integrates Four Key Elements

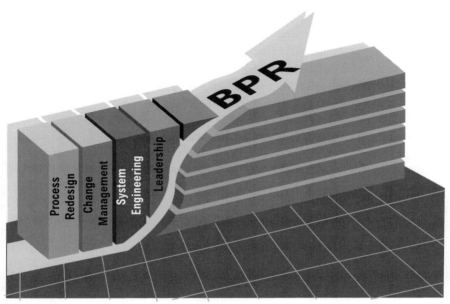

ball, these companies and agencies were forced to look for quantum leaps in performance; BPR provided the method.

Strategic, customer-focused BPR

Ideally, BPR begins with strategic decisions about where to invest in major process improvements. These decisions are based on extensive research about customer expectations, competitors, technology capabilities, and future environment. Wise organizations choose to invest first in core business processes that are most important to their customers, instead of in marginal processes with no direct customer impact. Within financial operations, these include the processes that are most critical to an agency being able to meet its mission and strategic goals. Simply saving money may not be reason enough to redesign a financial process. More important is improving financial performance or creating new value for the process customers.

Problems in BPR

Anyone who has attempted BPR, or who is familiar with the literature on the approach, knows that practitioners of it often run into problems that can be solved using ABC. For example:

- Data are not available to measure the current levels of performance of an agency's processes. Without these data, establishing priorities for improvement becomes guesswork.

- Few processes are mapped, so it is difficult to determine in what parts of an organization they exist and how their constituent activities are linked.

- Process cost and volume drivers and their effects on performance are not known or only vaguely understood.

- Criteria for judging the value of processes and their activities are not established, so that decisions about eliminating processes during BPR become subjective and often political.

Another set of problems is associated with managing human aspects of the radical changes brought about by BPR. A 1992 study by CSX/Index showed that most of the failures in BPR initiatives were the result of problems in this area. For example, a state revenue department asked C&L to assist in a major finance-related BPR project. Going in, we thought the project would center on technical issues. As the project got under way, we discovered that the technical plans were straightforward, well laid out, effective—and vehemently opposed by the department's field offices. For the next six months, we worked with the department to communicate the compelling need for change to the field offices and to involve them in planning and implementing the redesigned processes. This overcame their resistance and won their cooperation. The last section of this chapter, change management, addresses these issues.

Approaches to BPR

Some organizations take a "blank sheet" approach to BPR, which means totally scrapping the old process and building a new one from scratch. Others use a less extreme system of mapping the as-is process, then modifying major parts of it. All reliable approaches install new process infrastructures such as process performance measurement systems, continuous improvement practices, and internal controls.

C&L's BreakPoint BPR℠ approach is a good example of the logical stages of BPR. Also, it shows how to integrate the four key drivers of success in this method: leadership, process redesign, systems engineering, and change management. BreakPoint BPR has three phases: Discover, Redesign, and Realize.

Discover. This phase is a high-level examination of the total system and environment of a major process or processes. During Discover, teams of executives and senior managers supported by staff identify business improvement opportunities measured in terms of the gap between current performance and current or future customer requirements, strategic goals, competitor performance. The teams set "stretch" performance targets to close the gap, and these targets become the driving force of the BPR project. A key objective of Discover is to secure organizational buy-in for reaching the target, which is done by executives communicating the compelling need for this to personnel. Also, at this stage agencies look at how they will plan, acquire, and implement information technology that will enable radically new process redesigns. Often, it is important to analyze the business culture of the organization that owns a process that will be redesigned. This helps to identify possible barriers to successful change and enables agencies to start developing strategies for overcoming those barriers.

Redesign. The objective of this phase is to plan every facet of a redesigned process, including its core and support structures, management systems, human resources, workflow, and information technology. To do this, the selected process is taken apart and reassembled in better ways by redesign teams of agency managers, key employees, IT professionals, and often outside consultants. We recommend that most redesign team members be slated to manage or work in the redesigned process, which will increase their feeling of ownership for redesigns (and also motivate them to do their best). Finally, the teams develop transition plans for the technical and process aspects of change, plus change management plans for the personnel and organizations involved.

Realize. This phase develops refinements on the redesign and transition plan and implements them. Tasks include fleshing out redesigned process and information models, confirming resource requirements, technical fine-tuning, communications with other processes, and all the other details of putting the final touches on a new operation. A major part of change management during this phase is communicating the vision of the new process to its operators. Our approach calls for this to be done face to face with managers first, then with employees. Such sessions should explain the rationale for the change, its benefits to people and the organization, and steps being taken to assist personnel who will be adversely affected by the change.

Finally, it is critical that agencies include mechanisms for continuous improvement in their redesigned processes. This is because all new systems and processes must continuously make small improvements and other changes in order to stay current with changing (usually increasing) customer and stakeholder requirements. Methods for doing this include installing performance measurement and internal controls systems in processes and ensuring that their information flows to people who are authorized, trained, and capable of making control and improvement decisions.

Role of Financial Managers and Inspectors General in Reengineering

BPR projects should be based on a strong business case for investing substantial resources. Financial professionals can help to determine the costs and benefits of alternative solutions, the risks involved, and the means and schedule for funding the implementation of new processes and systems. If an outcome of BPR is to reduce process costs, then financial professionals can identify what costs are to go away and ensure that they do. Sometimes the costs do not go away, as we discovered with one organization in which BPR showed that a financial process obviated the need for eight clerks. However, the clerks were still in their office and were duplicating manually the work of information systems that automated the process. Finally, but not as an after-thought, financial managers, IGs, and auditors need to be involved in every phase of BPR to ensure that adequate internal controls are built into redesigned processes.

Change Management

Although we discuss change management last in this chapter, it is the most important aspect of every new method described in this book, especially financial management, performance measurement, and management controls processes. These processes are equivalent to a human nervous system, constantly acquiring and communicating vital information to managers and employees. When people cannot or do not use this information, then an agency has a nervous disorder or disease that will cripple and even kill it.

Human, Organizational, and Cultural Dimensions of Change

Change management is the process of aligning the human, organizational, and cultural elements of an agency with new ways of doing business. These three dimensions focus mostly on people, and include the following:

- **Human.** How people accept the new way of working, its effect on their lives, and their capabilities to operate under the new way, including skills, rewards, attitude, and motivation.
- **Organizational.** How an agency is structured to accommodate new ways, including authority levels, lines of communication, and infrastructure.
- **Cultural.** How an agency's culture fosters or hinders change in the right direction.

Organizations that include these dimensions in planning implement new ways of doing business that are both technically sound and accepted by workers. This process has become increasingly important to all sectors of the economy that are undergoing the wrenching changes of adjusting to the Information Age, other new technology, and, in government, a mandate to do more with less.

Inability to Change

The book *Activity-Based Management in Government* reports verbatim an interview with a financial officer about a new ABC system:

> *Coopers & Lybrand:* What types of ABC information do you give to managers and supervisors in the field?
>
> *Financial Officer* (pulling out thick book of computer printouts): We gave this cost analysis to all of them. It has detailed cost data by activity for each major process in each district.
>
> *C&L:* How have they used this information to improve their operations?
>
> *Financial Officer:* You know, they haven't used it, and I can't figure out why. It's detailed, accurate data, so it ought to be useful.
>
> *C&L:* Did you give them any training on how to use the information?
>
> *Financial Officer:* That sounds like a good idea.

This common mistake is what Robert S. Kaplan calls the "field of dreams" mentality: If we give managers and employees financial data, they will use it productively. The opposite is usually true. Unless organizations promote, enable, and reinforce new approaches to financial management, these will never be fully implemented.

Training in new financial tools is important, but so is ensuring that people can and will use the new skills they learn. For example, if operations managers have progressed in their careers without using managerial cost accounting, why should they bother now? An agency has to create incentives, rewards, and sanctions to make sure that they do. As important, executives must be committed to demanding that managers provide this information along with their reports and requests for funding. If these leaders do not use the information, no one else will.

Resistance to Change

Resistance is any overt or covert conduct by people that serves to maintain the status quo when an agency tries to change it. Resistance is a natural phase in the process of adopting an innovation, and is a function of fear and resentment. Usually, people do not resist an innovation per se. Instead, they resist the way they think it will change their lives. Thus, change management is in part directed at people's perceptions of an innovation.

> It's been said before, but I'll say it again: change is very difficult in an organization. People will invest incredible energy in fighting change, rather than participating in the movement to change. I always believe that I've planned for that when I initiate new programs or approaches—and I almost always underestimate how much people will resist.
> —Senior federal financial executive, C&L focus group, April 1996

A major, visceral fear of all human beings is of loss of control over their lives. Ambivalent situations where people do not know what the future holds for them produce a paralyzing sense of control loss. This most terrible of fears is most apparent in agencies that mishandle major restructuring and downsizing by keeping plans a secret and drawing out the process. People who are let go after a prolonged bout of such ambiguity actually feel a sense of relief, because now they can get on with planning and controlling the rest of their lives. Unfortunately, those who remain after such mishandled downsizing feel a debilitating sense of loss, which is called survival guilt.

People resent change imposed from without. Nobody likes to be ordered to change, especially if this means radically altering how their work is done. There are sound reasons for managers and employees to feel this way. For example, in the past, top management may have ordered them to do things that just did not work. Most organizations have a legacy of failed management initiatives such as quality circles, management by objectives, or zero-based budgeting. People remember these failures and resist new approaches that they perceive to be the same.

When people resist attempts to introduce an innovation, they are providing valuable information. This includes their resources and limitations and their attitudes toward new ideas and toward management, and also what management needs to do to introduce change successfully. This begins with communicating the compelling need for change.

Compelling Need

Technical change projects begin by identifying and defining a problem that must be solved or an opportunity to be gained. In change management, the reason to address the problem or opportunity becomes the compelling need for change that must be communicated to everyone. A compelling need may include that an agency may not survive without a specific change; that a major, visible problem has to be resolved; or that an excellent opportunity for growth and success will be attained by a specific change. The more "pain" people feel with the status quo, the more likely they are to accept a compelling need for change. A sharp pain, such as a sudden budget cut, is like appendicitis: Everyone knows it's there and wants to do something about it. Unfortunately, many management ills are more like cancer: people do not realize they have it until too late. In that case, executives must plan a careful communication campaign to educate people on the compelling need to change. This includes active involvement by executives, such as meeting with affected employees to discuss the issues and reasons surrounding an innovation.

Involving People

One way to break down resistance to change is to involve people in planning and implementing an innovation. Choosing the right people to be on teams that develop new financial processes is one way to do this. Team members should include managers and employees who have influence among their colleagues. If the influencers feel a sense of ownership for the new idea, they will promote it. Also, people can become involved in an innovation by observing and discussing the results of a pilot or demonstration project. Also, such "test runs" alleviate fears people may have that they cannot possibly master new technology.

Mapping the Change

We recommend that agencies contemplating a major change develop a change map to guide the transition from old to new ways of doing business. Figure 10-7 shows the variables involved in the map and the actions to be taken for each.

Figure 10-7

Change Map

Variable	Actions
Accountability	Develop specific roles, goals, and performance measures for change.
Adaptability	Learn from successful and unsuccessful change actions that are taken.
Communication	Plan for influencing those who will sponsor, support, implement, or be affected by the change. Plan for ensuring that those affected will participate in decisions and implementation.
Focus, Purpose, and Vision	Develop mission and guiding principles for the change. Specify results sought and criteria for evaluating progress and success.
Leadership	Plan for leadership actions that will promote and enable change. Plan for aligning the change with the existing culture, based on an assessment of the readiness to change.
Measurement and Results	Identify data to be used to track implementation. Specify the measurable improvements to be achieved by the change.
Momentum, Recognition, and Reward	Prepare leadership plan for responding to shifts in the pace of implementation of change actions or of acceptance of the change. Plan for recognizing and rewarding individuals and groups as they achieve results consistent with the change.
Skill Development	Plan for training people to enable them to participate effectively in the change.

Findings and plans developed as part of the change map process are as important, if not more, than any technical plans. Change maps tend to build on one another, which creates a profound understanding of the resilience of an agency's work force. Resilience is the capability of people to respond positively to repeated change. Good resilience is a critical variable in the success of organizations entering the 21st century, when the only constant will be change, change, and more change.

Summary

This chapter discussed five tools for improving financial management: 1) activity-based costing, 2) value analysis, 3) the COSO approach to controls, 4) BPR, and 5) change management. When federal financial managers master these tools, they will be well equipped for the many challenges of accounting's last frontier. Even more, they will be blazing trails for and guiding program managers into previously unknown or neglected practices that result in cost-effective decisions and sound fiscal management.

A CALL FOR ACTION

Good laws, if they are not obeyed, do not constitute good government.

–Aristotle, *Politics*

Throughout *Public Dollars, Common Sense* we have
demonstrated the power of financial management to
improve the quality, efficiency, and productivity of government. As well, we have shown how financial management
adds power to policy making and arms program managers
with information they can use to make cost-effective daily
decisions. Now, we conclude with recommendations aimed
at improving and accelerating the pace of federal financial
reform. These are our opinions, based on both Coopers &
Lybrand's corporate experience as an accounting and management consulting firm and on our own background as
auditors, federal financial officers, and consultants to government and industry.

The Executive Office and Congress

Senator John Glenn told us that the greatest threat to the
goals of the new reform legislation is public and political
apathy. "The trouble is that people don't find federal financial management as exciting as things like B-2 bombers or a
new federal highway. We buy goods and deliver services,
but how the money gets spent, with what kind of efficiency—that's measured by accounting, and is often ignored."

Use the New Financial and Performance Information to Establish Policy and Budgetary Priorities

In actuality, relatively few citizens will pressure Congress to
enforce the new reform legislation. As we said in Chapter 6,
this is all the more reason for government leaders to create
and sustain a disciplined approach to compliance with the
new laws. Compliance begins at the top, so sustaining the
push means the Executive Office and the Congress must
diligently use the financial information they require of federal agencies. However, elected leaders cannot delegate this
responsibility entirely to their budget analysts and other
support staff. Instead, the leaders must learn the meanings
of the numbers they receive from agencies, then use this

information to analyze the quality of stewardship and services federal organizations offer for the public dollar. Finally, Congress and the Executive Office must let the public know that sound financial and performance data play a strong part in making policy and budget decisions.

Include the Results of Financial Statement and Performance Measurement Audits in the Budget Formulation and Appropriations Processes

If the President and the Congress were a bank's loan committee, they would not dream of lending a fraction of the federal budget to an organization that could not produce an unqualified financial audit opinion. Likewise, the congressional and OMB processes for budget formulation and appropriations should begin with ascertaining the veracity of an agency's reported performance and financial condition. Without this information, much of what passes for sound stewardship during the appropriations process will continue to be guesswork.

Maintain Pressure on Agency Leaders to Comply With the New Reform Legislation

When elected officials take agency financial management information seriously, there will be much less need to consider "punishing" the agencies for lack of progress in complying with the new reform legislation by reducing their budgets. Budget reductions, although they send a powerful message to agency leaders, can be unfair to citizens who depend on government services. The more appropriate targets for the President, OMB, and Congress should be agency leaders themselves, who are ultimately accountable for their accounting and financial management practices.

Departmental Secretaries and Agency Directors

The new reform legislation makes it clear that the buck stops at the desk of departmental secretaries and agency directors. However, many of these leaders have "grown up," professionally speaking, without being exposed to the types of financial management information, tools, and techniques discussed in this book. Thus, they may not immediately perceive the importance of the new approach to fiscal stewardship. Other agency leaders may think that the new reforms will somehow fade away like so many other efforts to improve government management. The difference between the reforms and earlier, isolated, and sporadic Executive Branch or individual agency attempts at improvement is that the reforms are law. They are not going to disappear into some elephants' burial ground of management fads, both because the reforms are statutory and, more important, because sound financial management, accounting, and performance measurement practices make common sense.

Make Financial Management Improvement a Priority, and Get Started on It Now

Some deadlines for complying with the new reform legislation already have past, and others are looming. Directors of agencies that have not yet received unqualified audit opinions of their annual financial statements must make a top priority of complying with this most basic of all financial requirements. Agency leaders must use the process of developing the statements to identify financial management improvements, then move quickly to make the required changes.

Why move quickly on problems that have existed for decades? Because it will take years to correct these barriers to federal fiscal stewardship and cost-effective decision making, so wise leaders must start showing progress now. This is not a whole new ball game where the score is zero to zero. Instead, many federal agencies are playing financial management catch-up with other agencies, the private sector, and state and local governments. These other organizations often are in better shape in terms of fiscal stewardship to compete for federal budget dollars. For a federal agency to suffer budget cuts or even lose part of its mission for programmatic or political reasons is one thing. To lose because of deficiencies in financial management or performance measurement is an indictment of agency leadership.

Require Sound Financial and Performance Data From Program Managers, and Use It

Like the Executive Office and Congress, agency leaders must start requiring agency managers to provide sound financial and performance information when proposing funding for new and existing programs. This information should not be limited to justifying the potential benefits of new programs or increments of funding for current operations. This narrows the scope of executive attention to 5 or 10 percent of an agency's budget. An agency director is responsible for all the budget, and should regularly demand an accounting for ongoing programs and their related support and administrative functions.

Chief Financial Officers

To ensure that they are equipped to conquer the new accounting and financial management frontier, federal CFOs must assess their resources.

Assess the Culture and Readiness of the Agency to Determine Where to Start Making Changes

Complying with the spirit of the new reform legislation requires major changes in the way that most federal managers and employees do their work. For some, even the basic concept of using financial and performance information to make decisions will be foreign, much less mastering the fine points of managerial cost accounting practices. CFOs would do well to start with new practices that are most in keeping with current agency culture. Then, they can use the process of making the changes to build momentum for other innovations that would, if tried earlier, meet with resistance.

Assess the Skills and Style of the Financial Staff

A CFO can go only as far as the capability of his or her financial staff, and many agencies will require significant skill building in this area. Most federal financial personnel know everything about budget management and budgetary accounting but relatively little about the types of financial management and accrual accounting needed for the Team

Leader organizational role discussed in Chapter 3. More seriously, some financial managers view themselves mainly as the protectors of the agency purse, not as partners to program managers—and the Team Leader role is based on partnership.

Federal financial staffs are improving their skills in new financial management and accounting subjects, albeit slowly. The CFO's task is to enhance the quality of their technical training and to increase the pace of professional development. First, CFOs must determine what they want financial staff competence to be, then assess if current staff have the necessary training and experience. This should be followed by a human resources improvement plan that includes training, counseling, career paths, new hires, outsourcing, and other mechanisms for obtaining needed skills. Executing the plan must become the CFO's top priority, because all attempts to develop new financial organization capabilities will fail without capable personnel.

Changing the culture of the financial organization into one of Team Leader partnership means that the CFO must search for opportunities to put his or her people on program management teams that will benefit from new financial management capabilities. This starts at the top, with the CFO demonstrating the new skills and the partnership styles that are fundamental to such teamwork.

Assess the CFO's Own Skills and Style and Shore Up Weak Areas

Chapter 3 discussed seven roles a successful agency CFO must play: Strategist/Visionary, Information Manager, Networker, Innovator/Entrepreneur, Asset Manager, Change Manager, and Policy Maker. These roles cannot be delegated. CFOs must assess their skills and operating styles against the requirements of each role. Should a CFO be weak in one of the roles, he or she must shore up skills in that area through training. An alternative is to develop an exceptionally strong staff capability in the area, with regular monitoring by the CFO.

Take Control of the Budget Process

As stated in Chapter 3, CFOs should own their agencies' budget formulation process. This is the only way to ensure that, besides traditional program analysis and politics, budgets benefit from sound financial decisions and performance information. When in charge of the budget process, a CFO has the standing and clout to force consideration of financial aspects of program alternatives. This is not to say that financial numbers should be the only deciding points for budget decisions; there are other issues that may be more important. However, unless a CFO has budget authority, financial management issues will be too far down the priority list to affect budgetary decisions—which is not the intent of the new reform legislation.

Develop Intra-departmental CFO Councils to Integrate and Make Consistent Department-Wide Financial Management Policy and Practices

Departmental and agency CFOs must realize that they are or should be one of the principal unifying forces in their respective departments, and that together they can exercise much more influence. To provide a forum for discussing and reaching consensus on issues, department-level and agency CFOs should form councils that function in much the same way as the federal CFO Council. One mission of the departmental councils should be to bring, if not total uniformity, at least consistency to agency accounting, financial reporting, and financial management practices. Another should be to plan integrated action in areas such as systems development and new financial management improvement projects.

Financial Information Systems

Financial management begins and ends with information, which means that controlling relevant information systems is absolutely essential to a CFO's ability to make progress in financial reform.

Control the Development of Financial and Other Information Systems

Whether or not CFOs actually own their core financial systems, they are ultimately accountable for the accuracy and timeliness of the systems' information. Further, CFOs are responsible for bringing information needed for cost-effective decision making to all parts of an agency, which can include data in mixed or even nonfinancial systems. Therefore, we think that CFOs must control all aspects of core financial system development and should be involved as an equal partner in setting financial management objectives for other systems. Related to this recommendation is the need for CFOs and CIOs to define their respective roles and responsibilities for systems development and improvement.

Insist That Systems Development Be Driven by the Agency Strategic Plan

The Federal Financial Management Improvement Act of 1996 directs the head of an agency to prepare a plan by March 30, 1997, for bringing agency financial and mixed information systems into compliance with federal requirements in this area. The act mentions financial auditors' opinions about compliance as a driving force for systems development and improvement. In the rush to meet the March 30, 1997, deadline for the compliance plan, some CFOs and CIOs may focus too much on auditors' input, but fail even to glance at what should be the starting point for guidance on systems improvement: their agency's strategic plan.

FFMIA gives agencies three years to come into compliance, and more time if it can be justified. Three years is ample time to take a strategic approach to systems improvement. We think, in their roles as Information Managers, CFOs must insist on this approach, even if it means a slight delay in getting started with long-term corrective measures.

Have a Bias Toward COTS Solutions

In Chapter 4 we listed the advantages of COTS over custom software for financial management systems. COTS cost less and can be developed, installed, maintained, and upgraded more quickly; they provide better documentation; and COTS vendors have an economic motivation to enhance their products continually. Whereas there are a few exceptions that require custom software, COTS solutions are available for virtually every financial information requirement in an agency. Also, there are two hidden benefits to COTS that forward-looking CFOs will appreciate. First, the level of vendor and consultant support for many COTS packages is such that a CFO does not have to depend entirely on internal information service groups to use them. Second, COTS solutions usually require changes to internal processes, and many of the changes are marked improvements over existing financial processes. Approached in the right way, COTS is one more justification for improvement activities.

Annual Financial Statements and Audits

An audit is a financial service that must meet the requirements of law and stakeholder information needs. One of the major stakeholders is the CFO, who, along with the agency director, is accountable for audit results.

CFOs Must Take a Proactive Leadership Role in the Audit Process

Auditing financial statements is a complex process no matter where it takes place. This complexity is exacerbated in the federal government, where such audits are relatively new and where all those involved are still defining their roles and responsibilities. Auditor teams, be they from GAO, the agency's IG, or an independent public accounting firm, control the audit process. The team is responsible for establishing the methods and approaches they used to evaluate effectively the accuracy of the financial statements prepared by the CFO's organization.

Yet, though the audit team controls the audit, the CFO must take a proactive leadership role in the audit process. As the agent of the agency head, the CFO will be more successful in controlling the organization's financial affairs and reporting results if he or she is involved throughout the audit planning and execution phases. This includes preliminary discussions with the audit team and the agency's IG organization that address the audit scope, schedule, materiality, and related issues. The CFO's role in these discussions is critical to the auditor team's ability to be effective and efficient. For example, though the auditors actually determine what financial information they need to review in order to render an opinion on the financial statements or internal controls, the CFO can show them the best sources of that information. In this way the CFO acts as a facilitator for the auditors, helping to lead them through the organization and its financial management and accounting processes. Below, we describe some of the important actions that CFOs can take to facilitate the audit process and thereby help ensure that the results or both accurate and useful.

Form an audit committee. In Chapter 5 we said that CFOs should form audit committees that include agency heads, the CFO, the inspector general, senior representatives of audit organizations, and outside experts on in auditing and financial reporting. The purpose of such committees is to resolve issues between agency management and auditors. More important to the CFO, the committee elevates the status of the audit by directly involving the agency director and, through outside experts, provides a ready reference to the best practices of auditing. These resources put the CFO in much better position to debate audit issues with auditors.

Establish an ongoing, year-round partnership with auditors. Part of this relationship is done outside the audit committee, and includes direct communication among the agency head, CFO, and a senior executive in the audit organization. This relationship is especially important if the audit organization staff members who render the audit opinion are not the same as the field audit staff. Also, the CFO should meet regularly with the leader of the field auditor team, keeping that leader informed of changes in agency goals, programs, and other issues.

Develop communication protocols with auditors.
Before and during audits, the chief protocol is that all communication between auditors and agency staff must first go through the office of the CFO. This ensures that field auditors obtain the information they need, but that they are not going beyond the agreed-to scope of the audit.

Prepare Early for the Financial Statement and Audit Processes
There are several advantages to starting these processes early, only one of which is increasing the likelihood that they will be completed on time. As well, the first few years an agency follows the annual financial report development process are a period of discovery, learning, and improvement. Starting early in the year allows time to make changes in an orderly, considered manner that is integrated in other financial management improvement initiatives. For example, pre-audits are more valuable if enough time is allowed to act on their results. Also, an early start provides an opportunity to develop interim draft financial statements, which can be used both to identify improvements and to provide useful information to managers before the end of the year.

Individual CFOs and the Federal CFO Council Must Campaign Actively to Keep a Fairly Narrow Scope to Financial Statement Audits
In Chapter 6 we recognized that the scope of federal financial audits blends programmatic and financial issues, and that a certain amount of program information is needed to make the audits useful. However, the financial statement audit process was designed to do one thing well, and that is to attest to the veracity of the statements. Forcing such audits to address things like judging program effectiveness strains the original audit design and risks bogging financial audits down in issues best addressed through other means such as program audits and reviews. The result could become a hybrid that is ineffective for both financial and program audits.

Further, including too much program focus in financial audits invites auditors to critique routinely every single aspect of agency operations, without a specific, narrowly scoped directive to do so by the Executive Office or Congress. This adds a layer of annual program effectiveness reporting that neither branch of the government has spelled out in legislation or regulation—and for good reason. Sound, useful program reviews are an order of magnitude more complex and costly than financial statement auditing, and much more open to interpretation by both auditors and the users of audit information. Congress and the Executive Branch already have vehicles for both routine and special program reviews; if another vehicle is needed, it should be separate from financial statement audits.

Independent Public Accounting Firms Should Be the Federal Government's Primary Financial Statement Auditors

At this time few federal agencies have enough staff with the right training and experience to carry out the annual financial audit, and few have the budget or FTE authority to hire professionals with this background for their staff. These alone are good reasons to retain the services of independent public accounting firms to do most federal financial audits. Another is the demands on the time and resources of IG offices and the GAO. Independent public accounting firms have decades of experience in government agency auditing and are ready now to provide the needed services. Competition among the firms helps ensures that the price of their audits will be less than the cost of maintaining full-time internal audit staff, and that the firms will invest heavily in keeping their professionals and technology up to date in all aspects of the financial audit process.

Moreover, IG offices and the GAO are not as well equipped as independent accounting firms to give agencies technical assistance in correcting deficiencies discovered during audits. This has nothing to do with the financial management and financial systems knowledge of IG and GOA auditors, which is excellent. Instead, they simply do not have the staff resources to meet federal agency technical assistance needs. Most large, independent accounting firms do, because over the years they have, in response to client requirements, developed specialized divisions for financial management and financial systems consulting. Thus, while IG offices and the GAO can be superior partners in some aspects of process improvement, they cannot at this time replicate the partnership that has evolved over the years between audit clients and multiservice independent accounting firms.

Strategic Planning

CFOs should not wait for an invitation to participate in agency strategic planning. Just as finance is a part of strategy, the CFO is part of the strategy development process.

CFO Offices Must Develop the Capability to Support the Agency Strategy Process With Sound Financial Information

CFOs should designate and train some members of their staffs to support the agency strategy process with the data collection and analysis needed to assess the financial aspects of future scenarios. Also, these staff should be capable of conducting sound financial comparisons of the costs and results of alternate strategies for reaching agency goals. They should contribute financial projections and analyses to business plans needed to justify strategic investments, and otherwise provide information for cost-effective decisions.

CFOs Must Bring Solutions to the Strategy Table

The successful Strategist/Visionary CFO brings to the strategic planning table sound ideas for achieving agency goals. At a minimum, this includes developing ways to finance capital investments needed for executing strategies. More important, CFOs have at their fingertips the same basic information systems and tools as do most program managers; it is time these were applied to improving an agency's core business processes. With this in mind, the CFO must look for ways of using financial processes as vehicles for furthering an agency's mission, goals, and strategic areas of performance. For example, too often in the past financial processes have slowed down operations and created excessive overhead costs. Today, private companies and many government agencies have discovered that new approaches to financial processes can give them distinctive competitive advantages by significantly lowering cycle times and costs to customers.

Performance Measurement

CFOs should lead the way to integrating the performance measurement requirements of the Government Performance and Results Act into those of the CFO Act.

Tie Performance Planning to the Budget Process, and Manage It

Earlier, we recommended that CFOs should take charge of the agency budget formulation process. The GPRA makes it clear that consideration of agency performance measures and plans should be part of the congressional budgetary process, so it is logical for the CFO to manage the development of agency performance plans. This does not mean that the CFO should "own" the performance management process, which belongs to all agency executives. Instead, the CFO should be the performance planning team leader, responsible for giving this process the rigor and discipline required to meet the intent of Congress.

Apply Performance Measurement Within the Office of the CFO

CFOs who hope to become leaders in performance measurement must start by developing sound, effective performance measures for financial processes. This is not hard to do because most measures for financial processes already are well known and described in the literature. Doing a thorough job of measurement inside the CFO office gives financial managers the experience and credibility they need to become partners with program managers in developing agency-wide performance measures. To be truly effective and gain maximum credibility, a CFO also must use internal financial process performance measures to make business decisions about process improvement.

Use Innovative Tools to Integrate Financial and Program Performance Measures
This includes using activity-based costing, which provides a framework for defining and measuring the operations, financial and nonfinancial resources, and results of processes and their outputs. Other frameworks such as the balanced score card and hierarchy of measures enable agency executives and managers to readily see a variety of performance measures in order to have a holistic understanding of agency operations and results.

Plan to Audit Performance Measures
CFOs should approach the development of performance measures as they would the preparation of a financial statement that will be audited. This includes developing a set of criteria for choosing measures and ensuring that the measurement process is documented and has adequate internal controls. A good model for this is the system used in the State of Texas Government, which is described in Chapter 8.

Don't Wait Until June 1999 to Start Developing Performance Measures and Plans
We do not exaggerate when we say that financial tasks such as preparing auditable financial statements are child's play when compared to developing sound performance measurement systems and performance plans for an entire federal agency. Although it is good at measuring many things, the federal government as a whole has not had many positive experiences in developing measurement systems that depict agency performance in ways that are useful to Congress and citizens. Also, our experience is that agencies can easily become mired in internal dissension about what constitute the right measures, which all too often results in an executive-level measurement system of little use to program managers. CFOs need to start now to develop sound approaches to measurement that are acceptable and useful

to all users, including OMB, Congress, agency leaders, and managers.

Best Practices Benchmarking

The best ideas are those that someone else went through the sweat and expense to develop. For a tightly strapped government, capitalizing on this experience is a must.

Make Benchmarking a Routine Procedure in Most Major Financial Management Improvements

For purposes of best practices benchmarking, management processes are perhaps the best documented of all organizational functions. Accounting and financial management literature is replete with reports on best practices, and several government financial associations and groups report regularly on them. CFOs should insist that financial managers always look for information on best practices before making improvements, either in the literature or among potential benchmarking partners. Also, CFOs should routinely benchmark the performance of their processes against comparable outside operations. It is better to know today that a potential competitor is outperforming an internal financial organization than to discover this when being forced to outsource a financial process.

Provide Financial Analysis Support for Program Managers' Benchmarking Projects

Every agency benchmarking team should include a financial analyst from the CFO's office. The analyst should be skilled at calculating accurate cost data for internal and external processes, so that apples-to-apples comparisons can be used in selecting potential best practices.

Innovation, Creativity, and Discipline

In most chapters of *Public Dollars, Common Sense*, we reported innovations in financial management and performance measurement that, if adopted by and adapted to an agency, will improve its ability to achieve mission and goals. There are many other innovations, both financial and nonfinancial, that we did not have time to discuss. Most are amply detailed in the references in Appendix A, in other literature, and most especially through FinanceNet on the Internet. We hope we have inspired readers to dive into these sources for new ideas.

However, other people's ideas can take CFOs and financial managers only part way down the road to federal financial reform. Also needed is creativity, not so much in developing new concepts from scratch, but from making cross-connections among existing ideas. Much of this creativity will start to bloom when financial and program managers form the partnership we have advocated. In this relationship, financial managers will find new applications for existing financial tools and methods and will locate new tools to meet program managers' information needs. This is a natural process that occurs when people from different disciplines work together. However, that which blooms does not necessarily flourish, which is why CFOs must take extra care to provide resources to financial managers to develop and apply new tools.

This brings up our final point, which is about discipline. Every successful business needs someone to watch the pennies, which is the traditional role of the typical federal financial professional. Still, we think everyone will agree that penny watching is not going to pull the federal government out of a multi-trillion-dollar debt. Private companies understand this and insist that their CFOs think of ways to maximize profits, not just save costs. Likewise, agencies have plenty of penny-pinchers, but desperately need CFOs and financial managers who constantly think of new, more cost-effective ways to deliver services and products to citizens. This is a tough new role for federal financial managers, especially when it would be so easy to fall back into old work patterns. Pioneers have the discipline needed to take on a new challenge every day—and what we need in government are more financial pioneers.

Endnotes

1. Page 199: Association of Government Accountants, *Best Practices: The Association for Government Accountant's 45th Annual Professional Development Conference & Exposition,* 1995.)

2. Page 201: Gail B.Whitcomb, "Department of Defense: a breakthrough approach in EDI", *EDI World* (December 1994.)

3. Page 202: Association of Government Accountants, op cit.

4. Page 204: Ibid.

BIBLIOGRAPHY AND REFERENCES

Alwin, Lawrence F. "How far can we go? Measuring performance in government." Texas State Auditor's Office *Action Alert* (September 21, 1992).

Amos, Tracey, Cynthia A. Paolillo, and Denise Joseph. *Federal Financial Reform: Challenges, Issues, and Solutions: Enhancing CFO, GMRA, and GPRA Implementation with Activity-Based Management.* Washington, DC: Coopers & Lybrand. 1996.

Association of Government Accountants. *Best Practices: AGA's 45th Annual Professional Development Conference and Exposition.* June 1995.

Barr, Stephen and Mary C. Driscoll. "Best practices: the hallmarks of a world-class finance organization." *CFO* (September 1995): 31-44.

Birchard, Bill. "Closing the strategy gap." *CFO* (October 1996): 26-36.

Bolon, Meredith and Amy Weber. *Benchmarking: A Manager's Guide.* Washington, DC: Coopers & Lybrand. 1995.

Bowsher, Charles. *Managing the Cost of Government, Building an Effective Financial Management Structure.* U.S. General Accounting Office. GAO/AFMD-85-35. 1985.

– Speech before the Joint Financial Management Improvement Program Conference. March 19, 1996.

– Testimony before the U.S. Senate Committee on Governmental Affairs and the House of Representatives Committee on Government Reform and Oversight. March 6, 1996.

Brandeis, Louis. Testimony before the U.S. House of Representatives Committee on Interstate and Foreign Commerce. January 30, 1914.

Carr, David K. and Ian D. Littman. *Excellence in Government: Total Quality Management in the 1990s,* second edition. Washington, DC: Coopers & Lybrand. 1993.

Carr, David K., Ian D. Littman, and John K. Condon. *Improvement Driven Government: Public Service for the 21st Century.* Washington, DC: Coopers & Lybrand. 1995.

Chief Financial Officers Council, Human Resources Committee. "The CFO's Role in Strengthening Financial Management at the Component Organizational Level." September 1994.

– GPRA Implementation Committee. "Implementation of the Government Performance and Results Act (GPRA): A Report on the Chief Financial Officer's Role and Other Issues Critical to the Governmentwide Success of GPRA." May 1995.

Chief Financial Officers Council and the Joint Financial Management Improvement Program, "Framework for Financial Management Personnel in the Federal

Government." November 1995.

Clinton, Bill and Al Gore. *Putting Customers First: Standards for Serving the American People.* Report of the National Performance Review. September 1994.

Congressional Research Service, *Federal Budget, Accounting, and Financial Management Laws: Summaries of Selected Provisions.* Unpublished, July 16, 1996.

Coopers & Lybrand. *Internal Control–Integrated Framework.* Committee of Sponsoring Organizations of the Treadway Commission. New York: American Institute of Certified Public Accountants. 1992.

Coopers & Lybrand and the Association of Government Accountants. *Chief Financial Officers Act Survey Results: Examining Progress Toward Implementation of the Chief Financial Officers Act of 1990.* 1995.

Conyers, John. "Vigilance in government." *The Government Accountants Journal* (April 1995): 24-25.

Driscoll, Mary C. "Never stop learning." *CFO* (February 1995): 50-56.

Goldsmith, Stephen. "Moving Municipal Services Into the Marketplace." No. 14 in a series of papers by Carnegie Privatization Project, Carnegie Council, New York, NY. November 20, 1992.

Gore, Al. *Reinvention's Next Steps: Governing in a Balanced Budget World.* U.S. Government Printing Office. March 4, 1996.

– Remarks delivered at Harvard Commencement Day, Harvard University, Cambridge, MA. June 9, 1994.

– *Creating a Government That Works Better and Costs Less: Improving Financial Management.* National Performance Review. 1993.

Govoni, Stephen J. "Reinventing the federal CFO." *CFO* (October 1993): 46-53.

Graff, Stuart L. "The federal government: accounting's last frontier." *Management Accounting* (October 1995): 43-47.

The Hackett Group. "GSA Finance Benchmark Results." 1996: 1-24.

Harmon, Marion. "Is reinventing government for real?" *Quality Digest* (April 1995): 27.

Hayes, Heather B. "A vision too grand." *Government Executive* (February 1996): 26-29.

Hill, Eleanor J. Testimony before the U.S. House of Representatives Subcommittee on Government Management, Information, and Technology. November 14, 1995.

Hodsoll, Frank. "Brave new steps in implementing the CFO Act." *Government Accountants Journal* (Summer 1992): 9-12.

– "Office of Management and Budget plans for implementation of the Chief Financial Officers Act." *Government Accountants Journal* (April 1991): 12-13.

Horton, Frank: "Insights into the Chief Financial Officers Act of 1990." *Government Accountants Journal* (April 1991): 10-11.

International Institute for Management Development. "World Competitiveness Report." Lausanne, Switzerland. 1995.

Joint Financial Management Improvement Program. "Financial Management Systems Overview for Agency Leaders." No date.

– "Framework for Federal Financial Management Systems." January 1995.

– "Strategies to Improve Communication Between Program and Financial Managers." No date.

Kaplan, Robert S. and David P. Norton. "Using the balanced scorecard as a strategic management system." *Harvard Business Review* (January-February 1996): 75-85.

Kehoe, Joseph, William Dodson, Robert Reeve, and Gustav Plato, *Activity-Based Management in Government.* Washington, DC: Coopers & Lybrand. 1995.

Kehoe, Joseph. Testimony before the U.S. House of Representatives Subcommittee on Government Management, Information, and Technology. June 20, 1995.

Kent, Jill E. "Organization of the agency chief financial officer." *Government Accountants Journal* (April 1991): 27-32.

Kettl, Donald F. Testimony before the U.S. Senate Committee on Governmental Affairs and the House of Representatives Committee on Government Reform and Oversight. March 6, 1996.

Lau, Valerie, David F. Fiske and Carl Orne, "A consolidated financial statement for the federal government? Policy, problems, and potential." *GAO Review* (Winter 1995).

Longmire, Laura. Testimony before the U.S. House of Representatives Subcommittee on Government Management, Information, and Technology. June 20, 1996.

McCoy, Helen T. Testimony before the U.S. House of Representatives Subcommittee on Government Management, Information, and Technology. November 14, 1995.

Osborne, David. "Resurrecting government." *The Washington Post Magazine* (January 8, 1995): 12-32.

Osborne, David and Ted Gaebler. *Reinventing Government: How the Entrepreneurial Spirit Is Transforming the Public Sector.* New York: The Penguin Group. 1993.

Paine, Thomas. *Rights of Man, Common Sense, and Other Political Writings.* New York: Oxford University Press. 1995.

Quinn, James Brian et al., *The Strategy Process.* Englewood Cliffs, NJ: Prentice Hall. 1988. 3.

Richardson, Margaret Milner. Testimony before the U.S. House of Representatives Subcommittee on Government Management, Information, and Technology. March 6, 1996.

Riso, Gerald R. Testimony before the U.S. House of Representatives Subcommittee on Government Management, Information, and Technology. July 25, 1995.

Rivlin, Alice M. "Budgeting for performance." *Intergovernmental Perspective.* (Fall 1993/Winter 1994): 1-3 America Online.

Roberts, Alasdair. "Command performance." *Government Executive.* (August 1996): 21-26.

Steinberg, Harold. "The CFO Act: a look at federal accountability." *Journal of Accountancy* (March 1996): 5-60.

– "The time has come. The hour is at hand: performance measurement in the federal government–from resources to results." *AGA Journal* (Winter 1996): 26-30.

– Testimony before the U.S. House of Representatives Subcommittee on Government Management, Information, and Technology. July 25, 1995.

Steinhoff, Jeffrey C. "Challenges of the CFO Act." *Government Accountants Journal* (April 1991): 18-21.

Texas State Auditor's Office, Legislative Budget Board, and Governor's Office of Budget and Planning. *Guide to Performance Measurement for State Agencies, Universities, and Health-Related Institutions.* 1995 edition.

Tucker, Al. Testimony before the U.S. House of Representatives Subcommittee on Government Management, Information, and Technology. November 14, 1995.

Tully, Shawn, "Managing." *Fortune* (November 13, 1995): 160-172.

Turner, Frederick Jackson, *The Significance of the Frontier in American History.* Daniel Boorstin, ed. Chicago: The University of Chicago. 1996.

U.S. General Accounting Office. *GPRA Performance Reports.* GAO/GGD-96-66R. 1996.

– *Managing for Results: Status of the Government Performance and Results Act.* GAO/T-GGD-95-193. 1995.

– *Managing for Results: Critical Actions for Measuring Performance.* GAO/T-GGD/AIMD-95-187. 1995.

– *Managing for Results: Strengthening Financial and Budgetary Reporting.* GAO/T-GGD/AIMD-95-181. 1995

– *Managing for Results: Experiences Abroad Suggest Insights for Federal Management Reform.* GGD-95-120. 1995.

– *Government Reform: Goal Setting and Performance.* GAO/AIMD/GGD-95-130R. 1995.

– *Best Practices Methodology: A New Approach for Improving Government Operations.* GAO/NSIAD-95-154. 1995.

– *Financial Management: Continued Momentum Essential to Achieve CFO Act Goals.* GAO/T-AIMD-96-10. 1995.

– *Challenges Facing DoD in Meeting the Goals of the Chief Financial Officers Act.* GAO/T-AIMD-96-1. 1995.

– *Government Auditing Standards: 1994 Revision.* GAO/OCG-94-4. 1994.

– *Government Corporations: CFO Act Management Reporting Could Be Enhanced.* GAO/AIMD-94-73. 1994.

– *State Experiences Provide Insights for Federal Management Reforms.* GAO/GGD-95-22. 1994.

U.S. General Services Administration. *U.S. General Services Administration Accountability Report.* 1995.

U.S. Department of Justice, Justice Management Division. *DOJ Manager's Handbook on Developing Useful Performance Indicators.* April 1995.

U.S. Department of the Treasury, Financial Management Service. "Consolidated Financial Statements of the U.S. Government. 1994 Prototype." U.S. Government Printing Office. 1994.

U.S. Office of Management and Budget and Chief Financial Officers Council. *Federal Financial Management Status Report & Five-Year Plan.* June 1996.

Walters, Jonathan. "AuditPower!" *Governing* (April 1996): 25-29.

Walther, Thomas and Henry Johansson, John Dunleavy, and Elizabeth Hjelm. *Reinventing the CFO: Moving From Financial Management to Strategic Management.* New York, NY: McGraw-Hill. 1997.

Whitcomb, Gail B. "Department of Defense: A breakthrough approach in EDI." *EDI World* (December 1994): 21-22.

Whittaker, James B. "Get ready for GPRA." *Government Executive* (December 1996): 59-60.

Wilkerson, David and Clifton Cooksey. *Customer Service Measurement.* Washington, DC: Coopers & Lybrand. 1994.

APPENDIX A – RESOURCES

In this appendix, we list suggested reading on topics covered in *Public Dollars, Common Sens*e, contact information for resource groups, and Web site addresses for these and other groups and resources.

Suggested Reading

Federal Laws and Guidelines on Financial Management

Public Dollars, Common Sense: Federal Laws, Guidelines, and Resources Related to Financial Management. Washington, DC: Coopers & Lybrand, 1997. A full-text, searchable compilation of the principal federal laws (CFO Act, GPRA, GMRA, and FFMIA-96), OMB guidelines, and FASAB statements. Available in CD-ROM or diskette versions. Includes all resource information in this appendix, plus dozens more relevant Web site addresses that can be dialed automatically from the program.

Financial Management

Reinventing the CFO: Moving From Financial Management to Strategic Management, Thomas Walther, Henry Johansson, John Dunleavy, and Elizabeth Hjelm. New York, NY: McGraw-Hill, 1997. ISBN 0-07-012945-2.
A thorough review of the new roles of private sector CFOs and their offices. As well, the book presents a framework for financial professionals to reevaluate how they can move beyond internally focused analyses to truly add value to their business by providing insights that deliver competitive advantage. Includes illustrative case studies, benchmarks, and QuikGrids such as that shown in Chapter 3 of this book. The authors are C&L partners and senior managers.

CFO: The Magazine for Senior Financial Executives, CFO Publishing Corp., a subsidiary of The Economist Newspaper Group. ISSN 8756-7113.
This magazine is published and distributed monthly to chief financial officers and other senior financial executives. The annual subscription is $50, but it is free for CFOs and executives who qualify for this advertiser-supported periodical. *CFO* is an excellent way to stay up-to-date with the latest developments in corporate financial management. Includes occasional articles on federal financial management. To obtain ordering information, write to: *CFO,* P.O. Box 530, Mt Morris, IL 61054-0530 or call (800) 877-5416 or e-mail at GUS@CFO.ccmail.compuserve.com.

Improvement of Operations, Services, and Products

Improvement-Driven Government: Public Service for the 21st Century, by David K. Carr, Ian D. Littman, and John K. Condon. Washington, DC: Coopers & Lybrand, 1995. 592 pages.

An encyclopedic tour of the major organizational and process improvement approaches and methods used in government. This book provides detailed information on customer and organizational assessment, strategic planning, change management, tools for process control and improvement, service design, privatizing and outsourcing, performance measurement, activity-based costing, restructuring, internal controls, promoting teamwork, corporate culture, benchmarking, and continuous improvement. The authors are current and former partners with C&L's Government Consulting Practice.

Process Improvement: A Guide for Teams, Clifton Cooksey, Debra Eshelman, Richard Beans, Washington, DC: Coopers & Lybrand, 1993. 246 pages. ISBN 0-944533-06-X.

How do teams of managers and workers make improvements to the problems and opportunities identified in financial management processes? This is a how-to manual covering how to scope an improvement project, develop baseline data, analyze problems and opportunities, generate and test improvements, and introduce them to operations. Its tool box includes detailed instructions on more than 40 tools and techniques for improvement such as statistical process control tools, brainstorming, and affinity diagrams. Each manual includes a computer disk and user guide of software programs for dozens of statistical tools discussed in the text.

Activity-Based Costing and Management

Activity-Based Management in Government, Joseph Kehoe, William Dodson, Robert Reeve, Gustav Plato. Washington, DC: Coopers & Lybrand, 1995. 296 pages. ISBN 0-944533-10-8.

A thorough introduction to activity-based costing in government, this book shows how to apply the ABC approach to determining the actual costs of public sector products, services, and the processes that make them. Then, the book explains how to apply ABC methods to restructure and manage operations around core business processes, which is called Activity-Based Management. With dozens of examples from different levels of government, and from civilian and defense organizations. Lead author Joseph Kehoe was an adviser to the Federal Accounting Standards Advisory Board in developing developing FASAB Statement #4: *Managerial Cost Accounting Concepts and Standards for the Federal Government.*

Benchmarking

Benchmarking: A Manager's Guide, Meridith Bolon and Amy Weber. Washington, DC: Coopers & Lybrand, 1995. 110 pages.
This short, step-by-step guide takes the manager through the entire benchmarking procedure, from defining the scope of the project through institutionalizing the improved process. Authored by C&L managers who coach government teams in conducting benchmarking projects.

Change Management

Managing Change: Opening New Organizational Horizons, David K. Carr, Kelvin Hard, and William J. Trahant. Washington, DC: Coopers & Lybrand, 1994. 284 pages. ISBN 0-944533-12-4 (hardback) ISBN 0-944533-16-7 (paperback).
An in-depth exploration of the art and science of managing change in organization, this book provides dozens of examples from government and industry. The authors are partners in Coopers & Lybrand's Washington, DC and London, England offices.

Internal Controls

Internal Controls—Integrated Framework, Vincent M. O'Reilly et al.,. Committee of Sponsoring Organizations of the Treadway Commission. New York: American Institute of Certified Public Accountants. 1992.
The method described in this set of handbooks is based on a process viewpoint, enabling organizations to build internal controls into their operations, instead of adding them on afterwards. The set includes sample forms and scoring criteria for reviewing internal controls. Written by a Coopers & Lybrand team commissioned by the Treadway Commission. Order from the AICPA, listed below under Associations.

Performance Measurement

Customer Service Measurement, Monograph Series #1, David Wilkerson and Clifton Cooksey, Washington, DC: Coopers & Lybrand, 1994. 72 pages. ISBN 0-944533-08-6.
A handy guide to determining customer expectations and levels of satisfaction, then linking the results to performance measures at the process level. Geared toward government organizations, it contains examples from the public sector.

Survey Assessment, Monograph Series #2, David Wilkerson and Jefferson Kellogg, Washington, DC: Coopers & Lybrand, 1994. 63 pages. ISBN 0-944533-09-4.
This monograph discusses the steps involved in using survey instruments to collect information on customer expectations and satisfaction, and personnel morale, climate, and culture.

Managing Project Expectations, Monograph Series #3, David Wilkerson and Bonnie Brown, Washington, DC: Coopers & Lybrand, 1995. 61 pages. Organizations that carry out projects will appreciate this monograph on the Stakeholder Quality Process used by C&L to determine the expectations of the Firm's customers expectations, then develop performance measures to ensure that the expectations are met.

Business Process Redesign and Reengineering (BPR)

Best Practices in Reengineering: What Works and What Doesn't in the Reengineering Process, David K. Carr and Henry J. Johansson. New York: McGraw-Hill, 1995. 235 pages.
The authors base this book on a major survey of organizations that practice BPR. They use the results to explain how select strategic processes for reengineering, get the highest return on process improvement investment, and ensure continuous improvement in redesigned processes.

BreakPoint Business Process Redesign: How America's Top Companies Blast Past the Competition, David K. Carr, Kevin S. Dougherty, Henry J. Johansson, Robert E. King, and David E. Moran, Washington, DC: Coopers & Lybrand, 1992. 206 pages. ISBN 0-944533-04-3.
An overview of business process redesign or reengineering (BPR), discussed in Chapter 10, this book discusses the relationship of BPR to information technology, quality management, change management, and activity-based costing. It presents a methodology for developing, introducing, and sustaining major changes.

All books published by Coopers & Lybrand in Washington, DC, may be ordered from:

Bookmasters, Inc.
Distribution Center
1444 State Rt. 42
RD 11
Mansfield, Ohio 44903
Telephone: (800) 247-6553

Associations and Other Resource Groups

American Institute of Certified Accountants (AICPA)
1211 Avenue of the Americas
New York, NY. 10036-8775
(800) 862-4272
Web Address: http://www.aicpa.org
The AICPA is a professional society of accountants certified by the states and territories. AICPA responsibilities range from establishing auditing and reporting standards to conducting research on the continued development of educational programs. The group also maintains over 100 committees including Auditing Standards, Professional Ethics, and Information Technology. AICPA provides resources upon request.

American Management Association (AMA)
135 W. 50th St.
New York, NY. 10020
(212) 586-8100
Web Address: http://www.amanet.org
The AMA studies best practices of world class organizations, learning practical business skills through interaction with each other and expert faculty practitioners. Through these forums, members and their peers gain valuable professional growth and development outside of the classroom atmosphere. AMA provides resources upon request.

American Society of Military Comptrollers (ASMC)
P.O. Box 46575
Washington, D.C. 20050-6675
(800) 462-5637
Web Address: http://dubhe.cc.nps.navy.mil/~dbmu/asmc/members.htm
The ASMC provides educational information for the Army and its officers on their futures as it pertains to ranks and responsibilities. It also educates sister services as to some of ASMC's own personnel management issues.

Association of Government Accountants (AGA)
2200 Mount Vernon Ave.
Alexandria, VA. 22301
(703) 684-6931
Web Address: http://www.financenet.gov/aga.htm
The AGA is a professional society of financial managers that are employed by federal, state, and local governments in management and administrative positions.

They also conduct research to provide educational and professional development programs.

Chief Financial Officers Council (CFO Council)
Office of Management and Budget
17 St. and Pennsylvania Ave., NW
Washington, D.C. 20503
(202) 395-3000
Web Address: http://www.financenet.gov/cfo.htm
The CFO Council, consisting of the CFOs and Deputy CFOs of the largest federal agencies ad senior officials of the Office of Management and Budget and the Department of the Treasury, strives to make the government work better and cost less. They apply modern management techniques and integrated financial systems to best inform themselves and others on the best decisions to make to achieve desirable cost effective outcomes.

Federal Accounting Standards Advisory Board (FASAB)
750 1st St. NE, Rm. 1001
Washington, D.C. 20002
(202) 512-7350
Web Address: http://www.financenet.gov/fasab.htm
FASAB is a government organization created to consider and recommend accounting principles for the federal government. The boards recommendations are passed on through the publication of recommended accounting standards after the consideration of the financial and budgetary needs of congressional oversight committees, executive agencies, and related groups.

Financial Executives Institute (FEI)
10 Madison Ave.
P.O.Box 1938
Morristown, NJ. 07962-1938
(201) 898-4600
Web Address: http://www.fei.org
FEI is a professional organization of corporate financial executives who perform the duties of CFO, controller, treasurer, or vice-president-finance. They also sponsor research activities through their affiliated Financial Executives Research Foundation.

Institute of Management Accounting (IMA)
10 Paragon Drive, Montvale, NJ 07645-1760
(800) 638-4427
Web Address: http://www.imanet.org

A professional organization that focuses on management accounting. IMA oversees the certification of management accountants and related accounting sub-professions. Publishes or distributes related books and the monthly periodical Management Accounting.

Joint Financial Management Improvement Program (JFMIP)
666 11th St. NW, Suite 320
Washington, D.C. 20001-4542
(202) 512-9209
Web Address: http://www.financenet.gov/jfmip.htm
The JFMIP strives to make significant improvements to government programs to make them more effective and more efficient. The group also plays a key role in mobilizing resources in an effort to improve financial management practices.

National Performance Review (NPR)
750 17th St., NW, Suite 200
Washington, DC 20006
(202) 632-0150
Web Address: http://www.npr.gov
Central headquarters for reinventing the federal government, NPR has published dozens of reports useful to federal financial and program executives and managers for improving operations. To obtain e-mail catalogs of NPR publications, visit their Web site or send an e-mail to almanac@ace.esusda.gov with this message: "Send NPR catalog." No subject line is required.

Other Internet/Web Pages

FinanceNet. FinanceNet is a server created for finding information on federal financial management. Through it, users can obtain text of relevant laws, OMB Circulars, FASAB Statements, GAO reports, web sites for the CFO Council, GMRA, etc. The site also contains a link to the Library of Congress, information on government sales, and more.
Web Address: http://www.financenet.gov/

Coopers & Lybrand L.L.P. The C&L page provides useful information on CFO related topics, plus it gives an idea of our scope as an international organization.
Web Address: http://www.coopers.co.uk/coopers/fullindex.html

APPENDIX B
FEDERAL FINANCE LAWS, INSTRUCTIONS, AND GUIDELINES

When we asked senior federal financial executives for suggestions on contents for *Public Dollars, Common Sense,* many said to include the main laws that constitute the new reform legislation. In this appendix we present the relelvant text of the Chief Financial Officers Act, the Government Performance and Results Act, the Government Management Reform Act, and the most recent addition, the Federal Financial Management Improvement Act of 1996.

Also, in this appendix we provide summaries of key FASAB and OMB guidelines and instructions. Readers may obtain full text of the laws, guidelines, and instructions through FinanceNet or through our software package *Public Dollars, Common Sense: Federal Laws, Guidelines, and Resources Related to Financial Management (see* Appendix A). Figure B-1 is a map to the laws, guidelines, and instructions, indicating which documents have information that is relevant to a particular subject.

CONTENTS

Index to Federal Laws, Instructions, and Guidelines

Subject	Laws				FASAB Statements										OMB Circulars and Bulletins							
	CFO ACT	GPRA	GMRA	FFMIA	S1	S2	S3	S4	S5	S6	C1	C2	11	34	123	125	127	128	129	134	94-01	97-01
Assets/Liabilities					✓				✓	✓									✓		✓	✓
Financial Statements	✓		✓	✓			✓					✓								✓	✓	✓
Budget											✓		✓	✓								
Cost Accounting				✓				✓														
Loans/Loan Guarantees						✓													✓			
Excess Capacity								✓							✓							
Performance Measurements	✓	✓		✓				✓			✓						✓				✓	✓
Information Systems				✓							✓					✓						
Stewardship										✓	✓											
Internal Controls			✓								✓					✓						
Contractor Payments																		✓				
State and Local																						
Pay Adjustments			✓																			
Strategic Planning	✓	✓																				

Figure B-1

THE CHIEF FINANCIAL OFFICERS ACT OF 1996
P. L. 101-576, 104 STAT. 2838

AN ACT

To amend title 31, United States Code, to improve the general and financial management of the Federal Government. Be it enacted by the Senate and House of Representatives of the United States of America in Congress assembled,

TITLE I · GENERAL PROVISIONS

SEC. 101. SHORT TITLE.

This Act may be cited as the "Chief Financial Officers Act of 1990".

SEC. 102. FINDINGS AND PURPOSES.

(a) FINDINGS.—The Congress finds the following:

(1) General management functions of the Office of Management and Budget need to be significantly enhanced to improve the efficiency and effectiveness of the Federal Government.

(2) Financial management functions of the Office of Management and Budget need to be significantly enhanced to provide overall direction and leadership in the development of a modern Federal financial management structure and associated systems.

(3) Billions of dollars are lost each year through fraud, waste, abuse, and mismanagement among the hundreds of programs in the Federal Government.

(4) These losses could be significantly decreased by improved management, including improved central coordination of internal controls and financial accounting.

(5) The Federal Government is in great need of fundamental reform in financial management requirements and practices as financial management systems are obsolete and inefficient, and do not provide complete, consistent, reliable, and timely information.

(6) Current financial reporting practices of the Federal Government do not accurately disclose the current and probable future cost of operating and investment decisions, including the future need for cash or other resources, do not permit adequate comparison of actual costs among executive agencies, and do not provide the timely information required for efficient management of programs.

(b) PURPOSES.—The purposes of this Act are the following:

(1) Bring more effective general and financial management practices to the Federal Government through statutory provisions which would establish in the Office of Management and Budget a Deputy Director for Management, establish an Office of Federal Financial Management headed by a Controller, and designate a Chief Financial Officer in each executive department and in each major executive agency in the Federal Government.

(2) Provide for improvement, in each agency of the Federal Government, of systems of accounting, financial management, and internal controls to assure the issuance of reliable financial information and to deter fraud, waste, and abuse of Government resources.

(3) Provide for the production of complete, reliable, timely, and consistent financial information for use by the executive branch of the Government and the Congress in the financing, management, and evaluation of Federal programs.

TITLE II · ESTABLISHMENT OF CHIEF FINANCIAL OFFICERS

SEC. 201. DEPUTY DIRECTOR FOR MANAGEMENT.

Section 502 of title 31, United States Code, as amended by this Act, is amended—

(1) by redesignating subsections (c), (d), and (e), as amended by this section, as subsections (d), (e), and (f); and

(2) by inserting after subsection (b) the following:

"(c) The Office has a Deputy Director for Management appointed by the President, by and with the advice and consent of the Senate. The Deputy Director for Management shall be the chief official responsible for financial management in the United States Government."

SEC. 202. FUNCTIONS OF DEPUTY DIRECTOR FOR MANAGEMENT.

(a) CLERICAL AMENDMENTS.—Sections 503 and 504 of title 31, United States Code, are redesignated in order as sections 505 and 506, respectively.

(b) FUNCTIONS OF DEPUTY DIRECTOR FOR MANAGEMENT.—Subchapter I of chapter 5 of title 31, United States Code, is amended by inserting after section 502 the following:

"§ 503. Functions of Deputy Director for Management

"(a) Subject to the direction and approval of the Director, the Deputy Director for Management shall establish governmentwide financial management policies for executive agencies and shall perform the following financial management functions:

"(1) Perform all functions of the Director, including all functions delegated by the President to the Director, relating to financial management.

"(2) Provide overall direction and leadership to the executive branch on financial management matters by establishing financial management policies and requirements, and by monitoring the establishment and operation of Federal Government financial management systems.

"(3) Review agency budget requests for financial management systems and operations, and advise the Director on the resources required to develop and effectively operate and maintain Federal Government financial management systems and to correct major deficiencies in such systems.

"(4) Review and, where appropriate, recommend to the Director changes to the budget and legislative proposals of agencies to ensure that they are in accordance with financial management plans of the Office of Management and Budget.

"(5) Monitor the financial execution of the budget in relation to actual expenditures, including timely performance reports.

"(6) Oversee, periodically review, and make recommendations to heads of agencies on the administrative structure of agencies with respect to their financial management activities.

"(7) Develop and maintain qualification standards for agency Chief Financial Officers and for agency Deputy Chief Financial Officers appointed under sections 901 and 903, respectively.

"(8) Provide advice to agency heads with respect to the selection of agency Chief Financial Officers and Deputy Chief Financial Officers.

"(9) Provide advice to agencies regarding the qualifications, recruitment, performance, and retention of other financial management personnel.

"(10) Assess the overall adequacy of the professional qualifications and capabilities of financial management staffs throughout the Government and make recommendations on ways to correct problems which impair the capacity of those staffs.

"(11) Settle differences that arise among agencies regarding the implementation of financial management policies.

"(12) Chair the Chief Financial Officers Council established by section 302 of the Chief Financial Officers Act of 1990.

"(13) Communicate with the financial officers of State and local governments, and foster the exchange with those officers of information concerning financial management standards, techniques, and processes.

"(14) Issue such other policies and directives as may be necessary to carry out this section, and perform any other function prescribed by the Director.

"(b) Subject to the direction and approval of the Director, the Deputy Director for Management shall establish general management policies for executive agencies and perform the following general management functions:

"(1) Coordinate and supervise the general management functions of the Office of Management and Budget.

"(2) Perform all functions of the Director, including all functions delegated by the President to the Director, relating to—

"(A) managerial systems, including the systematic measurement of performance;

"(B) procurement policy;

"(C) grant, cooperative agreement, and assistance management;

"(D) information and statistical policy;

"(E) property management;

"(F) human resources management;

"(G) regulatory affairs; and

"(H) other management functions, including organizational studies, long-range planning, program evaluation, productivity improvement, and experimentation and demonstration programs.

"(3) Provide complete, reliable, and timely information to the President, the Congress, and the public regarding the management activities of the executive branch.

"(4) Facilitate actions by the Congress and the executive branch to improve the management of Federal Government operations and to remove impediments to effective administration.

"(5) Provide leadership in management innovation, through—

"(A) experimentation, testing, and demonstration programs; and

"(B) the adoption of modern management concepts and technologies.

"(6) Work with State and local governments to improve and strengthen intergovernmental relations, and provide assistance to such governments with respect to intergovernmental programs and cooperative arrangements.

"(7) Review and, where appropriate, recommend to the Director changes to the budget and legislative proposals of agencies to ensure that they respond to program evaluations by, and are in accordance with general management plans of, the Office of Management and Budget.

"(8) Provide advice to agencies on the qualification, recruitment, performance, and retention of managerial personnel.

"(9) perform any other functions prescribed by the Director."

SEC. 203. OFFICE OF FEDERAL FINANCIAL MANAGEMENT.

(a) ESTABLISHMENT.—Subchapter I of chapter 5 of title 31, United States Code, as amended by this Act, is amended by inserting after section 503 (as added by section 202 of this Act) the following:

"§ 504. Office of Federal Financial Management

"(a) There is established in the Office of Management and Budget an office to be known as the 'Office of Federal Financial Management'. The Office of Federal Financial Management, under the direction and control of the Deputy Director for Management of the Office of Management and Budget, shall carry out the financial management functions listed in section 503(a) of this title.

"(b) There shall be at the head of the Office of Federal Financial Management a Controller, who shall be appointed by the President, by and with the advice and consent of the Senate. The Controller shall be appointed from among individuals who possess—

"(1) demonstrated ability and practical experience in accounting, financial management, and financial systems; and

"(2) extensive practical experience in financial management in large governmental or business entities.

"(c) The Controller of the Office of Federal Financial Management shall be the deputy and principal advisor to the Deputy Director for Management in the performance by the Deputy Director for Management of functions described in section 503(a)."

(b) Statement of Appropriations in Budget.—Section 1105(a) of title 31, United States Code, is amended by adding at the end the following:

"(28) a separate statement of the amount of appropriations requested for the Office of Federal Financial Management."

(c) Clerical Amendment.—The table of contents at the beginning of chapter 5 of title 31, United States Code, is amended by striking the items relating to sections 503 and 504 and inserting the following:

"503. Functions of Deputy Director for Management.
"504. Office of Federal Financial Management.
"505. Office of Information and Regulatory Affairs.
"506. Office of Federal Procurement Policy."

SEC. 204. DUTIES AND FUNCTIONS OF THE DEPARTMENT OF THE TREASURY.

Nothing in this Act shall be construed to interfere with the exercise of the functions, duties, and responsibilities of the Department of the Treasury, as in effect immediately before the enactment of this Act.

SEC. 205. AGENCY CHIEF FINANCIAL OFFICERS.

(a) IN GENERAL.—Subtitle I of title 31, United States Code, is amended by adding at the end the following new chapter:

"CHAPTER 9—AGENCY CHIEF FINANCIAL OFFICERS

"Sec.

"901. Establishment of agency Chief Financial Officers.

"902. Authority and functions of agency Chief Financial Officers.

"903. Establishment of agency Deputy Chief Financial Officers.

"§ 901. Establishment of agency Chief Financial Officers

"(a) There shall be within each agency described in subsection (b) an agency Chief Financial Officer. Each agency Chief Financial Officer shall—

"(1) for those agencies described in subsection (b)(1)—

"(A) be appointed by the President, by and with the advice and consent of the Senate; or

"(B) be designated by the President, in consultation with the head of the agency, from among officials of the agency who are required by law to be so appointed;

"(2) for those agencies described in subsection (b)(2)—

"(A) be appointed by the head of the agency;

"(B) be in the competitive service or the senior executive service; and

"(C) be career appointees; and

"(3) be appointed or designated, as applicable, from among individuals who possess demonstrated ability in general management of, and knowledge of and extensive practical experience in financial management practices in large governmental or business entities.

"(b) (1) The agencies referred to in subsection (a)(1) are the following:

"(A) The Department of Agriculture.

"(B) The Department of Commerce.

"(C) The Department of Defense.

"(D) The Department of Education.

"(E) The Department of Energy.

"(F) The Department of Health and Human Services.

"(G) The Department of Housing and Urban Development.

"(H) The Department of the Interior.

"(I) The Department of Justice.

"(J) The Department of Labor.

"(K) The Department of State.

"(L) The Department of Transportation.

"(M) The Department of the Treasury.

"(N) The Department of Veterans Affairs.

"(O) The Environmental Protection Agency.

"(P) The National Aeronautics and Space Administration.

"(2) The agencies referred to in subsection (a)(2) are the following:

"(A) The Agency for International Development.

"(B) The Federal Emergency Management Agency.

"(C) The General Services Administration.

"(D) The National Science Foundation.

"(E) The Nuclear Regulatory Commission.

"(F) The Office of Personnel Management.

"(G) The Small Business Administration.

"§ 902. Authority and functions of agency Chief Financial Officers

"(a) An agency Chief Financial Officer shall—

"(1) report directly to the head of the agency regarding financial management matters;

"(2) oversee all financial management activities relating to the programs and operations of the agency;

"(3) develop and maintain an integrated agency accounting and financial management system, including financial reporting and internal controls, which—

"(A) complies with applicable accounting principles, standards, and requirements, and internal control standards;

"(B) complies with such policies and requirements as may be prescribed by the Director of the Office of Management and Budget;

"(C) complies with any other requirements applicable to such systems; and

"(D) provides for—

"(i) complete, reliable, consistent, and timely information which is prepared on a uniform basis and which is responsive to the financial information needs of agency management;

"(ii) the development and reporting of cost information;

"(iii) the integration of accounting and budgeting information; and

"(iv) the systematic measurement of performance;

"(4) make recommendations to the head of the agency regarding the selection of the Deputy Chief Financial Officer of the agency;

"(5) direct, manage, and provide policy guidance and oversight of agency financial management personnel, activities, and operations, including—

"(A) the preparation and annual revision of an agency plan to—

"(i) implement the 5-year financial management plan prepared by the Director of the Office of Management and Budget under section 3512(a)(3) of this title; and

"(ii) comply with the requirements established under sections 3515 and subsections (e) and (f) of section 3521 of this title;

"(B) the development of agency financial management budgets;

"(C) the recruitment, selection, and training of personnel to carry out agency financial management functions;

"(D) the approval and management of agency financial management systems design or enhancement projects;

"(E) the implementation of agency asset management systems, including systems for cash management, credit management, debt collection, and property and inventory management and control;

"(6) prepare and transmit, by not later than 60 days after the submission of the audit report required by section 3521(f) of this title, an annual report to the agency head and the Director of the Office of Management and Budget, which shall include—

"(A) a description and analysis of the status of financial management of the agency;

"(B) the annual financial statements prepared under section 3515 of this title;

"(C) the audit report transmitted to the head of the agency under section 3521(f) of this title;

"(D) a summary of the reports on internal accounting and administrative control systems submitted to the President and the Congress under the amendments made by the Federal Managers' Financial Integrity Act of 1982 (Public Law 97-255); and

"(E) other information the head of the agency considers appropriate to fully inform the President and the Congress concerning the financial management of the agency;

"(7) monitor the financial execution of the budget of the agency in relation to actual expenditures, and prepare and submit to the head of the agency timely performance reports; and

"(8) review, on a biennial basis, the fees, royalties, rents, and other charges imposed by the agency for services and things of value it provides, and make recommendations on revising those charges to reflect costs incurred by it in providing those services and things of value.

"(b) (1) In addition to the authority otherwise provided by this section, each agency Chief Financial Officer—

"(A) subject to paragraph (2), shall have access to all records, reports, audits, reviews, documents, papers, recommendations, or other material which are the property of the agency or which are available to the agency, and which relate to programs and operations with respect to which that agency Chief Financial Officer has responsibilities under this section;

"(B) may request such information or assistance as may be necessary for carrying out the duties and responsibilities provided by this section from any Federal, State, or local governmental entity; and

"(C) to the extent and in such amounts as may be provided in advance by appropriations Acts, may—

"(i) enter into contracts and other arrangements with public agencies and with private persons for the preparation of financial statements, studies, analyses, and other services; and

"(ii) make such payments as may be necessary to carry out the provisions of this section.

"(2) Except as provided in paragraph (1)(B), this subsection does not provide to an agency Chief Financial Officer any access greater than permitted under any other law to records, reports, audits, reviews, documents, papers, recommendations, or other material of any Office of Inspector General established under the Inspector General Act of 1978 (5 U.S.C. App.).

"§ 903. Establishment of agency Deputy Chief Financial Officers

"(a) There shall be within each agency described in section 901(b) an agency Deputy Chief Financial Officer, who shall report directly to the agency Chief Financial Officer on financial management matters. The position of agency Deputy Chief Financial Officer shall be a career reserved position in the Senior Executive Service.

"(b) Consistent with qualification standards developed by, and in consultation with, the agency Chief Financial Officer and the Director of the Office of Management and Budget, the head of each agency shall appoint as Deputy Chief Financial Officer an individual with demonstrated ability and experience in accounting, budget execution, financial and management analysis, and systems development, and not less than 6 years practical experience in financial management at large governmental entities."

(b) CLERICAL AMENDMENT.—The table of chapters at the beginning of subtitle I of title 31, United States Code, is amended by adding at the end the following:

"9. Agency Chief Financial Officers 901."

(c) CHIEF FINANCIAL OFFICERS OF DEPARTMENT OF VETERANS AFFAIRS AND DEPARTMENT OF HOUSING AND URBAN DEVELOPMENT.—

(1) DESIGNATION.—The Secretary of Veterans Affairs and the Secretary of Housing and Urban Development may each designate as the agency Chief Financial Officer of that department for purposes of section 901 of title 31, United States Code, as amended by this section, the officer designated, respectively, under section 4(c) of the Department of Veterans Affairs Act (38 U.S.C. 201 note) and section 4(e) of the Department of Housing and Urban Development Act (42 U.S.C. 3533(e)), as in effect before the effective date of this Act.

(2) CONFORMING AMENDMENT.—Section 4(c) of the Department of Veterans Affairs Act (38 U.S.C. 201 note) and section 4(e) of the Department of Housing and Urban Development Act (42 U.S.C. 3533(e)), as added by section 121 of Public Law 101-235, are repealed.

SEC. 206. TRANSFER OF FUNCTIONS AND PERSONNEL OF AGENCY CHIEF FINANCIAL OFFICERS.

(a) AGENCY REVIEWS OF FINANCIAL MANAGEMENT ACTIVITIES.—Not later than 120 days after the date of the enactment of this Act, the Director of the Office of Management and Budget shall require each agency listed in subsection (b) of section 901 of title 31, United States Code, as amended by this Act, to conduct a review of its financial management activities for the purpose of consolidating its accounting, budgeting, and other financial management activities under the agency Chief Financial Officer appointed under subsection (a) of that section for the agency.

(b) REORGANIZATION PROPOSAL.—Not later than 120 days after the issuance of requirements under subsection (a) and subject to all laws vesting functions in particular officers and employees of the United States, the head of each agency shall submit to the Director of the Office of Management and Budget a proposal for reorganizing the agency for the purposes of this Act. Such proposal shall include—

(1) a description of all functions, powers, duties, personnel, property, or records which the agency Chief Financial Officer is proposed to have authority over, including those relating to functions that are not related to financial management activities; and

(2) a detailed outline of the administrative structure of the office of the agency Chief Financial Officer, including a description of the responsibility and authority of financial management personnel and resources in agencies or other subdivisions as appropriate to that agency.

(c) REVIEW AND APPROVAL OF PROPOSAL.—Not later than 60 days after receiving a proposal from the head of an agency under subsection (b), the Director of the Office of Management and Budget shall approve or disapprove the proposal and notify the head of the agency of that approval or disapproval. The Director shall approve each proposal which establishes an agency Chief Financial Officer in conformance with section 901 of title 31, United States Code, as added by this Act, and which establishes a financial management structure reasonably tailored to the functions of the agency. Upon approving or disapproving a proposal of an agency under this section, the Director shall transmit to the head of the agency a written notice of that approval or disapproval.

(d) IMPLEMENTATION OF PROPOSAL.—Upon receiving written notice of approval of a proposal under this section from the Director of the Office of Management and Budget, the head of an agency shall implement that proposal.

SEC. 207. COMPENSATION.

(a) COMPENSATION, LEVEL II.—Section 5313 of title 5, United States Code, is amended by adding at the end the following:

"Deputy Director for Management, Office of Management and Budget."

(b) COMPENSATION, LEVEL III.—Section 5314 of title 5, United States Code, is amended by adding at the end the following:

"Controller, Office of Federal Financial Management, Office of Management and Budget."

(c) COMPENSATION, LEVEL IV.—Section 5315 of title 5, United States Code, is amended by adding at the end the following:

"Chief Financial Officer, Department of Agriculture.

"Chief Financial Officer, Department of Commerce.

"Chief Financial Officer, Department of Defense.

"Chief Financial Officer, Department of Education.

"Chief Financial Officer, Department of Energy.

"Chief Financial Officer, Department of Health and Human Services.

"Chief Financial Officer, Department of Housing and Urban Development.

"Chief Financial Officer, Department of the Interior.

"Chief Financial Officer, Department of Justice.

"Chief Financial Officer, Department of Labor.

"Chief Financial Officer, Department of State.

"Chief Financial Officer, Department of Transportation.

"Chief Financial Officer, Department of the Treasury.

"Chief Financial Officer, Department of Veterans Affairs.

"Chief Financial Officer, Environmental Protection Agency.

"Chief Financial Officer, National Aeronautics and Space Administration."

TITLE III - ENHANCEMENT OF FEDERAL FINANCIAL MANAGEMENT ACTIVITIES

SEC. 301. FINANCIAL MANAGEMENT STATUS REPORT; 5-YEAR PLAN OF DIRECTOR OF OFFICE OF MANAGEMENT AND BUDGET.

(a) IN GENERAL.—Section 3512 of title 31, United States Code, is amended by striking the heading thereof, redesignating subsections (a) through (f) in order as subsections (b) through (g), and by inserting before such subsection (b), as so redesignated, the following:

§ 3512, Executive agency accounting and other financial management reports and plans.

"(a) (1) The Director of the Office of Management and Budget shall prepare and submit to the appropriate committees of the Congress a financial management status report and a governmentwide 5-year financial management plan.

"(2) A financial management status report under this subsection shall include—

"(A) a description and analysis of the status of financial management in the executive branch;

"(B) a summary of the most recently completed financial statements—

"(i) of Federal agencies under section 3515 of this title; and

"(ii) of Government corporations;

"(C) a summary of the most recently completed financial statement audits and reports—

"(i) of Federal agencies under section 3521 (e) and (f) of this title; and

"(ii) of Government corporations;

"(D) a summary of reports on internal accounting and administrative control systems submitted to the President and the Congress under the amendments made by the Federal Managers' Financial Integrity Act of 1982 (Public Law 97-255); and

"(E) any other information the Director considers appropriate to fully inform the Congress regarding the financial management of the Federal Government.

"(3) (A) A governmentwide 5-year financial management plan under this subsection shall describe the activities the Director, the Deputy Director for Management, the Controller of the Office of Federal Financial Management, and agency Chief Financial Officers shall conduct over the next 5 fiscal years to improve the financial management of the Federal Government.

"(B) Each governmentwide 5-year financial management plan prepared under this subsection shall—

"(i) describe the existing financial management structure and any changes needed to establish an integrated financial management system;

"(ii) be consistent with applicable accounting principles, standards, and requirements;

"(iii) provide a strategy for developing and integrating individual agency accounting, financial information, and other financial management systems to ensure adequacy, consistency, and timeliness of financial information;

"(iv) identify and make proposals to eliminate duplicative and unnecessary systems, including encouraging agencies to share systems which have sufficient capacity to perform the functions needed;

"(v) identify projects to bring existing systems into compliance with the applicable standards and requirements;

"(vi) contain milestones for equipment acquisitions and other actions necessary to implement the 5-year plan consistent with the requirements of this section;

"(vii) identify financial management personnel needs and actions to ensure those needs are met;

"(viii) include a plan for ensuring the annual audit of financial statements of executive agencies pursuant to section 3521(h) of this title; and

"(ix) estimate the costs of implementing the governmentwide 5-year plan.

"(4) (A) Not later than 15 months after the date of the enactment of this subsection, the Director of the Office of Management and Budget shall submit the first financial management status report and governmentwide 5-year financial management plan under this subsection to the appropriate committees of the Congress.

"(B) (i) Not later than January 31 of each year thereafter, the Director of the Office of Management and Budget shall submit to the appropriate committees of the Congress a financial management status report and a revised governmentwide 5-year financial management plan to cover the succeeding 5 fiscal years, including a report on the accomplishments of the executive branch in implementing the plan during the preceding fiscal year.

"(ii) The Director shall include with each revised governmentwide 5-year financial management plan a description of any substantive changes in the financial statement audit plan required by paragraph (3)(B)(viii), progress made by executive agencies in implementing the audit plan, and any improvements in Federal Government financial management related to preparation and audit of financial statements of executive agencies.

"(5) Not later than 30 days after receiving each annual report under section 902(a)(6) of this title, the Director shall transmit to the Chairman of the Committee on Government Operations of the House of Representatives and the Chairman of the Committee on Governmental Affairs of the Senate a final copy of that report and any comments on the report by the Director."

(b) CLERICAL AMENDMENT.—The table of contents at the beginning of chapter 35 of title 31, United States Code, is amended by striking the item relating to section 3512 and inserting the following:

"3512. Executive agency accounting and other financial management reports and plans."

SEC. 302. CHIEF FINANCIAL OFFICERS COUNCIL.

(a) ESTABLISHMENT.—There is established a Chief Financial Officers Council, consisting of—

(1) the Deputy Director for Management of the Office of Management and Budget, who shall act as chairperson of the council;

(2) the Controller of the Office of Federal Financial Management of the Office of Management and Budget;

(3) the Fiscal Assistant Secretary of Treasury; and

(4) each of the agency Chief Financial Officers appointed under section 901 of title 31, United States Code, as amended by this Act.

(b) FUNCTIONS.—The Chief Financial Officers Council shall meet periodically to advise and coordinate the activities of the agencies of its members on such matters as consolidation and modernization of financial systems, improved quality of financial information, financial data and information standards, internal controls, legislation affecting financial operations and organizations, and any other financial management matter.

SEC. 303. FINANCIAL STATEMENTS OF AGENCIES.

(a) Preparation of Financial Statements.—

(1) IN GENERAL.—Subchapter II of chapter 35 of title 31, United States Code, is amended by adding at the end the following:

"§ 3515. Financial statements of agencies

"(a) Not later than March 31 of 1992 and each year thereafter, the head of each executive agency identified in section 901(b) of this title shall prepare and submit to the Director of the Office of Management and Budget a financial statement for the preceding fiscal year, covering—

"(1) each revolving fund and trust fund of the agency; and

"(2) to the extent practicable, the accounts of each office, bureau, and activity of the agency which performed substantial commercial functions during the preceding fiscal year.

"(b) Each financial statement of an executive agency under this section shall reflect—

"(1) the overall financial position of the revolving funds, trust funds, offices, bureaus, and activities covered by the statement, including assets and liabilities thereof;

"(2) results of operations of those revolving funds, trust funds, offices, bureaus, and activities;

"(3) cash flows or changes in financial position of those revolving funds, trust funds, offices, bureaus, and activities; and

"(4) a reconciliation to budget reports of the executive agency for those revolving funds, trust funds, offices, bureaus, and activities.

(c) The Director of the Office of Management and Budget shall prescribe the form and content of the financial statements of executive agencies under this section, consistent with applicable accounting principles, standards, and requirements.

"(d) For purposes of this section, the term 'commercial functions' includes buying and leasing of real estate, providing insurance, making loans and loan guarantees, and other credit programs and any activity involving the provision of a service or thing of value for which a fee, royalty, rent, or other charge is imposed by an agency for services and things of value it provides.

"(e) Not later than March 31 of each year, the head of each executive agency designated by the President may prepare and submit to the Director of the Office of Management and Budget a financial statement for the preceding fiscal year, covering accounts of offices, bureaus, and activities of the agency in addition to those described in subsection (a)."

(2) EFFECTIVE DATE OF SUBSECTION.—Subsection (e) of section 3515 of title 31, United States Code, as added by paragraph (1), shall take effect on the date on which a resolution described in subsection (b)(1) of this section is passed by the Congress and approved by the President.

(3) WAIVER OF REQUIREMENT.—The Director of the Office of Management and Budget may, for fiscal year 1991, waive the application of section 3515(a) of title 31, United States Code, as amended by this subsection, with respect to any revolving fund, trust fund, or account of an executive agency.

(b) RESOLUTION APPROVING DESIGNATION OF AGENCIES.—

(This strictly procedural section not included in *Public Dollars, Common Sense*)

(c) REPORT ON SUBSTANTIAL COMMERCIAL FUNCTIONS.—Not later than 180 days after the date of the enactment of this Act, the Director of the Office of Management and Budget shall determine and report to the Congress on which executive agencies or parts thereof perform substantial commercial functions for which financial statements can be prepared practicably under section 3515 of title 31, United States Code, as added by this section.

(d) PILOT PROJECT.—(1) Not later than March 31 of each of 1991, 1992, and 1993, the head of the Departments of Agriculture, Labor, and Veterans Affairs, the General Services Administration, and the Social Security Administration shall each prepare and submit to the Director of the Office of Management and Budget financial statements for the preceding fiscal year for the accounts of all of the offices, bureaus, and activities of that department or administration.

(2) Not later than March 31 of each of 1992 and 1993, the head of the Departments of Housing and Urban Development and the Army shall prepare and submit to the Director of the Office of Management and Budget financial

statements for the preceding fiscal year for the accounts of all of the offices, bureaus, and activities of that department.

(3) Not later than March 31, 1993, the head of the Department of the Air Force, the Internal Revenue Service, and the United States Customs Service, shall each prepare and submit to the Director of the Office of Management and Budget financial statements for the preceding fiscal year for the accounts of all of the offices, bureaus, and activities of that department or service.

(4) Each financial statement prepared under this subsection shall be audited in accordance with section 3521 (e), (f), (g), and (h) of title 31, United States Code.

(e) REPORT ON INITIAL FINANCIAL STATEMENTS.—Not later than June 30, 1993, the Director of the Office of Management and Budget shall report to the Congress on the financial statements prepared for fiscal years 1990, 1991, and 1992 under subsection (a) of section 3515 of title 31, United States Code (as added by subsection (a) of this section) and under subsection (d) of this section. The report shall include analysis of—

(1) the accuracy of the data included in the financial statements;

(2) the difficulties each department and agency encountered in preparing the data included in the financial statements;

(3) the benefits derived from the preparation of the financial statements; and

(4) the cost associated with preparing and auditing the financial statements, including a description of any activities that were foregone as a result of that preparation and auditing.

(f) CLERICAL AMENDMENT.—The table of sections at the beginning of chapter 35 of title 31, United States Code, is amended by inserting after the item relating to section 3514 the following:

"3515. Financial statements of agencies."

SEC. 304. FINANCIAL AUDITS OF AGENCIES.

(a) IN GENERAL.—Section 3521 of title 31, United States Code, is amended by adding at the end the following new subsections:

"(e) Each financial statement prepared under section 3515 by an agency shall be audited in accordance with applicable generally accepted government auditing standards—

"(1) in the case of an agency having an Inspector General appointed under the Inspector General Act of 1978 (5 U.S.C. App.), by the Inspector General or by an independent external auditor, as determined by the Inspector General of the agency; and

"(2) in any other case, by an independent external auditor, as determined by the head of the agency.

"(f) Not later than June 30 following the fiscal year for which a financial statement is submitted under section 3515 of this title by an agency, the person who audits the statement for purpose of subsection (e) shall submit a report on the audit to the head of the agency. A report under this subsection shall be prepared in accordance with generally accepted government auditing standards.

"(g) The Comptroller General of the United States—

"(1) may review any audit of a financial statement conducted under this subsection by an Inspector General or an external auditor;

"(2) shall report to the Congress, the Director of the Office of Management and Budget, and the head of the agency which prepared the statement, regarding the results of the review and make any recommendation the Comptroller General considers appropriate; and

"(3) may audit a financial statement prepared under section 3515 of this title at the discretion of the Comptroller General or at the request of a committee of the Congress.

An audit the Comptroller General performs under this subsection shall be in lieu of the audit otherwise required by subsection (e) of this section. Prior to performing such audit, the Comptroller General shall consult with the Inspector General of the agency which prepared the statement.

"(h) Each financial statement prepared by an executive agency for a fiscal year after fiscal year 1991 shall be audited in accordance with this section and the plan required by section 3512(a)(3)(B)(viii) of this title."

(b) WAIVER OF REQUIREMENTS.—The Director of the Office of Management and Budget may waive application of subsections (e) and (f) of section 3521 of title 31, United States Code, as amended by this section, to a financial statement submitted by an agency for fiscal years 1990 and 1991.

SEC. 305. FINANCIAL AUDITS OF GOVERNMENT CORPORATIONS.

Section 9105 of title 31, United States Code, is amended to read as follows:

"§ 9105. Audits

"(a) (1) The financial statements of Government corporations shall be audited by the Inspector General of the corporation appointed under the Inspector General Act of 1978 (5 U.S.C. App.) or by an independent external auditor, as determined by the Inspector General or, if there is no Inspector General, by the head of the corporation.

"(2) Audits under this section shall be conducted in accordance with applicable generally accepted government auditing standards.

"(3) Upon completion of the audit required by this subsection, the person who audits the statement shall submit a report on the audit to the head of the

Government corporation, to the Chairman of the Committee on Government Operations of the House of Representatives, and to the Chairman of the Committee on Governmental Affairs of the Senate.

"(4) The Comptroller General of the United States—

"(A) may review any audit of a financial statement conducted under this subsection by an Inspector General or an external auditor;

"(B) shall report to the Congress, the Director of the Office of Management and Budget, and the head of the Government corporation which prepared the statement, regarding the results of the review and make any recommendation the Comptroller General of the United States considers appropriate; and

"(C) may audit a financial statement of a Government corporation at the discretion of the Comptroller General or at the request of a committee of the Congress. An audit the Comptroller General performs under this paragraph shall be in lieu of the audit otherwise required by paragraph (1) of this subsection. Prior to performing such audit, the Comptroller General shall consult with the Inspector General of the agency which prepared the statement.

"(5) A Government corporation shall reimburse the Comptroller General of the United States for the full cost of any audit conducted by the Comptroller General under this subsection, as determined by the Comptroller General. All reimbursements received under this paragraph by the Comptroller General of the United States shall be deposited in the Treasury as miscellaneous receipts.

"(b) Upon request of the Comptroller General of the United States, a Government corporation shall provide to the Comptroller General of the United States all books, accounts, financial records, reports, files, workpapers, and property belonging to or in use by the Government corporation and its auditor that the Comptroller General of the United States considers necessary to the performance of any audit or review under this section.

"(c) Activities of the Comptroller General of the United States under this section are in lieu of any audit of the financial transactions of a Government corporation that the Comptroller General is required to make under any other law."

SEC. 306. MANAGEMENT REPORTS OF GOVERNMENT CORPORATIONS.

(a) **IN GENERAL.**—Section 9106 of title 31, United States Code, is amended to read as follows:

"§ 9106. Management reports

"(a) (1) A Government corporation shall submit an annual management report to the Congress not later than 180 days after the end of the Government corporation's fiscal year.

"(2) A management report under this subsection shall include—

"(A) a statement of financial position;

"(B) a statement of operations;

"(C) a statement of cash flows;

"(D) a reconciliation to the budget report of the Government corporation, if applicable;

"(E) a statement on internal accounting and administrative control systems by the head of the management of the corporation, consistent with the requirements for agency statements on internal accounting and administrative control systems under the amendments made by the Federal Managers' Financial Integrity Act of 1982 (Public Law 97-255);

"(F) the report resulting from an audit of the financial statements of the corporation conducted under section 9105 of this title; and

"(G) any other comments and information necessary to inform the Congress about the operations and financial condition of the corporation.

"(b) A Government corporation shall provide the President, the Director of the Office of Management and Budget, and the Comptroller General of the United States a copy of the management report when it is submitted to Congress."

(b) CLERICAL AMENDMENT.—The table of sections for chapter 91 of title 31, United States Code, is amended by striking the item relating to section 9106 and inserting the following:

"9106. Management reports."

SEC. 307. ADOPTION OF CAPITAL ACCOUNTING STANDARDS.

No capital accounting standard or principle, including any human capital standard or principle, shall be adopted for use in an executive department or agency until such standard has been reported to the Congress and a period of 45 days of continuous session of the Congress has expired.

Approved November 15, 1990.

GOVERNMENT PERFORMANCE AND RESULTS OF ACT OF 1993
P. L. 103-66, 107 STAT. 285

AN ACT

To provide for the establishment of strategic planning and performance measurement in the Federal Government, and for other purposes. Be it enacted by the Senate and House of Representatives of the United States of America in Congress assembled,

SECTION 1. SHORT TITLE.

This Act may be cited as the "Government Performance and Results Act of 1993".

SEC. 2. FINDINGS AND PURPOSES.

(a) FINDINGS.—The Congress finds that—

(1) waste and inefficiency in Federal programs undermine the confidence of the American people in the Government and reduces the Federal Government's ability to address adequately vital public needs;

(2) Federal managers are seriously disadvantaged in their efforts to improve program efficiency and effectiveness, because of insufficient articulation of program goals and inadequate information on program performance; and

(3) congressional policymaking, spending decisions and program oversight are seriously handicapped by insufficient attention to program performance and results.

(b) PURPOSES.—The purposes of this Act are to—

(1) improve the confidence of the American people in the capability of the Federal Government, by systematically holding Federal agencies accountable for achieving program results;

(2) initiate program performance reform with a series of pilot projects in setting program goals, measuring program performance against those goals, and reporting publicly on their progress;

(3) improve Federal program effectiveness and public accountability by promoting a new focus on results, service quality, and customer satisfaction;

(4) help Federal managers improve service delivery, by requiring that they plan for meeting program objectives and by providing them with information about program results and service quality;

(5) improve congressional decisionmaking by providing more objective information on achieving statutory objectives, and on the relative effectiveness and efficiency of Federal programs and spending; and

(6) improve internal management of the Federal Government.

SEC. 3. STRATEGIC PLANNING.

Chapter 3 of title 5, United States Code, is amended by adding after section 305 the following new section:

"§ 306. Strategic plans

"(a) No later than September 30, 1997, the head of each agency shall submit to the Director of the Office of Management and Budget and to the Congress a strategic plan for program activities. Such plan shall contain—

"(1) a comprehensive mission statement covering the major functions and operations of the agency;

"(2) general goals and objectives, including outcome—related goals and objectives, for the major functions and operations of the agency;

"(3) a description of how the goals and objectives are to be achieved, including a description of the operational processes, skills and technology, and the human, capital, information, and other resources required to meet those goals and bjectives;

"(4) a description of how the performance goals included in the plan required by section 1115(a) of title 31 shall be related to the general goals and objectives in the strategic plan;

"(5) an identification of those key factors external to the agency and beyond its control that could significantly affect the achievement of the general goals and objectives; and

"(6) a description of the program evaluations used in establishing or revising general goals and objectives, with a schedule for future program evaluations.

(b) The strategic plan shall cover a period of not less than five years forward from the fiscal year in which it is submitted, and shall be updated and revised at least every three years.

(c) The performance plan required by section 1115 of title 31 shall be consistent with the agency's strategic plan. A performance plan may not be submitted for a fiscal year not covered by a current strategic plan under this section.

(d) When developing a strategic plan, the agency shall consult with the Congress, and shall solicit and consider the views and suggestions of those entities potentially affected by or interested in such a plan.

(e) The functions and activities of this section shall be considered to be inherently Governmental functions. The drafting of strategic plans under this section shall be performed only by Federal employees.

(f) For purposes of this section the term 'agency' means an Executive agency defined under section 105, but does not include the Central Intelligence Agency, the General Accounting Office, the Panama Canal Commission, the United States Postal Service, and the Postal Rate Commission."

SEC. 4. ANNUAL PERFORMANCE PLANS AND REPORTS.

(a) Budget Contents and Submission to Congress.—Section 1105(a) of title 31, United States Code, is amended by adding at the end thereof the following new paragraph:

"(29) beginning with fiscal year 1999, a Federal Government performance plan for the overall budget as provided for under section 1115."

(b) Performance Plans and Reports.—Chapter 11 of title 31, United States Code, is amended by adding after section 1114 the following new sections:

"§ 1115. Performance plans

"(a) In carrying out the provisions of section 1105(a)(29), the Director of the Office of Management and Budget shall require each agency to prepare an annual performance plan covering each program activity set forth in the budget of such agency. Such plan shall—

"(1) establish performance goals to define the level of performance to be achieved by a program activity;

"(2) express such goals in an objective, quantifiable, and measurable form unless authorized to be in an alternative form under subsection (b);

"(3) briefly describe the operational processes, skills and technology, and the human, capital, information, or other resources required to meet the performance goals;

"(4) establish performance indicators to be used in measuring or assessing the relevant outputs, service levels, and outcomes of each program activity;

"(5) provide a basis for comparing actual program results with the established performance goals; and

"(6) describe the means to be used to verify and validate measured values.

"(b) If an agency, in consultation with the Director of the Office of Management and Budget, determines that it is not feasible to express the performance goals for a particular program activity in an objective, quantifiable, and measurable form, the Director of the Office of Management and Budget may authorize an alternative form. Such alternative form shall—

"(1) include separate descriptive statements of—

"(A)(i) a minimally effective program, and

"(ii) a successful program, or

"(B) such alternative as authorized by the Director of the Office of Management and Budget, with sufficient precision and in such terms that would allow for an accurate, independent determination of whether the program activity's performance meets the criteria of the description; or

"(2) state why it is infeasible or impractical to express a performance goal in any form for the program activity.

(c) For the purpose of complying with this section, an agency may aggregate, disaggregate, or consolidate program activities, except that any aggregation or consolidation may not omit or minimize the significance of any program activity constituting a major function or operation for the agency.

(d) An agency may submit with its annual performance plan an appendix covering any portion of the plan that—

"(1) is specifically authorized under criteria established by an Executive order to be kept secret in the interest of national defense or foreign policy; and

"(2) is properly classified pursuant to such Executive order.

(e) The functions and activities of this section shall be considered to be inherently Governmental functions. The drafting of performance plans under this section shall be performed only by Federal employees.

(f) For purposes of this section and sections 1116 through 1119, and sections 9703 and 9704 the term—

"(1) 'agency' has the same meaning as such term is defined under section 306(f) of title 5;

"(2) 'outcome measure' means an assessment of the results of a program activity compared to its intended purpose;

"(3) 'output measure' means the tabulation, calculation, or recording of activity or effort and can be expressed in a quantitative or qualitative manner;

"(4) 'performance goal' means a target level of performance expressed as a tangible, measurable objective, against which actual achievement can be compared, including a goal expressed as a quantitative standard, value, or rate;

"(5) 'performance indicator' means a particular value or characteristic used to measure output or outcome;

"(6) 'program activity' means a specific activity or project as listed in the program and financing schedules of the annual budget of the United States Government; and

"(7) 'program evaluation' means an assessment, through objective measurement and systematic analysis, of the manner and extent to which Federal programs achieve intended objectives.

"§ 1116. Program performance reports

"(a) No later than March 31, 2000, and no later than March 31 of each year thereafter, the head of each agency shall prepare and submit to the President and the Congress, a report on program performance for the previous fiscal year.

"(b)(1) Each program performance report shall set forth the performance indicators established in the agency performance plan under section 1115, along with the actual program performance achieved compared with the performance goals expressed in the plan for that fiscal year.

"(2) If performance goals are specified in an alternative form under section 1115(b), the results of such program shall be described in relation to such specifications, including whether the performance failed to meet the criteria of a minimally effective or successful program.

"(c) The report for fiscal year 2000 shall include actual results for the preceding fiscal year, the report for fiscal year 2001 shall include actual results for the two preceding fiscal years, and the report for fiscal year 2002 and all subsequent reports shall include actual results for the three preceding fiscal years.

"(d) Each report shall—

"(1) review the success of achieving the performance goals of the fiscal year;

"(2) evaluate the performance plan for the current fiscal year relative to the performance achieved toward the performance goals in the fiscal year covered by the report;

"(3) explain and describe, where a performance goal has not been met (including when a program activity's performance is determined not to have met the criteria of a successful program activity under section 1115(b)(1)(A)(ii) or a corresponding level of achievement if another alternative form is used)—

"(A) why the goal was not met;

"(B) those plans and schedules for achieving the established performance goal; and

"(C) if the performance goal is impractical or infeasible, why that is the case and what action is recommended;

"(4) describe the use and assess the effectiveness in achieving performance goals of any waiver under section 9703 of this title; and

"(5) include the summary findings of those program evaluations completed during the fiscal year covered by the report.

"(e) An agency head may include all program performance information required annually under this section in an annual financial statement required under section 3515 if any such statement is submitted to the Congress no later than March 31 of the applicable fiscal year.

"(f) The functions and activities of this section shall be considered to be inherently Governmental functions. The drafting of program performance reports under this section shall be performed only by Federal employees.

"§ 1117. Exemption

"The Director of the Office of Management and Budget may exempt from the requirements of sections 1115 and 1116 of this title and section 306 of title 5, any agency with annual outlays of $20,000,000 or less."

SEC. 5. MANAGERIAL ACCOUNTABILITY AND FLEXIBILITY.

(a) Managerial Accountability and Flexibility.—Chapter 97 of title 31, United States Code, is amended by adding after section 9702, the following new section:

"§ 9703. Managerial accountability and flexibility

"(a) Beginning with fiscal year 1999, the performance plans required under section 1115 may include proposals to waive administrative procedural requirements and controls, including specification of personnel staffing levels, limitations on compensation or remuneration, and prohibitions or restrictions on funding transfers among budget object classification 20 and subclassifications 11, 12, 31, and 32 of each annual budget submitted under section 1105, in return for specific individual or organization accountability to achieve a performance goal. In preparing and submitting the performance plan under section 1105(a)(29), the Director of the Office of Management and Budget shall review and may approve any proposed waivers. A waiver shall take effect at the beginning of the fiscal year for which the waiver is approved.

"(b) Any such proposal under subsection (a) shall describe the anticipated effects on performance resulting from greater managerial or organizational flexibility, discretion, and authority, and shall quantify the expected improvements in performance resulting from any waiver. The expected improvements shall be compared to current actual performance, and to the projected level of performance that would be achieved independent of any waiver.

"(c) Any proposal waiving limitations on compensation or remuneration shall precisely express the monetary change in compensation or remuneration amounts, such as bonuses or awards, that shall result from meeting, exceeding, or failing to meet performance goals.

"(d) Any proposed waiver of procedural requirements or controls imposed by an agency (other than the proposing agency or the Office of Management and Budget) may not be included in a performance plan unless it is endorsed by the agency that established the requirement, and the endorsement included in the proposing agency's performance plan.

"(e) A waiver shall be in effect for one or two years as specified by the Director of the Office of Management and Budget in approving the waiver. A waiver may be renewed for a subsequent year. After a waiver has been in effect for three consecutive years, the performance plan prepared under section 1115 may propose that a waiver, other than a waiver of limitations on compensation or remuneration, be made permanent.

"(f) For purposes of this section, the definitions under section 1115(f) shall apply."

SEC. 6. PILOT PROJECTS.

(a) **PERFORMANCE PLANS AND REPORTS.**—Chapter 11 of title 31, United States Code, is amended by inserting after section 1117 (as added by section 4 of this Act) the following new section:

"§ 1118. Pilot projects for performance goals

"(a) The Director of the Office of Management and Budget, after consultation with the head of each agency, shall designate not less than ten agencies as pilot projects in performance measurement for fiscal years 1994, 1995, and 1996. The selected agencies shall reflect a representative range of Governmentfunctions and capabilities in measuring and reporting program performance.

"(b) Pilot projects in the designated agencies shall undertake the preparation of performance plans under section 1115, and program performance reports under section 1116, other than section 1116(c), for one or more of the major functions and operations of the agency. A strategic plan shall be used when preparing agency performance plans during one or more years of the pilot period.

"(c) No later than May 1, 1997, the Director of the Office of Management and Budget shall submit a report to the President and to the Congress which shall—

"(1) assess the benefits, costs, and usefulness of the plans and reports prepared by the pilot agencies in meeting the purposes of the Government Performance and Results Act of 1993;

"(2) identify any significant difficulties experienced b the pilot agencies in preparing plans and reports; and

"(3) set forth any recommended changes in the requirements of the provisions of Government Performance and Results Act of 1993, section 306 of title 5, sections 1105, 1115, 1116, 1117, 1119 and 9703 of this title, and this section."

(b) **MANAGERIAL ACCOUNTABILITY AND FLEXIBILITY.**—Chapter 97 of title 31, United States Code, is amended by inserting after section 9703 (as added by section 5 of this Act) the following new section:

"§ 9704. Pilot projects for managerial accountability and flexibility

"(a) The Director of the Office of Management and Budget shall designate not less than five agencies as pilot projects in managerial accountability and flexibility for fiscal years 1995 and 1996. Such agencies shall be selected from those designated as pilot projects under section 1118 and shall reflect a representative range of Government functions and capabilities in measuring and reporting program performance.

"(b) Pilot projects in the designated agencies shall include proposed waivers in accordance with section 9703 for one or more of the major functions and operations of the agency.

"(c) The Director of the Office of Management and Budget shall include in the report to the President and to the Congress required under section 1118(c)—

"(1) an assessment of the benefits, costs, and usefulness of increasing managerial and organizational flexibility, discretion, and authority in exchange for improved performance through a waiver; and

"(2) an identification of any significant difficulties experienced by the pilot agencies in preparing proposed waivers.

"(d) For purposes of this section the definitions under section 1115(f) shall apply."

(c) **PERFORMANCE BUDGETING.**—Chapter 11 of title 31, United States Code, is amended by inserting after section 1118 (as added by section 6 of this Act) the following new section:

"§ 1119. Pilot projects for performance budgeting

"(a) The Director of the Office of Management and Budget, after consultation with the head of each agency shall designate not less than five agencies as pilot projects in performance budgeting for fiscal years 1998 and 1999. At least three of the agencies shall be selected from those designated as pilot projects under section 1118, and shall also reflect a representative range of Government functions and capabilities in measuring and reporting program performance.

"(b) Pilot projects in the designated agencies shall cover the preparation of performance budgets. Such budgets shall present, for one or more of the major functions and operations of the agency, the varying levels of performance, including outcome—related performance, that would result from different budgeted amounts.

"(c) The Director of the Office of Management and Budget shall include, as an alternative budget presentation in the budget submitted under section 1105 for fiscal year 1999, the performance budgets of the designated agencies for this fiscal year.

"(d) No later than March 31, 2001, the Director of the Office of Management and Budget shall transmit a report to the President and to the Congress on the performance budgeting pilot projects which shall—

"(1) assess the feasibility and advisability of including a performance budget as part of the annual budget submitted under section 1105;

"(2) describe any difficulties encountered by the pilot agencies in preparing a performance budget;

"(3) recommend whether legislation requiring performance budgets should be proposed and the general provisions of any legislation; and

"(4) set forth any recommended changes in the other requirements of the Government Performance and Results Act of 1993, section 306 of title 5, sections 1105, 1115, 1116, 1117, and 9703 of this title, and this section.

"(e) After receipt of the report required under subsection (d), the Congress may specify that a performance budget be submitted as part of the annual budget submitted under section 1105."

SEC. 7. UNITED STATES POSTAL SERVICE.

(Not included in *Public Dollars, Common Sense.*)

SEC. 8. CONGRESSIONAL OVERSIGHT AND LEGISLATION.

(a) **IN GENERAL.**—Nothing in this Act shall be construed as limiting the ability of Congress to establish, amend, suspend, or annul a performance goal. Any such action shall have the effect of superseding that goal in the plan submitted under section 1105(a)(29) of title 31, United States Code.

(b) **GAO REPORT.**— No later than June 1, 1997, the Comptroller General of the United States shall report to Congress on the implementation of this Act, including the prospects for compliance by Federal agencies beyond those participating as pilot projects under sections 1118 and 9704 of title 31, United States Code.

SEC. 9. TRAINING.

The Office of Personnel Management shall, in consultation with the Director of the Office of Management and Budget and the Comptroller General of the United States, develop a strategic planning and performance measurement training component for its management training program and otherwise provide managers with an orientation on the development and use of strategic planning and program performance measurement.

SEC. 10. APPLICATION OF ACT.

No provision or amendment made by this Act may be construed as—

(1) creating any right, privilege, benefit, or entitlement for any person who is not an officer or employee of the United States acting in such capacity, and no person who is not an officer or employee of the United States acting in such capacity shall have standing to file any civil action in a court of the United States to enforce any provision or amendment made by this Act; or

(2) superseding any statutory requirement, including any requirement under section 553 of title 5, United States Code.

SEC. 11. TECHNICAL AND CONFORMING AMENDMENTS.

(a) Amendment to Title 5, United States Code.—The table of sections for chapter 3 of title 5, United States Code, is amended by adding after the item relating to section 305 the following: "306. Strategic plans."

(b) Amendments to Title 31, United States Code.—

(1) Amendment to chapter 11.—The table of sections for chapter 11 of title 31, United States Code, is amended by adding after the item relating to section 1114 the following:

"1115. Performance plans.
"1116. Program performance reports.
"1117. Exemptions.
"1118. Pilot projects for performance goals.
"1119. Pilot projects for performance budgeting."

(2) Amendment to chapter 97.—The table of sections for chapter 97 of title 31, United States Code, is amended by adding after the item relating to section 9702 the following:

"9703. Managerial accountability and flexibility.

"9704. Pilot projects for managerial accountability and flexibility."

(c) Amendment to Title 39, United States Code.—The table of chapters for part III of title 39, United States Code, is amended by adding at the end thereof the following new item: "28. Strategic planning and performance management 2801".

Approved August 3, 1993

GOVERNMENT MANAGEMENT REFORM ACT OF 1994
P. L. 103-356, 108 STAT. 3410

AN ACT

To provide a more effective, efficient, and responsive Government. Be it enacted by the Senate and House of Representatives of the United States of America in Congress assembled,

SECTION 1. SHORT TITLE AND TABLE OF CONTENTS.

(a) SHORT TITLE: This Act may be cited as the "Government Management Reform Act of 1994".

(b) TABLE OF CONTENTS: (Note: the table of contents and Titles 1, 2, and 3 of the Act, which are not relevant to financial management, are not included in *Public Dollars, Common Sense.*)

TITLE IV – FINANCIAL MANAGEMENT

SEC. 401. SHORT TITLE.

This title may be cited as the "Federal Financial Management Act of 1994".

SEC. 402. ELECTRONIC PAYMENTS.

(a) IN GENERAL: Section 3332 of title 31, United States Code, is amended to read as follows:

"§3332. Required direct deposit

"(a)(1) Notwithstanding any other provision of law, all Federal wage, salary, and retirement payments shall be paid to recipients of such payments by electronic funds transfer, unless another method has been determined by the Secretary of the Treasury to be appropriate.

"(2) Each recipient of Federal wage, salary, or retirement payments shall designate one or more financial institutions or other authorized payment agents and provide the payment certifying or authorizing agency information necessary for the recipient to receive electronic funds transfer payments through each institution so designated.

"(b)(1) The head of each agency shall waive the requirements of subsection (a) of this section for a recipient of Federal wage, salary, or retirement payments authorized or certified by the agency upon written request by such recipient.

"(2) Federal wage, salary, or retirement payments shall be paid to any recipient granted a waiver under paragraph (1) of this subsection by any method determined appropriate by the Secretary of the Treasury.

"(c)(1) The Secretary of the Treasury may waive the requirements of subsection (a) of this section for any group of recipients upon request by the head of an agency under standards prescribed by the Secretary of the Treasury.

"(2) Federal wage, salary, or retirement payments shall be paid to any member of a group granted a waiver under paragraph (1) of this subsection by any method determined appropriate by the Secretary of the Treasury.

"(d) This section shall apply only to recipients of Federal wage or salary payments who begin to receive such payments on or after January 1, 1995, and recipients of Federal retirement payments who begin to receive such payments on or after January 1, 1995.

"(e) The crediting of the amount of a payment to the appropriate account on the books of a financial institution or other authorized payment agent designated by a payment recipient under this section shall constitute a full acquittance to the United States for the amount of the payment."

(b) Technical and Conforming Amendment: The table of sections for chapter 33 of title 31, United States Code, is amended by amending the item for section 3332 to read:

"3332. Required direct deposit."

SEC. 403. FRANCHISE FUND PILOT PROGRAMS.

(a) ESTABLISHMENT—There is authorized to be established on a pilot program basis in each of six executive agencies a franchise fund. The Director of the Office of Management and Budget, after consultation with the chairman and ranking members of the Committees on Appropriations and Governmental Affairs of the Senate, and the Committees on Appropriations and Government Operations of the House of Representatives, shall designate the agencies.

(b) USES—Each such fund may provide, consistent with guidelines established by the Director of the Office of Management and Budget, such common administrative support services to the agency and to other agencies as the head of such agency, with the concurrence of the Director, determines can be provided more efficiently through such a fund than by other means. To provide such services, each such fund is authorized to acquire the capital equipment, automated data processing systems, and financial management and management information systems needed. Services shall be provided by such funds on a competitive basis.

(c) FUNDING—(1) There are authorized to be appropriated to the franchise fund of each agency designated under subsection (a) such funds as are necessary to carry out the purposes of the fund, to remain available until expended. To the extent that unexpended balances remain available in other accounts for the purposes to be carried out by the fund, the head of the agency may transfer such balances to the fund.

(2) Fees for services shall be established by the head of the agency at a level to cover the total estimated costs of providing such services. Such fees shall be deposited in the agency's fund to remain available until expended, and may be used to carry out the purposes of the fund.

(3) Existing inventories, including inventories on order, equipment, and other assets or liabilities pertaining to the purposes of the fund may be transferred to the fund.

(d) REPORT ON PILOT PROGRAMS—Within 6 months after the end of fiscal year 1997, the Director of the Office of Management and Budget shall forward a report on the results of the pilot programs to the Committees on Appropriations of the Senate and of the House of Representatives, and to the Committee on Governmental Affairs of the Senate and the Committee on Government Operations of the House of Representatives. The report shall contain the financial and program performance results of the pilot programs, including recommendations for—

(1) the structure of the fund;

(2) the composition of the funding mechanism;

(3) the capacity of the fund to promote competition; and

(4) the desirability of extending the application and implementation of franchise funds to other Federal agencies.

(e) PROCUREMENT—Nothing in this section shall be construed as relieving any agency of any duty under applicable procurement laws.

(f) TERMINATION—The provisions of this section shall expire on October 1, 1999.

SEC. 404. SIMPLIFICATION OF MANAGEMENT REPORTING PROCESS.

(a) IN GENERAL—To improve the efficiency of executive branch perfor- mance in implementing statutory requirements for financial management reporting to the Congress and its committees, the Director of the Office of Management and Budget may adjust the frequency and due dates of or consolidate any statutorily required reports of agencies to the Office of Management and Budget or the President and of agencies or the Office of Management and Budget to the Congress under any laws for which the Office of Management and Budget has financial management responsibility, including—

(1) chapters 5, 9, 11, 33, 35, 37, 39, 75, and 91 of title 31, United States Code;

(2) the Federal Civil Penalties Inflation Adjustment Act of 1990 (28 U.S.C. 2461 note; Public Law 101—410; 104 Stat. 890).

(b) APPLICATION—The authority provided in subsection (a) shall apply only to reports of agencies to the Office of Management and Budget or the President and of agencies or the Office of Management and Budget to the Congress required by statute to be submitted between January 1, 1995, and September 30, 1997.

(c) ADJUSTMENTS IN REPORTING—The Director may consolidate or adjust the frequency and due dates of any statutorily required reports under subsections (a) and (b) only after—

(1) consultation with the Chairman of the Senate Committee on Governmental Affairs and the Chairman of the House of Representatives Committee on Government Operations; and

(2) written notification to the Congress, no later than February 8 of each fiscal year covered under subsection (b) for those reports required to be submitted during that fiscal year.

SEC. 405. ANNUAL FINANCIAL REPORTS.

(a) FINANCIAL STATEMENTS—Section 3515 of title 31, United States Code, is amended to read as follows:

"§ 3515. Financial statements of agencies

"(a) Not later than March 1 of 1997 and each year thereafter, the head of each executive agency identified in section 901(b) of this title shall prepare and submit to the Director of the Office of Management and Budget an audited financial statement for the preceding fiscal year, covering all accounts and associated activities of each office, bureau, and activity of the agency.

"(b) Each audited financial statement of an executive agency under this section shall reflect—

"(1) the overall financial position of the offices, bureaus, and activities covered by the statement, including assets and liabilities thereof; and

"(2) results of operations of those offices, bureaus, and activities.

"(c) The Director of the Office of Management and Budget shall identify components of executive agencies that shall be required to have audited financial statements meeting the requirements of subsection (b).

"(d) The Director of the Office of Management and Budget shall prescribe the form and content of the financial statements of executive agencies under this section, consistent with applicable accounting and financial reporting principles, standards, and requirements.

"(e) The Director of the Office of Management and Budget may waive the application of all or part of subsection (a) for financial statements required for fiscal years 1996 and 1997.

"(f) Not later than March 1 of 1995 and 1996, the head of each executive agency identified in section 901(b) of this title and designated by the Director of the Office of Management and Budget shall prepare and submit to the Director of the Office of Management and Budget an audited financial statement for the preceding fiscal year, covering all accounts and associated activities of each office, bureau, and activity of the agency.

"(g) Not later than March 31 of 1995 and 1996, for executive agencies not designated by the Director of the Office of Management and Budget under subsection (f), the head of each executive agency identified in section 901(b) of this title shall prepare and submit to the Director of the Office of Management and Budget a financial statement for the preceding fiscal year, covering—

"(1) each revolving fund and trust fund of the agency; and

"(2) to the extent practicable, the accounts of each office, bureau, and activity of the agency which performed substantial commercial functions during the preceding fiscal year.

"(h) For purposes of subsection (g), the term "commercial functions" includes buying and leasing of real estate, providing insurance, making loans and loan guarantees, and other credit programs and any activity involving the provision of a service or thing for which a fee, royalty, rent, or other charge is imposed by an agency for services and things of value it provides."

(b) AUDITS BY AGENCIES—Subsection 3521(f) of title 31, United States Code, is amended to read as follows:

"(f)(1) For each audited financial statement required under subsections (a) and (f) of section 3515 of this title, the person who audits the statement for purpose of subsection (e) of this section shall submit a report on the audit to the head of the agency. A report under this subsection shall be prepared in accordance with generally accepted government auditing standards.

"(2) Not later than June 30 following the fiscal year for which a financial statement is submitted under subsection (g) of section 3515 of this title, the person who audits the statement for purpose of subsection (e) of this section shall submit a report on the audit to the head of the agency. A report under this subsection shall be prepared in accordance with generally accepted government auditing standards."

(c) GOVERNMENTWIDE FINANCIAL STATEMENT—Section 331 of title 31, United States Code, is amended by adding the following new subsection:

"(e)(1) Not later than March 31 of 1998 and each year thereafter, the Secretary of the Treasury, in coordination with the Director of the Office of Management and Budget, shall annually prepare and submit to the President and the Congress an audited financial statement for the preceding fiscal year, covering all accounts and associated activities of the executive branch of the United States Government. The financial statement shall reflect the overall financial position, including assets and liabilities, and results of operations of the executive branch of the United States Government, and shall be prepared in accordance with the form and content requirements set forth by the Director of the Office of Management and Budget.

"(2) The Comptroller General of the United States shall audit the financial statement required by this section."

Approved October 13, 1994.

THE FEDERAL FINANCIAL MANAGEMENT IMPROVEMENT ACT OF 1996
P.L. 104-208
TITLE VIII—FEDERAL FINANCIAL MANAGEMENT IMPROVEMENT

SEC. 801. SHORT TITLE

This title may be cited as the 'Federal Financial Management Improvement Act of 1996.'

SEC. 802. FINDINGS AND PURPOSES

(a) FINDINGS— The Congress finds the following:

(1) Much effort has been devoted to strengthening Federal internal accounting controls in the past. Although progress has been made in recent years, Federal accounting standards have not been uniformly implemented in financial management systems for agencies.

(2) Federal financial management continues to be seriously deficient, and Federal financial management and fiscal practices have failed to—

(A) identify costs fully;

(B) reflect the total liabilities of congressional actions; and

(C) accurately report the financial condition of the Federal Government.

(3) Current Federal accounting practices do not accurately report financial results of the Federal Government or the full costs of programs and activities. The continued use of these practices undermines the Government's ability to provide credible and reliable financial data and encourages already widespread Government waste, and will not assist in achieving a balanced budget.

(4) Waste and inefficiency in the Federal Government undermine the confidence of the American people in the government and reduce the federal Government's ability to address vital public needs adequately.

(5) To rebuild the accountability and credibility of the Federal Government, and restore public confidence in the Federal Government, agencies must incorporate accounting standards and reporting objectives established for the Federal Government into their financial management systems so that all the assets and liabilities, revenues, and expenditures or expenses, and the full costs of programs and activities of the Federal Government can be consistently and accurately recorded, monitored, and uniformly reported throughout the Federal Government.

(6) Since its establishment in October 1990, the Federal Accounting Standards Advisory Board (hereinafter referred to as the 'FASAB') has made substantial progress toward developing and recommending a comprehensive set of

accounting concepts and standards for the Federal Government. When the accounting concepts and standards developed by FASB are incorporated into Federal financial management systems, agencies will be able to provide cost and financial information that will assist the Congress and financial managers to evaluate the cost and performance of Federal programs and activities, and will therefore provide important information that has been lacking, but is needed for improved decision making by financial managers and the Congress.

(7) The development of financial management systems with the capacity to support these standards and concepts will, over the long term, improve Federal financial management.

(b) PURPOSE—The purposes of this Act are to—

(1) provide for consistency of accounting by an agency from one fiscal year to the next, and uniform accounting standards throughout the Federal Government;

(2) require Federal financial management systems to support full disclosure of Federal financial data, including the full costs of Federal programs and activities, to the citizens, the Congress, the President, and agency management, so that programs and activities can be considered based on their full costs and merits;

(3) increase the accountability and credibility of federal financial management;

(4) improve performance, productivity and efficiency of Federal Government financial management;

(5) establish financial management systems to support controlling the cost of Federal Government;

(6) build upon and complement the Chief Financial Officers Act of 1990 (Public Law 101-576; 104 Stat. 2838), the Government Performance and Results Act of 1993 (Public Law 103-62; 107 Stat. 285) and the Government Management Reform Act of 1994 (Public Law 103-356; 108 Stat. 3410); and

(7) increase the capability of agencies to monitor execution of the budget by more readily permitting reports that compare spending of resources to results of activities.

SEC. 803 IMPLEMENTATION OF FEDERAL FINANCIAL MANAGEMENT IMPROVEMENTS.

(a) IN GENERAL—Each agency shall implement and maintain financial management systems that comply substantially with Federal financial management systems requirements, applicable Federal accounting standards, and the United States Government Standard General Ledger at the transaction level.

(b) AUDIT COMPLIANCE FINDING—

(1) IN GENERAL—Each audit required by section 3521(e) of title 31, United States Code, shall report whether the agency financial management systems comply with the requirements of subsection (a).

(2) **CONTENT OF REPORTS**—When the person performing the audit required by section 3521(e) of title 31, United States Code, reports that the agency financial management systems do not comply with the requirements of subsection (a), the person performing the audit shall include in the report on the audit—

(A) the entity or organization responsible for the financial management systems that have been found not to comply with the requirements of subsection (a);

(B) all facts pertaining to the failure to comply with the requirements of subsection (a), including—

(i) the nature and extent of the noncompliance including areas in which there is substantial but not full compliance;

(ii) the primary reason or cause of the noncompliance;

(iii) the entity or organization responsible for the non-compliance; and

(iv) any relevant comments from any responsible officer or employee; and

(C) a statement with respect to the recommended remedial actions and the time frames to implement such actions.

(c) **COMPLIANCE IMPLEMENTATION**—

(1) **DETERMINATION**—No later than the date described under paragraph (2), the Head of an agency shall determine whether the financial management systems of the agency comply with the requirements of subsection (a). Such determination shall be based on—

(A) a review of the report on the applicable agency-wide audited financial statement;

(B) any other information the Head of the agency considers relevant and appropriate.

(2) **DATE OF DETERMINATION**—The determination under paragraph (1) shall be made no later than 120 days after the earlier of—

(A) the date of the receipt of an agency-wide audited financial statement; or

(B) the last day of the fiscal year following the year covered by such statement.

(3) **REMEDIATION PLAN**—

(A) If the Head of an agency determines that the agency's financial management systems do not comply with the requirements of subsection (a), the head of the agency, in consultation with the Director, shall establish a remediation plan that shall include resources, remedies, and intermediate target dates necessary to bring the agency's financial management systems into substantial compliance.

(B) If the determination of the head of the agency differs from the audit compliance findings required in subsection (b), the Director shall review such determinations and provide a report on the findings to the appropriate committees of the Congress.

(4) **Time Period for Compliance**—A remediation plan shall bring the agency's financial management systems into substantial compliance no later than 3 years after the date a determination is made under paragraph (1), unless the agency, with concurrence of the Director—

(A) determines that the agency's financial management systems cannot comply with the requirements of subsection (a) within 3 years;

(B) specifies the most feasible date for bringing the agency's financial management systems into compliance with the requirements of subsection (a); and

(C) designates an official of the agency who shall be responsible for bringing the agency's financial management systems into compliance with the requirements of subsection (a) by the date specified under subparagraph (B).

SEC. 804. REPORTING REQUIREMENTS.

(a) **Reports by the Director**—No later than March 31 of each year, the Director shall submit a report to the Congress regarding implementation of this Act. The Director may include the report in the financial management status report and the 5-year financial management plan submitted under section 3512(a)(1) of title 31, United States Code.

(b) **Reports by the Inspector General**—Each Inspector General who prepares a report under section 5(a) of the Inspector General Act of 1978 (5 U.S.C. App.) shall report to Congress instances and reasons when an agency has not met the intermediate target dates established in the remediation plan required under section 3. Specifically the report shall include—

(1) the entity or organization responsible for the non-compliance;

(2) the facts pertaining to the failure to comply with the requirements of subsection (a), including the nature and extent of the non-compliance, the primary reason or cause for the failure to comply, and any extenuating circumstances; and

(3) a statement of the remedial actions needed to comply.

(c) **Reports by the Comptroller General**—No later than October 1, 1997, and October 1, of each year thereafter, the Comptroller General of the United States shall report to the appropriate committees of the Congress concerning—

(1) compliance with the requirements of section 3(a) of this Act, including whether the financial statements of the Federal Government have been prepared in accordance with applicable accounting standards; and

(2) the adequacy of applicable accounting standards for the Federal Government.

SEC. 805. CONFORMING AMENDMENTS.

(a) AUDITS BY AGENCIES—Section 3521(f)(1) of title 31, United States Code, is amended in the first sentence by inserting 'and the Controller of the Office of Federal Financial Management' before the period.

(b) FINANCIAL MANAGEMENT STATUS REPORT—Section 3512(a)(2) of title 31, United States Code, is amended by—

(1) in subparagraph (D) by striking 'and' after the semicolon;

(2) by redesignating subparagraph (E) as subparagraph (F); and

(3) by inserting after subparagraph (D) the following:

'(E) a listing of agencies whose financial management systems do not comply substantially with the requirements of Section 3(a) the Federal Financial Management Improvement Act of 1996, and a summary statement of the efforts underway to remedy the noncompliance; and'

(c) INSPECTOR GENERAL ACT OF 1978—Section 5(a) of the Inspector General Act of 1978 is amended—

(1) in paragraph (11) by striking 'and' after the semicolon;

(2) in paragraph (12) by striking the period and inserting '; and'; and

(3) by adding at the end the following new paragraph:

'(13) the information described under section 05(b) of the Federal Financial Management Improvement Act of 1996.'

SEC. 806. DEFINITIONS.

For purposes of this title:

(1) AGENCY—The term 'agency' means a department or agency of the United States Government as defined in section 901(b) of title 31, United States Code.

(2) DIRECTOR—The term 'Director' means the Director of the Office of Management and Budget.

(3) FEDERAL ACCOUNTING STANDARDS—The term 'Federal accounting standards' means applicable accounting principles, standards, and requirements consistent with section 902(a)(3)(A) of title 31, United States Code.

(4) FINANCIAL MANAGEMENT SYSTEMS—The term 'financial management systems' includes the financial systems and the financial portions of mixed systems necessary to support financial management, including automated and manual processes, procedures, controls, data, hardware, software, and support personnel dedicated to the operation and maintenance of system functions.

(5) FINANCIAL SYSTEM—The term 'financial system' includes an information system, comprised of one or more applications, that is used for (A) collecting, processing, maintaining, transmitting, or reporting data about financial events; (B) supporting financial planning or budgeting activities; (C) accumulating and

reporting costs information; or (D) supporting the preparation of financial statements.

(6) **MIXED SYSTEM**—The term 'mixed system' means an information system that supports both financial and nonfinancial functions of the Federal Government or components thereof.

SEC. 807. EFFECTIVE DATE.

This title shall take effect for the fiscal year ending September 30, 1997.

SEC. 808. REVISION OF SHORT TITLES.

(a) Section 4001 of Public Law 104-106 (110 Stat. 642; 41 U.S.C. 251 note) is amended to read as follows:

"§ 4001. Short Title.

'This division and division E may be cited as the 'Clinger-Cohen Act of 1996'.'

(b) Section 5001 of Public Law 104-106 (110 Stat. 679; 40 U.S.C. 1401 note) is amended to read as follows:

"§ 5001. Short Title.

'This division and division D may be cited as the 'Clinger-Cohen Act of 1996'.'

(c) Any reference in any law, regulation, document, record, or other paper of the United States to the Federal Acquisition Reform Act of 1996 or to the Information Technology Management Reform Act of 1996 shall be considered to be a reference to the Clinger-Cohen Act of 1996.

This Act may be cited as the 'Treasury, Postal Service, and General Government Appropriations Act, 1997'.

Approved September 30, 1996.

Concept Statements

Federal Accounting Standards Advisory Board statements on concepts differ from statements of recommended accounting standards. Concept statements are more general and do not contain specific recommendations that would, when issued by FASAB's sponsors (GAO, OMB, and Treasury), become authoritative requirements for federal agencies and auditors. Instead, statements on concepts, once approved by the sponsors, provide general guidance to FASAB itself as it deliberates on specific issues. The statements also help others to understand federal accounting and financial reports.

Statement of Federal Financial Accounting Concepts #1: Objectives of Federal Financial Reporting, September 2, 1993
This is a conceptual statement on the objectives of federal financial reporting. It focuses on the uses, user needs, and objectives of such reporting. Users of financial information about the federal government are classified in four major groups: citizens, Congress, executives, and program managers. The objectives of financial reporting include budgetary integrity, stewardship, and ensuring that financial management systems and internal accounting and administrative controls are adequate.

Statement of Federal Financial Accounting Concepts #2: Entity and Display June 5, 1995
This statement provides guidance as to what would be encompassed by a federal government entity's financial report. The statement specifies the types of entities for which there ought to be financial reports, establishes guidelines for defining the makeup of each type of reporting entity, identifies types of financial reports for communicating the information for each type of reporting entity, and suggests the types of information each type of report would convey.

Statements of Federal Financial Accounting Standards

Abbreviated as SSFAS, these are standards that FASAB recommends to its sponsors. FASAB communicates its recommendations by publishing recommended accounting standards after considering the financial and budgetary information needs of congressional oversight groups, executive agencies, and other users of federal financial information. The FASAB also considers comments from the public on its proposed recommendations, which are published for comment as "exposure drafts." When issued in final form, SFFASs are considered "GAAP" for federal agencies to use in preparing financial statements in accordance with the requirements of the CFO Act. Auditors are to consider SFFASs as authoritative references when auditing financial statements. FASAB's sponsors may also decide to adopt the recommendations as part of other guidelines such as OMB circulars.

Statement #1: Accounting For Selected Assets and Liabilities, March 30, 1993
In this statement, FASAB recommends accounting standards for selected assets and liabilities. The assets are cash, fund balance with Treasury, accounts receivable, interest receivable, advances and prepayments, and investments in Treasury securities. The liabilities are accounts payable, interest payable, and other current liabilities.

Statement #2: Accounting For Direct Loans And Loan Guarantees, July 15, 1993
This statement provides accounting standards for federal direct loans and loan guarantees. The standards require that direct loans obligated and loan guarantees committed after September 30, 1991, be accounted for on a present value basis, consistent with the intent of the Federal Credit Reform Act of 1990.

Statement #3: Accounting For Inventory and Related Property, October 27, 1993
The standards presented in this document apply to several types of tangible property, other than long term fixed assets, held by federal government agencies. The property types include: inventory (i.e., items held for sale); operating materials and supplies; stockpile materials; seized and forfeited property; foreclosed property; and goods held under price support and stabilization programs (including nonrecourse loans and purchase agreements).

Statement #4: Managerial Cost Accounting Concepts and Standards for the Federal Government, July 31, 1995
The managerial cost accounting concepts and standards contained in this statement are aimed at providing reliable and timely information on the full cost of federal programs, their activities, and outputs. The concepts and standards describe the relationship among cost accounting, financial reporting, and budgeting. The five standards set forth the fundamental elements of managerial cost accounting: (1) accumulating and reporting costs of activities on a regular basis for management information purposes, (2) establishing responsibility segments to match costs with outputs, (3) determining full costs of government goods and services, (4) recognizing the costs of goods and services provided among federal entities, and (5) using appropriate costing methodologies to accumulate and assign costs to outputs.

Statement #5: Accounting for Liabilities of the Federal Government, September 1995
These standards apply to general purpose financial reports of U.S. government reporting entities. This statement establishes accounting standards for liabilities of the federal government not covered in SSFAS #1 or SSFAS #2 above. The statement defines "liability" as a probable future outflow or other sacrifice of resources as a result of past transactions or events. As well as providing a general liability recognition principle, the Statement includes several specific federal liability accounting standards, including for contingencies, capital leases, federal debt,

pensions and other retirement or postemployment benefits, and insurance and guarantee programs.

Statement #6: Accounting For Property, Plant, and Equipment, September 1995
This statement contains accounting standards for cleanup costs for hazardous waste removal, containment, or disposal; federally owned property, plant, and equipment (PP&E); and deferred maintenance on PP&E. The statement identifies four categories of PP&E:

- General: PP&E used to provide general government services or goods;
- Federal mission: Weapons systems, space exploration equipment, and similar PP&E for which applying depreciation accounting would not contribute to measuring the cost of outputs produced, or to assessing operating performance, in any given accounting period.
- Heritage assets: Assets possessing significant educational, cultural, or natural characteristics; and
- Stewardship land: Land other than that included in general PP&E.

Office of Management and Budget Circulars and Bulletins

OMB circulars are statements of standards to be followed by federal agencies in their financial accounting and reporting.

Circular No. A-11: Preparation and Submission of Budget Estimates, June 1995
This circular details the changes to the federal budget submission process for a particular fiscal year. It includes information on implementing the Government Performance and Results Act

Circular No. A-34: Instructions on Budget Execution, November 1994
Provides guidance and instructions on budget execution, monitoring federal outlays, etc.

Circular No. A-123: Management Accountability and Control, Revised June 21, 1995
This circular provides guidance to federal managers on improving the accountability and effectiveness of federal programs and operations by establishing, assessing, correcting, and reporting on management controls. The circular requires agencies and individual federal managers must take systematic and proactive measures to (i) develop and implement appropriate, cost-effective management controls for results-oriented management; (ii) assess the adequacy of management controls in federal programs and operations; (iii) identify needed improvements; (iv) take corresponding corrective action; and (v) report annually on management controls.

Circular No. A-125: Prompt Payment, Revised December 12, 1989
This circular prescribes policies and procedures to be followed by Executive departments and agencies in paying for property and services acquired under

federal contracts pursuant to the Prompt Payment Act of 1982, as amended, and for entitlement payments under the Agricultural Act of 1949.

Circular No. A-127: Financial Management Systems, Revised July 23, 1993

This circular prescribes policies and standards for executive departments and agencies to follow in developing, operating, evaluating, and reporting on financial management systems. The circular was issued pursuant to the CFO Act and the Federal Managers' Financial Integrity Act. It requires each agency to establish and maintain a single, integrated financial management system that complies with:

- Applicable accounting principles, standards, and related requirements as defined by OMB and the Department of the Treasury;
- Internal control standards as defined in Circular A-123 or successor documents;
- Information resource management policy as defined in Circular A-130 or successor documents; and
- Operating policies and related requirements prescribed by OMB, the Department of the Treasury and the agency.

Circular No. A-128: Audits of State and Local Governments, April 12, 1985

This circular was issued pursuant to the Single Audit Act of 1984. It establishes audit requirements for State and local governments that receive federal aid, and defines federal responsibilities for implementing and monitoring those requirements.

Circular No. A-129: Policies For Federal Credit Programs and Non-Tax Receivables, Revised

This circular prescribes policies and procedures for justifying, designing, and managing federal credit programs and for collecting non-tax receivables. It sets principles for designing credit programs, including the preparation and review of legislation and regulations; budgeting for the costs of credit programs and minimizing unintended costs to the government; and improving the efficiency and effectiveness of federal credit programs. It also sets standards for extending credit, managing lenders participating in the government's guaranteed loan programs, servicing credit and non-tax receivables, and collecting delinquent debt.

Circular No. A-134: Financial Accounting Principles and Standards, May 20, 1993

This circular establishes the policies and procedures for approving and publishing financial accounting principles and standards. It also establishes the policies to be followed by Executive Branch agencies and OMB in seeking and providing interpretations and other advice related to the standards.

OMB Bulletin No. 94-01: Form and Content of Agency Financial Statements, November 13, 1993

This bulletin defines the form and content of financial statements of executive departments and agencies for financial statements beginning with the year ending September 30, 1993, (FY 1993). It incorporates the reporting and disclosure requirements contained in SFFAS #1, 2, and 3, listed above.

OMB Bulletin No. 97-01: Form and Content of Agency Financial Statements, October 24, 1996

This bulletin establishes the form and content of financial statements of executive departments and agencies for financial statements beginning with the year ending September 30, 1998, (FY 1998). In addition to some previous requirements defined in OMB Bulletin 94-01, agencies will prepare a Statement of Net Cost, Statement of Changes in Net Position, Statement of Budgetary Resources, Statement of Financing, and for some agencies, a Statement of Custodial Activity. Chapter 5 summarizes these and other requirements of the new bulletin.

GLOSSARY

Where possible, we provide an official definition of a term, citing the specific federal law, regulation, or other document in which the term is defined. Notes in parentheses show the cited law or rule; please refer to Appendix B for a description of the source. Terms in italics are defined in the glossary.

Accrual-based Accounting. An accounting method which uses accruals to measure the financial status of an entity. (C&L)

Accruals. Entries in a chart of accounts which indicate obligations made and payments that are expected. (C&L)

Accounting Standards or Principles. Those conventions, rules, and procedures necessary to define acceptable accounting practice at a particular time. Accounting standards include broad guidelines of general application and may also include detailed practices and procedures. (OMB Circular 134)

Activity. The actual work task or step performed in producing and delivering products and services. An aggregation of actions performed within an organization that is useful for purposes of activity-based costing (FASAB 4). An activity is the same as a simple process.

Activity Analysis. The identification and description of activities in an organization. Activity analysis involves determining what activities are done within a department, how many people perform the activities, how much time they spend performing the activities, what resources are required to perform the activities, what operational data best reflect the performance of the activities, and what customer value the activity has for the organization. Activity analysis is accomplished with interviews, questionnaires, observation, and review of physical records of work. It is the foundation for agency process value analysis, which is key to overall review of program delivery. (FASAB 4)

Activity-Based Costing (ABC). A cost accounting method that measures the cost and performance of process related activities and cost objects. It assigns cost to cost objects, such as products or customers, based on their use of activities. It recognizes the causal relationship of cost drivers to activities. (FASAB 4)

Activity Budgeting. The use of activity-based costing methods to prepare operations budgets to show the amount of resources that identified activities are expected to consume, based on forecasted demand for their outputs. (C&L)

Adverse Opinion. In an audit report, a statement by auditors that financial statements do not represent fairly the reporting entity's financial position and operations.

Assets. Tangible or intangible items owned by the federal government which would have probable economic benefits that can be obtained or controlled by a federal government entity. (FASAB 1)

Audit, Financial. A review of the accuracy and validity of the financial records, reports, and statements of an organization for the purpose of verifying that the organization has conformed to established accounting procedures and principles.

Audit Opinions. See adverse opinion, disclaimer opinion, qualified opinion, and unqualified opinion.

Cash-based Accounting. A method of accounting which records cash transactions only and does not involve accruals. (C&L)

Change Management. The process of aligning the human, organizational and cultural elements of an agency with new ways of doing business. (C&L)

Core Business Process. A cross-functional process that produces an organization's main products or services. (C&L)

Cost. The monetary value of resources used or sacrificed or liabilities incurred to achieve an objective, such as to acquire or produce a good or to perform an activity or service. (FASAB 4)

Cost Allocation. A method of assigning costs to activities, outputs, or other cost objects. The allocation base used to assign a cost to objects is not necessarily the cause of the cost. For example, assigning the cost of power to machine activities by machine hours is an allocation because machine hours are an indirect measure of power consumption. (FASAB 4)

Cost Assignment. A process that identifies costs with activities, outputs, or other cost objects. In a broad sense, costs can be assigned to processes, activities, organizational divisions, products, and services. There are three methods of cost assignment: (a) directly tracing costs wherever economically feasible, (b) cause-and-effect, and (c) allocating costs on a reasonable and consistent basis. (FASAB 4)

Cost Driver. Any factor that causes a change in the cost of an activity or output. For example, the quality of parts received by an activity, or the degree of complexity of tax returns to be reviewed by the IRS. (FASAB 4)

Cost Object (also referred to as Cost Objective). An Activity, output, or item whose cost is to be measured. In a broad sense, a cost object can be an organizational division, a function, task, product, service, or a customer. (FASAB 4)

Critical Success Factor (CSF). In developing strategic plans or performance measures, CSFs are those few critical areas where things must go right in order for an agency to achieve its mission. (C&L)

Cross-functional Process. A Process that involves employees, products, or processes from more than one department or functional area.

Culture. The basic assumptions and beliefs that are shared by members of an organization, that operate unconsciously, and define in a basic, "taken for granted" fashion an organization's view of itself and its environment. (C&L)

Customer. The person, group, or organization that receives products and services from an agency. External customers are outside the agency; internal customers are the next operation, office, or user downstream from a specific process. (C&L).

Customer Satisfaction. The level of satisfaction expressed by Customers on a range of issues they consider significant, as measured by a survey, focus group, interviews, or some other formal means. (C&L)

Cycle Time. The time required for a process to produce one unit of output. (C&L)

Direct Cost. The cost of resources directly consumed by an Activity. Direct costs are assigned to activities by direct tracing of units of resources consumed by individual activities. A cost that is specifically identified with a single Cost object. (FASAB 4)

Disclaimer Opinion. In an audit, a statement that the auditors feel that they cannot express an opinion on financial statements for various reasons, most commonly because of data quality, data availability, or unreliable financial systems, but also because the scope of the audit was severely limited by the audit client or by circumstances. (C&L)

Disclosure. An explanation, or exhibit, attached to a financial statement, or embodied in a report (e.g., an auditor's) containing a fact, opinion, or detail required or helpful in the interpretation of the statement or report; an expanded heading or a footnote. (Kohler's Dictionary for Accountants, as cited in FASAB 3)

Entity. A unit within the federal government, such as a department, agency, bureau, or program, for which a set of financial statements would be prepared. Entity also encompasses a group of related or unrelated commercial functions, revolving funds, trust funds, and/or other accounts for which financial statements will be prepared in accordance with OMB annual guidance on Form and Content of Financial Statements. (FASAB 1).

Expense. Outflow or other using up of resources or incurring liabilities (or a combination of both), the benefits from which apply to an entity's operations for the current accounting period, but do not extend to future periods. (FASAB 4)

Financial System. An information system, comprised of one or more applications, that is used for any of the following: collecting, processing, maintaining, transmitting, and reporting data about financial events; supporting financial planning or budgeting activities; accumulating and reporting cost information; or supporting the preparation of financial statements. (FFMIA-96). The term "financial management systems" means the financial systems and the financial portions of mixed systems necessary to support financial management. (OMB Circular A-127)

Financial Reporting. The process of recording, reporting, and interpreting, in terms of money, an entity's financial transactions and events with economic consequences for the entity. Reporting in the federal government also deals with nonfinancial information about service efforts and accomplishments of the government, i.e., the inputs of resources used by the government, the outputs of goods and services provided by the government, the outcomes and impacts of governmental programs, and the relationships among these elements. (FASAB Concept #1)

Full Cost. The sum of all costs required by a Cost Object including the costs of activities performed by other entities regardless of funding sources. (FASAB 4)

Full-time-equivalent (FTE). A measure of labor hours, e.g., two people who work half time make one FTE. (C&L)

Generally Accepted Accounting Principles (GAAP). Those accounting principles that have substantial authoritative support. Specifically, they represent the consensus at any time as to which economic resources and obligations should be recorded as assets and liabilities, which changes in them should be recorded, when these changes should be recorded, how the recorded assets and liabilities and changes in them should be measured, what information should be disclosed and how, and which financial statements should be prepared. (Accounting Principles Board Statement No. 4)

Indirect Cost. A cost that cannot be identified specifically with or traced to a given cost object in an economically feasible way. (FASAB 4) Also called "overhead cost."

Information System. The organized collection, processing, transmission, and dissemination of information in accordance with defined procedures. Information systems include non-financial, financial, and mixed systems. (OMB Circular a-11)

Internal Controls. A subset of management controls used to assure that there is prevention or timely detection of unauthorized acquisition, use, or disposition of an entity's assets. (OMB Circular 123)

Interpretation of Federal Financial Accounting Standards. A document of narrow scope that provides clarifications of original meaning, additional definitions, or other guidance pertaining to an existing Statement of Federal Financial Accounting Standards (SFFAS). (OMB Circular 134)

Joint Financial Management Improvement Program (JFMIP). A joint and cooperative undertaking of OMB, GAO, the Department of the Treasury and OPM, working in cooperation with each other and with operating agencies to improve financial management. (C&L)

Liability. A probable and measurable future outflow of resources arising from past transactions or events. (FASAB 1)

Management Controls. The organization, policies, and procedures used by agencies to reasonably ensure that (i) programs achieve their intended results; (ii) resources are used consistent with agency mission; (iii) programs and resources are protected from waste, fraud, and mismanagement; (iv) laws and regulations are followed; and (v) reliable and timely information is obtained, maintained, reported and used for decision making. (OMB Circular 123)

Managerial Cost Accounting System. The organization and procedures, whether automated or not, and whether part of the general ledger or stand-alone, that accumulates and reports consistent and reliable cost information and performance data from various agency feeder systems. The accumulated and reported data enable management and other interested parties to measure and make decisions about the agency's (or its component units') ability to improve operations, safeguard assets, control its resources, and determine if mission objectives are being met. (FASAB 4)

Mapping. Creating a flow chart that depicts the tasks required to operate a process, or the processes required to operate a core business process. (C&L)

Mixed System. An information system that supports both financial and nonfinancial functions of the federal government or components thereof. (FFMIA-96)

Obligations. In federal accounting, a reservation of appropriated spending authority that will be used to pay for a specific contract, a purchase order, or another item (FASAB 4 Concept #1). Binding agreements that will result in outlays, immediately or in the future (OMB A-11).

Opinions, Audit. See adverse opinion, disclaimer opinion, qualified opinion, and unqualified opinion.

Outcome. The results of a program activity compared to its intended purposes. Program results may be evaluated in terms of service or product quantity and quality, customer satisfaction, and effectiveness. (FASAB 4)

Outcome Measure. An assessment of the results of a program activity compared to its intended purpose (GPRA). The tabulation, calculation, or recording of activity or effort and can be expressed in a quantitative or qualitative manner (OMB Circular A-11).

Outputs. Any product or service generated from the consumption of resources. It can include information or paper work generated by the completion of the tasks of an activity. (FASAB 4)

Output Measure. The tabulation, calculation, or recording of activity or effort that can be expressed in a quantitative or qualitative manner. (GPRA)

Performance Goal. A target level of performance expressed as a tangible, measurable objective, against which actual achievement can be compared, including a goal expressed as a quantitative standard, value, or rate. (GPRA)

Performance Indicator. A particular value or characteristic used to measure output or outcome. (GPRA)

Performance Measurement. A means of evaluating efficiency, effectiveness, and results. A balanced performance measurement scorecard includes financial and nonfinancial measures focusing on quality, cycle time, and cost. Performance measurement should include program accomplishments in terms of outputs (quantity of products or services provided, e.g., How many items efficiently produced?) and outcomes (results of providing outputs, e.g., are outputs effectively meeting intended agency mission objectives?).

Performance Plan. An annual plan that establishes performance goals defined in an objective, quantifiable, and measurable form that show the level of performance to be achieved by a program activity; describes the operational processes and resources required to meet the goals; establishes performance indicators to be used in measuring or assessing the relevant outputs, service levels, and outcomes of each program activity; provides a basis for comparing actual program results with the goals; and describes the means to be used to verify and validate measured values. (GPRA)

Process. The organized method of converting inputs (people, equipment, methods, materials, and environment), to outputs (products or services). The natural aggregation of work activities and tasks performed for program delivery. (FASAB 4)

Process Value Analysis. Tools and techniques for studying processes through customer value analysis. Its objective is to identify opportunities for lasting improvement in the performance of an organization. It provides an in-depth review of work activities and tasks, through activity analysis, which aggregate to form processes for agency program delivery. In addition to activity-based costing, quality and cycle time factors are studied for a complete analysis of performance measurement. Each activity within the process is analyzed, including whether or not the activity adds value for the customer. (FASAB 4) See Value-Added Activity.

Product. Any discrete, traceable, or measurable good or service provided to a customer. Often goods are referred to as tangible products, and services are referred to as intangible products. A good or service is the product of a process resulting from the consumption of resources. (FASAB 4)

Qualified Opinion. A statement that auditors believe that financial statements fairly present the operations and financial position of a reporting entity, except for certain areas for which they have material concerns. (C&L)

Recognition (or Recognize). The process of formally recording or incorporating an item into the financial statements of an entity as an asset, liability, revenue, expense, or the like. A recognized item is depicted in both words and numbers, with the amount included in the statement totals. Recognition comprehends both initial recognition of an item and recognition of subsequent changes in or removal of a previously recognized item. (FASAB 1, as derived from FASB Statement of Financial Accounting Concepts No. 5, para. 6)

Service. An intangible product or task rendered directly to a customer. (FASAB 4)

Stakeholder. A person, group, or organization who have a vested interested in how an agency performs. Stakeholders may include customers, Congress, oversight agencies, employees, suppliers, and the community. (C&L)

Strategic Plan. A five-year agency plan that includes its mission statement; general goals and objectives and a description of how they will be achieved; an identification of those key factors external to the agency and beyond its control that could significantly affect the achievement of the goals and objectives; and a description of the program evaluations used in establishing or revising general goals and objectives. (Edited from GPRA)

Support Costs. Costs of activities not directly associated with production. Typical examples are the costs of automation support, communications, postage, process engineering, and purchasing. (FASAB 4)

Traceability. The ability to assign a cost directly to a specific Activity or Cost Object by identifying or observing specific resources consumed by the activity or cost object. (FASAB 4)

Unit Cost. The cost of a selected unit of a good or service. Examples include dollar cost per ton, machine hour, labor hour, or department hour. (FASAB 4)

Unqualified Opinion. In an audit report, an unqualified opinion expresses the auditor's belief that financial statements fairly present the operations and financial position of the reporting entity, that the financial statements conform to accounting principles and standards, that the scope of the audit was not significantly limited, and that the examination of evidence revealed no material misstatements. (C&L)

Value-Added Activity. An activity that is judged to contribute to customer value or satisfy an organizational need. The attribute "value-added" reflects a belief that the activity cannot be eliminated without reducing the quantity, responsiveness, or quality of output required by a customer or organization. Value-added activities should physically change the product or service in a manner that meets customer expectations. (FASAB 4)

Value Analysis. See Process Value Analysis.

ABOUT THE AUTHORS

The authors are members of the Coopers & Lybrand L.L.P. Government Consulting Practice in Washington, D.C.

William R. Phillips, CGFM

Mr. Phillips, a Partner, leads C&L's services to federal chief financial officers, and has 17 years experience in government consulting in the fields of financial operations and business practice improvement. He has testified to Congressional committees on the implementation of federal financial management reform initiatives such as the CFO Act, the GMRA, and the GPRA. Mr. Phillip's consulting clients include the Federal Bureau of Investigation, the Defense Finance and Accounting Service, the National Science Foundation, National Public Radio, NASA, the Social Security Administration, the Federal Deposit Insurance Corporation, the Department of Education, and the Departments of the Air Force, Army, Navy, Interior, Education, and Energy. He holds a BA in history and international studies from Dickinson College and an MBA in finance from the College of William and Mary.

Bonnie L. Brown, CGFM

Ms. Brown is an engagement director and advisor for several financial management improvement and CFO Act implementation projects, including the Departments of the Army and Air Force, and the Defense Finance and Accounting Service's Navy and headquarters operations. During her 25 years as a government manager and consultant, Ms. Brown has worked at the federal, state and local levels in providing financial process improvement, financial systems design and development, and training. Her other clients include the General Services Administration, the Department of Energy, the Department of Defense, the Department of the Navy, the Federal Bureau of Investigation, National Public Radio, and national security organizations. She co-authored the monograph, Managing Project Expectations, which describes a methodology for effective project management and quality assurance. Ms. Brown holds a BS in business administration from East Carolina University.

C. Morgan Kinghorn, Jr., CGFM

Before joining C&L in 1995, Mr. Kinghorn worked with the federal government for 25 years in positions such as the CFO of the Internal Revenue Service; comptroller, budget director, and deputy assistant administrator of the Environmental Protection Agency; and Director of Financial Management at the Office of Management and Budget. He is the recipient of the Distinguished and Meritorious Executive Awards and the Donald L. Scantlebury Award for federal financial management, and is a Fellow of the National Academy of Public Administration. Mr. Kinghorn led the Federal Accounting Standards Advisory Board team that developed new managerial cost accounting standards. He holds a BA in government from the University of Redlands and an MPIA from the Maxwell School of Syracuse University.

Andrew C. West, CGFM

Mr. West is a former career Army officer with 20 years experience in training, logistics, operations and financial management. Before joining C&L, he taught strategic planning and organizational management at Vanderbilt University. Mr. West's federal clients include the Patent and Trademark Office, the Social Security Administration, the Coast Guard, the Federal Bureau of Investigation, and the Departments of Defense, Army, and Air Force. In 1995, he managed the C&L/Association of Government Accountants survey of progress in CFO Act, GPRA, and GMRA implementation, and has published several articles on the results. He holds a BS in business administration from the University of North Carolina at Chapel Hill and an MBA from Syracuse University. He is a member of Beta Gamma Sigma, the honor society for collegiate schools of business.

About Coopers & Lybrand L.L.P.

Coopers & Lybrand L.L.P. is one of the "Big Six" accounting and management consulting firms, with an large and growing Government Consulting Practice headquartered in the Washington, DC area. C&L professionals are currently assisting many federal agencies address the requirements of the CFO, GPRA, and GMRA Acts. We help our clients tackle the vast array of business and auditability issues, such as systems limitations, data integrity, control processes, accounting standards, and reporting requirements. Our integrated full-service approach to financial management improvements includes:

- Assessing financial management and control environments
- Evaluating data integrity
- Reviewing systems controls
- Interpreting and applying accounting guidance and policy
- Preparing financial statements and producing annual reports
- Evaluating and developing relevant performance measures
- Identifying and employing federal best practices in financial management reform
- Providing support before, during, and after the financial statement audit
- Conducting activity-based costing pilots and activity-based management implementations

For more information on how C&L can assist in financial management improvements, please contact the authors at:

Coopers & Lybrand L.L.P.
1751 Pinnacle Drive
McClean, Virginia 22102
Phone: 703-918-3000

INDEX